Digital Evidence

2015

Jeffrey B. Welty

UNC
SCHOOL OF
GOVERNMENT

The School of Government at the University of North Carolina at Chapel Hill works to improve the lives of North Carolinians by engaging in practical scholarship that helps public officials and citizens understand and improve state and local government. Established in 1931 as the Institute of Government, the School provides educational, advisory, and research services for state and local governments. The School of Government is also home to a nationally ranked graduate program in public administration and specialized centers focused on information technology and environmental finance.

As the largest university-based local government training, advisory, and research organization in the United States, the School of Government offers up to 200 courses, webinars, and specialized conferences for more than 12,000 public officials each year. In addition, faculty members annually publish approximately 50 books, manuals, reports, articles, bulletins, and other print and online content related to state and local government. Each day that the General Assembly is in session, the School produces the *Daily Bulletin Online*, which reports on the day's activities for members of the legislature and others who need to follow the course of legislation.

The Master of Public Administration Program is offered in two formats. The full-time, two-year residential program serves up to 60 students annually. In 2013 the School launched MPA@UNC, an online format designed for working professionals and others seeking flexibility while advancing their careers in public service. The School's MPA program consistently ranks among the best public administration graduate programs in the country, particularly in city management. With courses ranging from public policy analysis to ethics and management, the program educates leaders for local, state, and federal governments and nonprofit organizations.

Operating support for the School of Government's programs and activities comes from many sources, including state appropriations, local government membership dues, private contributions, publication sales, course fees, and service contracts. Visit www.sog.unc.edu or call 919.966.5381 for more information on the School's courses, publications, programs, and services.

Printed in the United States of America

21 02 19 18 17 2 3 4 5 6

ISBN 978-1-56011-837-4

Contents

Preface

This is a new book about a relatively new topic: digital evidence. It's a topic of personal interest to me, perhaps because it allows me to count surfing the Internet for information about new technologies as "work." But it's also a topic of increasing importance to the criminal justice system. I am grateful to work at the School of Government, an institution that encourages faculty members to create new resources to address emerging legal issues that matter to the courts.

It's strange to write an old-fashioned paper book about a high-tech topic like digital evidence. However, recent surveys conducted by the School of Government suggest that our client groups still value this format for legal resources. Perhaps future editions will be available in electronic form.

Although my name is on the cover, this book was a team effort. It would not have been possible without the research assistance of Christopher Tyner, funded in part by an IBM faculty development grant. The book is much better as a result of the comments I received from my colleagues Bob Farb, Jessie Smith, Shea Denning, and Jamie Markham. The writing is clearer and the footnoting more complete thanks to the work of Melissa Twomey. More fundamentally, the book would not have existed at all were it not for the questions I have received over the years from officers, lawyers, and judges about various aspects of the law as it relates to digital evidence. Thanks to everyone who has contributed to this book, whether named above or not.

I have worked hard to make the book useful, but I am sure that it could be better. If you think that I have omitted an important topic, missed a significant case, erred in my analysis, or made other mistakes, please let me know so that future editions may benefit from your insight. I may be reached at (919) 843-8474 or by email at welty@sog.unc.edu.

Introduction

This is a book about digital evidence in criminal cases. It addresses how such evidence may be obtained and the rules that govern its introduction in court. As discussed below, it was written mainly for North Carolina judges, lawyers, and officers, though it may be of use to officials in other states as well.

I. Digital Evidence as an Emerging Issue

For years, courts and commentators have viewed digital evidence as an important emerging issue in criminal cases.[1] It has now emerged. Consider the following data:

- Courts across the country issued opinions in more than 1,500 criminal cases involving searches of digital devices in the past three years.[2] The volume of such decisions is up more than threefold from

1. *See, e.g.,* Orin S. Kerr, *Digital Evidence and the New Criminal Procedure,* 105 Colum. L. Rev. 279, 280 (2005) (arguing that "the use of computers in criminal activity has popularized a new form of evidence, digital evidence" and that "the new methods of collecting digital evidence should . . . lead to reforms in the law of criminal procedure"); U.S. Dep't of Justice, Crim. Div., Computer Crime & Intellectual Prop. Section, Searching and Seizing Computers and Obtaining Electronic Evidence in Criminal Investigations xii (3d ed. 2009), *available at* www.justice.gov/criminal/cybercrime/docs/ssmanual2009.pdf (hereinafter Searching and Seizing Computers) (stating that "[c]omputer crime investigations raise many novel issues"); Tara McGraw Swaminatha, *The Fourth Amendment Unplugged: Electronic Evidence Issues & Wireless Defenses,* 7 Yale J.L. & Tech. 51, 53 (2004–2005) (discussing "unsettled" law regarding "novel electronic evidence issues"); State v. Jones, 102 A.3d 694, 702 (Conn. 2014) (noting the "issues raised by the ever increasing prevalence of digital evidence").

2. The author submitted a Westlaw query for "search! /5 (computer cell! laptop!)" on February 3, 2015, and limited the results to state and federal criminal cases, resulting in 1,632 responsive cases.

a decade ago.[3] North Carolina has also seen an increase in such cases.[4]
- There has been an even sharper increase in the number of opinions in criminal cases that address GPS tracking. Westlaw contains just thirty-seven such opinions from the state and federal courts in 2004, while the database contains 702 such opinions from 2014, nearly a twenty-fold increase.[5] North Carolina has also seen an increase in GPS tracking cases.[6]
- Court opinions referring to the Stored Communications Act,[7] the principal federal statute regulating law enforcement access to email and other electronic communications, have also ballooned in number.[8]

These written opinions are just the tip of the iceberg. Most criminal cases, particularly in state court, do not result in any written orders—certainly none that are selected for inclusion in Westlaw. In cases large and small, courts are seeing more disputes about how the evidence rules apply to digital evidence, magistrates are seeing more search warrant applications targeting digital devices, and law enforcement officers are obtaining digital evidence more often. The *New York Times* reported that officers requested data from cell phone service providers more than a million times in 2012.[9]

This explosion in the collection of, and litigation over, digital evidence is a direct result of the ever-increasing role that digital devices play in our society. Criminals, crime victims, witnesses, and others use digital devices every day and leave digital trails that may contain critical evidence. More than 80 percent of American households, and more than 90 percent of

---

3. In 2004 there were only 174 such cases, while in 2014 there were 598.

4. In 2004, North Carolina's appellate courts issued five opinions in criminal cases matching the search criteria, while in 2014, there were eleven such opinions.

5. The author submitted a Westlaw query for "GPS" on February 3, 2015, and limited the results to state and federal criminal cases.

6. In 2004, North Carolina's appellate courts did not issue any opinions in criminal cases in which the term "GPS" was used. In 2014, the appellate division issued ten such opinions.

7. 18 U.S.C. §§ 2701 *et seq.*

8. The results of a Westlaw query revealed that in 2004 there were just three cases nationwide that contained the phrase "Stored Communications Act", while in 2014, there were 118 such cases.

9. Brian X. Chen, *A Senator Plans Legislation to Narrow Authorities' Cellphone Data Requests*, N.Y. Times (Dec. 9, 2013), www.nytimes.com/2013/12/09/technology/a-senator-plans-legislation-to-narrow-authorities-cellphone-data- requests.html.

households headed by younger adults, contain at least one computer, and a significant majority of Americans have Internet access at home.[10]

In some respects, though, computers are yesterday's technology. Almost all American adults have a cell phone, and among younger adults, almost all have a smartphone. These phones are used to do nearly everything that can be done on a computer, including sending and receiving emails, text messages, and photographs; engaging with social networks; and accessing the Internet.[11] In short, as the United States Supreme Court recently observed, "[c]ell phones have become important tools in facilitating coordination and communication among members of criminal enterprises, and can provide valuable incriminating information about dangerous criminals."[12]

Of course, it is not just computers and cell phones that have become important to criminal investigations and prosecutions. Websites, peer-to-peer networks, chat rooms, social media, email, text messaging, and a thousand other features of the digital landscape are also relevant.

II. Purpose and Structure of This Book

This book is a guide to the legal issues presented by the collection and introduction of digital evidence in criminal cases. It does not address civil cases and electronic discovery under the civil procedure rules.

Although there are other resources on the general topic of digital evidence, this book differs from existing works in important ways. For example, the Computer Crime and Intellectual Property Section of the Criminal Division of the United States Department of Justice wrote an influential early manuscript on searching digital devices.[13] The document is available online free of charge, but it was last updated in 2009, focuses exclusively on the federal courts, and is written strictly from a prosecutorial perspective. Professor Wayne LaFave's widely-used treatise on criminal procedure has been revised

---

10. Thom File & Camille Ryan, U.S. Census Bureau, Computer and Internet Use in the United States: 2013 (Nov. 2014), *available at* www.census.gov/content/dam/Census/library/publications/2014/acs/acs-28.pdf.

11. Pew Research Internet Project, *Mobile Technology Fact Sheet*, pewinternet.org (last visited Feb. 2, 2015), http://www.pewinternet.org/fact-sheets/mobile-technology-fact-sheet/.

12. Riley v. California, ___ U.S. ___, ___, 134 S. Ct. 2473, 2493 (2014).

13. *See* Searching and Seizing Computers, *supra* note 1.

to include material on digital searches and seizures,[14] but it is written for an academic audience and does not address the introduction of digital evidence under the evidence rules.

By contrast, this book is intended to address the full sweep of digital evidence issues that arise in criminal cases. Therefore, it covers both how digital evidence may be obtained and the rules that govern the admissibility of electronic evidence.

Furthermore, the book is intended to be more practical than theoretical. It is meant to be useful for three main audiences. First, law enforcement officers must make search and seizure decisions in the field, often under time pressure. This book should help them to do that. Second, lawyers need to raise and litigate issues concerning digital evidence. This book is intended to be a resource that provides valuable information to lawyers on both sides of criminal cases. Third, judges must rule on the issues that lawyers raise, and this book should help them as well.

Although the book is intended to be useful for multiple actors in the criminal justice system, in certain sections it naturally emphasizes certain roles. For example, much of the material about search warrant applications is directed principally to the officers who draft them. Of course, that same material may be of interest to a judge or a magistrate considering such an application, or to a prosecutor or a defense lawyer litigating the validity of a search warrant issued based upon such an application.

As to the organization of the book, it contains this introductory section and the following substantive chapters:

- Chapter 1, concerning search warrants for digital devices
- Chapter 2, concerning warrantless searches of digital devices
- Chapter 3, concerning law enforcement access to and interception of electronic communications, from phone calls to email and text messages
- Chapter 4, concerning GPS tracking
- Chapter 5, concerning the law of evidence and the introduction of digital evidence in criminal trials

The book also contains appendices, in which several frequently referenced statutes are reproduced:

- Appendix A, the Stored Communications Act

---

14. Wayne R. LaFave et al., Criminal Procedure (3d ed. 2007). Chapter 4 of the treatise, entitled "Network Surveillance," is an example of digital-specific material.

- Appendix B, North Carolina's wiretapping statutes
- Appendix C, North Carolina's pen register statutes

In many areas, especially where the law is unclear or still emerging, the book provides summaries of leading cases. The cases often reach different results, and this book usually describes the competing approaches without endorsing any of them. (There are a few exceptions, where the author believes that a particular approach is clearly misguided.) In some instances, virtually every case on an issue is summarized in the text, while for other issues, enough cases exist on a point of law that the book is necessarily selective. The book is generally current through the end of 2014.

III. Extent to Which This Book Focuses on North Carolina

This book is published by the UNC School of Government, where the author is a member of the faculty. The mission of the School is to "improve the lives of North Carolinians by engaging in practical scholarship that helps public officials and citizens understand and improve state and local government."[15] Because the School's mission is focused on North Carolina, this book has been written with North Carolina officials in mind. So, for example, the discussion of wiretapping in chapter 3 contains a close analysis of the North Carolina wiretapping statute. And North Carolina cases, where they exist, are given special attention.

However, there are many important issues concerning digital evidence on which there is not yet any North Carolina law, and on which North Carolina courts would be likely to look to out-of-state authorities for guidance. Furthermore, there are legal issues regarding digital evidence that are governed mainly by federal law, such as the Stored Communications Act. Therefore, this book analyzes many statutes, and cites and summarizes many cases, that are not from North Carolina. Because so many of the authorities cited in this book are not from North Carolina, the book may be of interest to some court actors from other jurisdictions, and of course, they are more than welcome to use it.

---

15. *See* UNC School of Government, *About the School: Mission and History,* http://www.sog.unc.edu/node/257.

Chapter 1: Search Warrants

This chapter addresses the use of search warrants to obtain digital evidence. It covers the need for a search warrant, issues relating to probable cause and particularity, the authority of various types of judicial officials to issue search warrants, and considerations in executing search warrants. Generally, the chapter focuses on search warrants for digital devices. Search warrants may also be used to obtain evidence from telecommunications service providers, and that topic is addressed in chapter 3.

I. Need for a Search Warrant

The Fourth Amendment to the United States Constitution protects individuals against unreasonable searches and seizures of their "persons, houses, papers, and effects."[1] A search within the meaning of the Fourth Amendment takes place "when an expectation of privacy that society is prepared to consider reasonable is infringed."[2] Courts have interpreted the Fourth Amendment to mean that searches are reasonable only when conducted pursuant to a search warrant, unless one of a "few specifically established and well-delineated exceptions" to the warrant requirement applies.[3] Because individuals have a reasonable expectation of privacy in the contents of their digital devices, such as cellular phones, tablets, and computers,[4] the Fourth Amendment requires a law enforcement officer to obtain a search warrant to search such a device unless an exception to the warrant requirement applies. Exceptions to the warrant requirement are discussed in chapter 2.

---

1. U.S. Const. amend. IV.
2. United States v. Jacobsen, 466 U.S. 109, 113 (1984).
3. Katz v. United States, 389 U.S. 347, 357 (1967).
4. In *Riley v. California*, 573 U.S. ___, 134 S. Ct. 2473 (2014), the U.S. Supreme Court ruled that a search warrant was necessary to search the cell phone of an arrestee, a ruling that makes sense only if there is a reasonable expectation of privacy in digital devices. Although *Riley* involved cell phones, the Court's reasoning clearly applies to other types of digital devices. Indeed, the Court once referred to cell phones as "minicomputers that also happen to have the capacity to be used as a telephone." *Id.* at 2489.

II. Probable Cause

A. Generally

In order to obtain a search warrant, an officer must present a judicial official with *probable cause*, which the United States Supreme Court has defined as a "fair probability that contraband or evidence of a crime will be found in a particular place."[5] This standard applies to search warrants for digital devices as it does to other search warrants. However, the application of the standard to digital devices raises a number of recurrent issues, discussed below. Because the North Carolina appellate courts have decided just a handful of cases involving probable cause, search warrants, and digital devices,[6] the discussion relies heavily on out-of-state cases, especially those from the federal appellate courts.

Probable cause to believe that a suspect committed a crime does not always provide probable cause to search the suspect's digital devices. Several years ago, the North Carolina Court of Appeals ruled that although there was probable cause to search a defendant's residence for evidence of a homicide, there was not probable cause to search any computers at the residence because "[t]he [search warrant] affidavit does not include any indication . . . that would suggest a search of defendant's computer would lead to information regarding the . . . homicide."[7]

However, more and more human activity is being conducted through, or documented on, digital devices, making it increasingly reasonable to believe that evidence of a crime will be found on a suspect's digital devices. In *United States v. Doe*,[8] a federal district court case from North Carolina, an officer seeking a warrant to search a defendant's cellular phone for evidence of gun and theft offenses stated in the application that "individuals often take pictures, videos, send text messages, and [make] other uses of

---

5. Illinois v. Gates, 462 U.S. 213, 238 (1983).

6. *See, e.g.*, State v. Dexter, 186 N.C. App. 587 (2007) (finding ample probable cause based on defendant's girlfriend's report that defendant received "child porn" on the computer; his membership in a website called lolitateens.com; and his history of sex crimes); State v. Peterson, 179 N.C. App. 437 (2006) (finding probable cause to search defendant's house in connection with a homicide, but not his computer), *aff'd*, 361 N.C. 587 (2007); State v. Pickard, 178 N.C. App. 330 (2006) (finding probable cause to search defendant's home for digital media based on multiple reports of defendant's sexual abuse of children while recording his activities).

7. State v. Peterson, 179 N.C. App. 437, 449 (2006), *aff'd*, 361 N.C. 587 (2007).

8. No. 1:12-CR-00128-MR-DLH, 2013 WL 4212400 (W.D.N.C. Aug. 14, 2013).

digital media which will implicate or document the crimes in which they take part."[9] Ruling on a subsequent motion to suppress, the court agreed:

> [G]iven the plethora of offenses the [defendant and others] allegedly committed . . . it is not an imaginary stretch to believe that the Defendant's cell phone might contain incriminating evidence in image form, [such] as photographs or movies, documenting the [unlawfully possessed] firearm or the stolen property. . . . Similarly, the evidence presented provided . . . probable cause to believe that the Defendant's phone might contain incriminating evidence in written form, [such] as texts or emails, documenting correspondence between the Defendant and others . . . offering for sale the gun or the stolen property. . . .[10]
>
> . . . .
>
> With the popularity of social media sites like Twitter, Facebook, and Instagram, together with cell phones' capability to send text messages and pictures, common sense would lead a practical person to conclude that human behavior includes the making of [self-portraits that may include criminal activity].[11]

One lesson from *Doe* is that when an officer seeks a search warrant for electronic devices in connection with a crime that is not necessarily computer-related, it may be helpful to set forth the officer's past experience with finding evidence on digital devices.

It is also important to keep in mind the type of crime at issue. Certain types of offenses may be so likely to be facilitated by electronic devices that probable cause to believe that a defendant committed those crimes will nearly always provide probable cause to search the defendant's digital devices. For example, drug dealers very often use cell phones, and Medicare fraud is almost certain to involve computerized billing systems. By contrast, other types of crimes may often occur with little or no digital trail. For example, searching a defendant's computer for evidence of an assault that took place in a nightclub likely will require a specific showing that the computer contains such evidence.[12]

---

9. 2013 WL 4212400, at *3.

10. 2013 WL 4212400, at *7.

11. 2013 WL 4212400, at *8.

12. *Cf.* United States v. Hunter, 13 F. Supp. 2d 574 (D. Vt. 1998) (in a money laundering investigation, it was proper for a search warrant to authorize the search of a suspect's computers although nothing in the warrant application

A related issue concerns whether a showing of probable cause extends to all of a suspect's digital devices or only to some. Because digital files are easily transferred among devices, probable cause to support a search of one of a suspect's devices often will provide probable cause to search the suspect's other devices as well.[13] An officer seeking authority to search all of a suspect's digital devices should explain the transferability of digital evidence in the warrant application.

B. Child Pornography Cases

Child pornography cases present several unique issues concerning probable cause. Because such a large proportion of search warrants issued for electronic devices are obtained in child pornography cases, those issues are considered in some detail below.

1. Describing/Identifying Child Pornography

Sometimes a search warrant application will state that the applicant or another witness saw "child pornography" or "pictures of nude children" on a suspect's computer. Sometimes the application will contain a detailed description of an image or will refer to the *hash value*[14] of a known child

---

showed that the records the police sought were specifically likely to be stored on computer; most business records and documents are stored that way).

13. *See, e.g.*, United States v. Summage, 481 F.3d 1075, 1077 (8th Cir. 2007) (police suspected that the defendant had paid a mentally disabled man to engage in a sex act with a woman, and had videotaped and photographed the encounter; officers obtained a warrant for "[a]ll video tapes and DVD[]s . . . [a]ll video and/or digital recording devices and equipment . . . [and] computer(s)"; officers found child pornography during the search; the court held that there was probable cause to believe that the video and photographs would be stored digitally, that the officer had no way to know the format or device in which the video and photographs would be found, and that it was therefore reasonable to believe that the video and photographs might be present in any of the digital media). *But cf.* United States v. Hill, 459 F.3d 966, 968 (9th Cir. 2006) (after computer repair technician reported finding child pornography on defendant's computer, police obtained warrant for, inter alia, "all storage media belonging to either the computer or the individual identifying himself as defendant" at defendant's home; defendant argued that the warrant was overbroad, i.e., that it authorized the seizure of items for which there was no probable cause; the court agreed, holding that blanket seizures of all computer-related items in a particular place will often be justified because there is no way to know where a specific file or image is located, but that the affiant must say as much, and since the affiant did not do so here, the warrant was overbroad). The material in section III.A of this chapter concerning descriptions of the property to be searched is also relevant to this discussion.

14. "A 'hash value' [sometimes called an "SHA1 value"] is an alphanumeric string that serves to identify an individual digital file as a kind of 'digital

pornography file. In some cases, an image may be attached to the application and filed under seal. How much detail is required before a judicial official may find probable cause to believe that an image possessed or viewed by a suspect contains child pornography?

Courts have not agreed completely on this issue. It is clearly sufficient to (1) attach an image to the application under seal or (2) provide a detailed description of what the image contains—e.g., "the image shows a naked prepubescent female who appears to be approximately eight years old performing oral sex on an adult male."[15] Identifying a known child pornography image by its hash value, when possible, is also likely sufficient.

Conclusory statements that an image "is child pornography" are questionable. Such statements arguably do not provide the basic facts that a judicial official needs to make an independent determination of probable cause. Finally, descriptions that refer to child nudity but fail to establish that the nudity is sexual in nature clearly are inadequate, by themselves, to provide probable cause. They could as easily refer to an innocent bathtub picture as to child pornography.

Case Summaries on Describing/Identifying Child Pornography

DESCRIPTION/IDENTIFICATION SUFFICIENT

State v. Letoile, 94 A.3d 851, 855 (N.H. 2014) (a search warrant for the defendant's computer was supported by probable cause when it was based on his ex-wife's statement that the computer contained links to "pornographic websites . . . [that] had images of adult males engaging in genital contact with minor females . . . [or] depicted minor females engaged in sexual acts with each other").

United States v. Miknevich, 638 F.3d 178, 183, 184 (3d Cir. 2011) (finding probable cause even though "the state magistrate was presented with an affidavit that provided no factual details regarding the substance of the images in question"; although the "better practice for an applicant seeking a warrant based on images of alleged child pornography [is] to append the images or to provide a description of the images," probable cause was established here based on the descriptive

---

fingerprint.'" United States v. Wellman, 663 F.3d 224, 226 n.2 (4th Cir. 2011).

15. The U.S. Supreme Court ruled that a detailed description of the contents of pornographic movies was sufficient to establish probable cause for violations of obscenity laws in *New York v. P.J. Video, Inc.*, 475 U.S. 868, 876 (1986) (affidavits provided "more than enough information" to make it "clear beyond peradventure that the warrant was supported by probable cause to believe that the five films at issue were obscene under New York law").

and explicit file name listed in the application, as well as on the file's hash value).

United States v. Wellman, 663 F.3d 224, 228 (4th Cir. 2011) (not reaching the question of whether a search warrant which neither described nor provided an example of child pornography allegedly possessed by defendant was supported by probable cause and instead assuming that, even if the warrant was deficient, officers acted in good faith; the court did, however, state that it "decline[d] to impose a requirement that a search warrant application involving child pornography must include an image of the alleged pornography").

United States v. Cartier, 543 F.3d 442 (8th Cir. 2008) (warrant application contained probable cause where it identified an image as child pornography based on its hash value).

United States v. Battershell, 457 F.3d 1048, 1051, 1053 (9th Cir. 2006) (defendant's girlfriend showed a police officer several pictures she had found on defendant's computer; the officer then applied for a warrant to search the computer for child pornography; he did not attach the images but described them as showing "a young female (8-10 YOA) naked in a bathtub" and "another young female having sexual intercourse with an adult male"; the reviewing court found that the former description was insufficient to show probable cause that the computer contained child pornography, as opposed to, say, a family photograph, but that the latter was sufficient, especially combined with the girlfriend's statement that the computer had pictures of "kids having sex"; although it "would have been preferable if the affiant in this case had included copies of the photographs in the warrant application," an officer's failure "to include a photograph in a warrant application is not fatal to establishing probable cause").

Ferrick v. State, 217 P.3d 418, 422 (Alaska Ct. App. 2009) (a search warrant application stated that "a particular folder on the [defendant's] computer contained several images of naked young children . . . well under puberty. One of the images depicted a girl with her legs spread . . . and this image was labeled 'Fill me up' . . . . [while] [t]he other two images were pictures of naked boys with their penises displayed"; this description, albeit not totally ruling out the possibility that the images were artistic or were not of real children, was adequate to provide probable cause).

United States v. Simpson, 152 F.3d 1241 (10th Cir. 1998) (warrant application established probable cause to believe that the defendant's computer would contain child pornography despite failure to attach or describe images, where the defendant had engaged in online "chat" with undercover officer and had offered to supply computer disks with images of pre-pubescent children engaged in sexual activity).

DESCRIPTION/IDENTIFICATION INSUFFICIENT

United States v. Pavulak, 700 F.3d 651, 661 (3d Cir. 2012) (a warrant was not supported by probable cause even though, among other facts, investigators stated that they had seen defendant "viewing child pornography"; the term "child pornography" was conclusory and "does not present any facts from which the magistrate could discern . . . that what is depicted in the images meets the statutory definition of child pornography and complies with constitutional limits . . . the most the magistrate could infer was that *the affiant* concluded that the images constitute child pornography").

United States v. Krupa, 658 F.3d 1174, 1178 (9th Cir. 2011) (a search warrant application stated that an officer began searching a computer pursuant to the defendant's consent and saw "an image of suspected contraband," namely, an image that "appeared to be . . . of a nude 15 to 17 year old female with a web site label of *www.nude-teens.com*"; this description "did not necessarily support the conclusion that the photograph constituted child pornography"; however, the affidavit still provided probable cause for a search warrant for child pornography based on the additional facts that the applicant "set forth his qualifications as a trained investigator of computers for computer crimes and child pornography" and that an officer obtained the computers when he responded to a report of child neglect at the defendant's residence and found the defendant in a home with fifteen computers and two children who were not his own).

United States v. Doyle, 650 F.3d 460, 473 (4th Cir. 2011) (warrant application lacked probable cause to support a search for child pornography where it indicated that three children reported being sexually assaulted by the defendant at his home and that one reported being shown "pictures of nude children"; "nothing in the affidavit support[ed] a belief that the alleged pictures" constituted child pornography, as "[t]he mere presence of nudity in a photograph, even child nudity, does not constitute child pornography").

United States v. Brunette, 256 F.3d 14, 18 (1st Cir. 2001) (an officer determined that the defendant had posted several images online; the officer applied for a search warrant for the defendant's computer, describing the images only as "a prepubescent boy lasciviously displaying his genitals," parroting the language of 18 U.S.C. § 2256(2)(E), which defines such genital displays as child pornography; the reviewing court held that the description was conclusory and failed to provide probable cause; generally, "[a] judge cannot . . . make this determination without either a look at the allegedly pornographic images, or at least an assessment based on a detailed, factual description of them").

2. Staleness

When an officer applies for a search warrant, the judicial official must consider whether the information is recent enough to provide probable cause or whether it has become outdated, or "stale." Many courts have recognized that staleness is a less serious concern in child pornography cases than in other cases, as people who obtain child pornography tend to retain it, and as child pornography is often stored digitally and digital materials are easily retained for long periods of time. Thus, information that is months or even years old may be sufficient to provide probable cause. Officers preparing search warrant applications in child pornography cases should consider including a discussion of offenders' propensity to hoard or collect child pornography over time.[16]

Case Summaries on Staleness/Child Pornography

INFORMATION STALE

United States v. Doyle, 650 F.3d 460, 474 (4th Cir. 2011) (although staleness is rare in child pornography cases, where there was a "complete absence of any indication as to when the pictures were possessed," a search warrant application was stale).

United States v. Greathouse, 297 F. Supp. 2d 1264 (D. Or. 2003) (evidence that, thirteen months prior to the issuance of a search warrant, the defendant shared child pornography from his computer with other people over the internet was stale; there was no evidence of more recent, or ongoing, criminal activity; no evidence that the defendant

---

16. For a general discussion of staleness in computer search cases, see U.S. Dep't of Justice, Computer Crime & Intellectual Prop. Section, Searching & Seizing Computers & Obtaining Electronic Evidence in Criminal Investigations 68 (3d ed. 2009) (hereinafter Searching & Seizing Computers), *available at* www.justice.gov/criminal/cybercrime/docs/ssmanual2009.pdf.

was a pedophile and so especially likely to hoard such material; and computer technology evolves quickly, so that whole hard drives become obsolete or are replaced frequently; the court also noted that the government presented no empirical evidence that people who obtain child pornography are prone to keep it for protracted periods).

United States v. Zimmerman, 277 F.3d 426 (3d Cir. 2002) (police suspected that the defendant had showed a single adult pornography video to minors six, ten, or more months earlier; officers applied for and obtained a search warrant authorizing a search of the defendant's computers for child and adult pornography; the Third Circuit ruled that there was nothing at all to support a search for child pornography and that, as to adult pornography, the evidence was stale; there was no reason to believe that the defendant would have kept the video for a long period of time, since unlike child pornography, it was presumably legal and easy to obtain; the court also expressed doubt about the utility of boilerplate affidavits about the tendency of pedophiles to hoard child pornography absent some knowledge of the specific defendant and case).

INFORMATION NOT STALE

State v. Rayfield, ___ N.C. App. ___, ___, 752 S.E.2d 745, 753 (2014) (finding that the information supporting a search warrant application was not stale even though a key piece of evidence was a victim's statement that the defendant had showed her images of himself having sex with a 10-year-old girl several years before the search warrant application was submitted; the court stated that "the items sought by the search warrant—magazines, videos, computers, cell phones, hard drives, gaming systems, MP3 players, a camera, a video recorder, thumb drives, and other pictures or documents—were not incriminating in and of themselves and were of enduring utility to Defendant").

State v. Valley, 755 F.3d 581, 586 (7th Cir. 2014) (search warrant based on evidence that the defendant had downloaded child pornography eight months earlier was not stale; the application stated that "in 'almost every instance' when multiple months separate discovery of child pornography and issuance of a warrant, the images remain on the computer").

United States v. Carroll, 750 F.3d 700, 704 (7th Cir. 2014) (search warrant based on evidence that the defendant had child pornography on his digital devices five years earlier was not stale where the "affidavit made clear that [the investigating officer] had learned through training and experience that collectors of child pornography hoard their images for long periods of time because of the great personal value the images have for sexual gratification, the difficulty in obtaining the images as a result of their illegality, and their value to other collectors such that the images may be traded for new images").

United States v. Robinson, 741 F.3d 588, 597 (5th Cir. 2014) (search warrant based on evidence that the defendant had child pornography on his computer two years earlier was not stale, in part because "evidence of child pornography often is found in the secrecy of a defendant's home and the criminal activity is carried out over a long period").

United States v. Seiver, 692 F.3d 774, 778 (7th Cir. 2012) (reviewing relevant cases and finding that a seven-month delay between defendant uploading child pornography to the internet and submission of an application for a search warrant did not render the information supporting the warrant stale; stating that "[t]he most important thing to keep in mind for future cases is the need to ground inquiries into 'staleness' and 'collectors' in a realistic understanding of modern computer technology and the usual behavior of its users" and concluding that "[o]nly in the exceptional case should a warrant to search a computer for child pornography be denied on [staleness] grounds").

United States v. Richardson, 607 F.3d 357 (4th Cir. 2010) (a four-month delay between the defendant's sending of an email containing child pornography and an officer's application for a search warrant did not render supporting information stale; there is a "consensus" that collectors of child pornography tend to retain it for long periods of time).

United States v. Burkhart, 602 F.3d 1202, 1206 (10th Cir. 2010) (information supporting a warrant application was not stale despite the fact that "two years and four months had passed since . . . the date of the most recent email between the Italian child porn distributor and [an email address associated with defendant]"; the court stated that defendant was "charged with *possession* of child pornography, not acquiring it," so his "offense did not cease with his last purchase, but continued as long as he possessed the videos").

United States v. Vosburgh, 602 F.3d 512, 529 (3d Cir. 2010) (information not stale after lapse of four months; information regarding child pornography crimes "has a relatively long shelf life").

United States v. Morales-Aldahondo, 524 F.3d 115, 119 (1st Cir. 2008) (the "passage of more than three years from the acquisition of the evidence until the warrant application" did not render evidence supporting the warrant stale because "customers of child pornography sites do not quickly dispose of their cache").

United States v. Allen, 625 F.3d 830 (5th Cir. 2010) (evidence of possession of child pornography that was eighteen months old was not stale where officer's affidavit asserted (a) that people who possess child pornography tend to maintain their collections over time and (b) that deleted files can often be recovered much later).

United States v. Potts, 586 F.3d 823 (10th Cir. 2009) (evidence that defendant possessed child pornography ten months prior to the issuance of the warrant was not stale because (a) the defendant vaguely acknowledged a continued interest in child pornography just before the warrant issued and (b) the court found that collectors of child pornography tend to hoard it).

United States v. Frechette, 583 F.3d 374 (6th Cir. 2009) (evidence that defendant subscribed to a child pornography website fifteen months prior to the issuance of a search warrant was not stale and provided probable cause).

State v. Pickard, 178 N.C. App. 330, 336 (2006) (information contained in an application seeking a warrant to search "computers, computer equipment and accessories, cassette videos or DVDs, video cameras, digital cameras, [and] film cameras and accessories" was not stale despite the fact that some information was eighteen to nineteen months old and other information did not have a specific time reference; because the items sought were "of enduring utility" to the defendant, who was creating child pornography, there was no reason to think that the defendant would have disposed of them).

United States v. Riccardi, 405 F.3d 852, 861 (10th Cir. 2005) (internal quotation marks, citation omitted) ("Since the materials are illegal to distribute and possess, initial collection is difficult. Having succeeded in obtaining images, collectors are unlikely to destroy them.").

3. Visits/Subscriptions to Child Pornography Websites

Several courts have considered whether the fact that a suspect has visited, or has subscribed to, a child pornography website is sufficient to provide probable cause. While courts have ruled uniformly that joining or subscribing to a website or internet group focused on child pornography is sufficient, the mere fact that a suspect has visited a public website related to child pornography is less conclusive. Determining probable cause in such a case may require a careful analysis of the content visible or available on the portions of the website that are likely to be encountered by members of the public.[17] To the extent possible, officers applying for a search warrant in such a case should provide detailed information about the specific pages visited by the suspect. The duration of the suspect's visit, if known, may also be relevant, as it may bear on whether the visit was inadvertent or intentional.

Case Summaries on Visits/Subscriptions to Child Pornography Websites

SUFFICIENT PROBABLE CAUSE

State v. Letoile, 94 A.3d 851, 855, 856 (N.H. 2014) (a search warrant for the defendant's computer was supported by probable cause when it was based on his ex-wife's statement that the computer contained links to "pornographic websites . . . [that] had images of adult males engaging in genital contact with minor females . . . [or] depicted minor females engaged in sexual acts with each other"; although the defendant argued that "evidence of a visit to a website cannot support the conclusion that child pornography was downloaded on a computer," the court ruled that the mere possibility that the content of the website changed between the time the defendant visited it and when his ex-wife visited it, or the mere possibility that he downloaded nothing from the website, were not sufficiently likely to defeat probable cause).

United States v. Clayton, 68 M.J. 419, 425 (C.A.A.F. 2010) (defendant belonged to a Google group entitled "Preteen–Bestiality–and–Anything–Taboo," which was used to exchange child pornography; although there was "no evidence . . . that he posted messages to the Google site, participated in discussions, or uploaded or downloaded child pornography," nor any indication "how long he belonged to the group, how often he accessed the website, or whether he received the digests he requested," the defendant's membership in the group was sufficient to provide probable cause).

United States v. Frechette, 583 F.3d 374, 381 (6th Cir. 2009) (probable cause existed to support a search warrant because common sense dictated that it was "not likely that the defendant [was] someone who was innocently surfing the internet and accidentally paid $79.95 for a

---

17. *See generally* SEARCHING & SEIZING COMPUTERS, *supra* note 16, at 67.

subscription to [a child pornography] website" and who then did not use the subscription).

United States v. Gourde, 440 F.3d 1065, 1068, 1070 (9th Cir. 2006) (en banc) (internal quotation marks omitted) (a search warrant application established probable cause where it stated that the defendant joined and paid for access to a website that "advertised pictures of young girls" and provided images of young girls engaged in sexually explicit conduct; the defendant remained a member of the site for more than two months, and any time he visited the website he had to have seen images of "naked prepubescent females with a caption that described them as twelve to seventeen-year-old girls"; his "status as a member manifested his intention and desire to obtain illegal images"; there was probable cause even though the site offered some legal content, including adult pornography, and even though the affidavit did not describe specific images in a way that identified them as child pornography).

United States v. Wagers, 452 F.3d 534, 540 (6th Cir. 2006) (a checking card with a billing address linked to the defendant's office was used to purchase subscriptions to illegal pornography websites; this provided probable cause to search the defendant's home; "evidence that a person has visited or subscribed to websites containing child pornography supports the conclusion that he has likely downloaded, kept, and otherwise possessed the material").

United States v. Froman, 355 F.3d 882, 891 (5th Cir. 2004) (the fact of defendant's voluntary membership in an online "e-group" that had the "predominant purpose . . . to engage in collection and distribution of child pornography," combined with the fact that defendant's registered email addresses contained terms indicative of his specific interest in child pornography, provided probable cause for a search warrant).

United States v. Martin, 426 F.3d 68, 75 (2d Cir. 2005) (the majority had "no difficulty" concluding that an affidavit provided probable cause where it included evidence that an occupant of defendant's house was a member of an online group whose "primary reason for existence, was the trading and collection of child pornography").

INSUFFICIENT PROBABLE CAUSE

United States v. Falso, 544 F.3d 110, 121 (2d Cir. 2008) (there was evidence that the defendant may have "'gained access or attempted to gain access' to the non-member" portion of a child pornography website, but he was not a subscriber and there was no indication of the accessibility of the few images of child pornography available on the non-member portion of the site; the "[affiant's] inconclusive statements about whether [the defendant] even accessed the . . . website, coupled with the absence of details about the features and nature of the non-member site, falls short of establishing probable cause").

4. Sexual Misconduct

When an officer has evidence that a suspect has engaged in, or has attempted to engage in, sexual misconduct, especially with children, the officer may wish to search the suspect's computer and other electronic devices for child pornography. The courts have divided regarding whether evidence of actual or attempted sexual misconduct is alone sufficient to establish probable cause to believe that the suspect possesses child pornography. (Clearly it is a factor that may be considered together with other evidence.) If an officer's experience or training suggests a nexus between sexual misconduct and the possession of child pornography, that information should be included in the officer's affidavit.

Case Summaries on Sexual Misconduct

SUFFICIENT PROBABLE CAUSE

United States v. Clark, 668 F.3d 934, 937 (7th Cir. 2012) (search warrant application alleged that the defendant sexually assaulted his niece, made advances on other children, and showed a child some pornography on a computer; it also asserted that individuals who commit "sex offenses involving minors will often collect and/or view images on the computer"; this provided probable cause that the defendant possessed child pornography).

United States v. Colbert, 605 F.3d 573, 578 (8th Cir. 2010) (defendant approached a 5-year-old at a park and attempted to entice her to his home; this provided probable cause to search his home for evidence of child pornography because "[t]here is an intuitive relationship between acts such as child molestation or enticement and possession of child pornography").

United States v. Kapordelis, 569 F.3d 1291, 1311–12, 1312 (11th Cir. 2009) (an affidavit provided probable cause for the search of the defendant's home where it provided a reasonable basis for a magistrate to conclude that "Defendant could be engaged in sex tourism and that Defendant would reasonably keep evidence of such activities, including sexually explicit images of children, in his home, a place where one might ordinarily orchestrate travel, keep information about one's travel, and make plans for activities—whether legal or illegal—while on a trip"; the court further stated that common sense established a nexus between "Defendant's travel to Russia, the facts which suggested that he met and engaged in sexual activity with young boys and the assertion that evidence of sex tourism and child pornography would be found in Defendant's home").

United States v. Paton, 535 F.3d 829, 836 (8th Cir. 2008) (suspicion that the defendant was involved in the sexual exploitation of children was first raised when the defendant was found in the woods at a park with a group of boys and a digital camera, and was reinforced when two of the boys indicated that the defendant had been taking nude photographs of them in secluded locations over a two-year period; there was a sufficient nexus between the defendant's home, digital media, and child pornography because "just as law enforcement officers would expect to find tools of the drug trade . . . in the residence of a suspected drug trafficker, investigators expect to find computer systems and Internet access, among other things, in the home of an individual who is known to get sexual gratification from children").

INSUFFICIENT PROBABLE CAUSE

United States v. Needham, 718 F.3d 1190, 1195 (9th Cir. 2013) (the defendant, a registered sex offender, touched the penis of a 5-year-old boy in a public bathroom; officers obtained a warrant to search the defendant's home, including his digital devices, for child pornography, based on his "unnatural sexual interest in children"; the court ruled that "the bare inference that those who molest children are likely to possess child pornography . . . does not establish probable cause to search a suspected child molester's home for child pornography"; however, the court applied the federal good faith exception to the exclusionary rule).

United States v. Galpin, 720 F.3d 436, 448 (2d Cir. 2013) (a warrant was facially overbroad and violated the Fourth Amendment where "[t]he only crime that [was] specified in the warrant . . . [was a] registration offense" yet the warrant "nonetheless authorized a search for images depicting child sexual activity").

United States v. Doyle, 650 F.3d 460, 472 (4th Cir. 2011) (stating that "evidence of child molestation alone does not support probable cause to search for child pornography," even where the abuse is alleged to have taken place in the suspect's home).

United States v. Hodson, 543 F.3d 286, 292 (6th Cir. 2008) (during an online chat with an officer posing as a young boy, the defendant admitted molesting his nephew; based on this acknowledgment, an officer obtained a search warrant to search the defendant's home for child pornography; the court ruled that the warrant "was defective for lack of probable cause—[it] established probable cause for one crime (child molestation) but designed and requested a search for evidence of an entirely different crime (child pornography)").

C. Based on IP Address

Another recurrent issue in computer search cases is whether there is probable cause when an officer determines that a computer at a particular IP address[18] is involved in criminal activity and obtains subscriber records from an internet service provider that tie the IP address to a physical address. Generally, courts have ruled that this is sufficient to establish probable cause to search the digital devices located at that physical address, even when it is not possible to rule out the possibility that the subscriber could have had an unsecured wireless network and that a neighbor or passer-by could have used the network to commit the criminal activity in question.[19]

---

18. "[A]n IP address, also sometimes referred to as [an] Internet Protocol address, is a unique number identifying the location of an end-user's computer. When an end-user logs onto [an] internet service provider, they are assigned a unique IP number that will be used for that entire . . . session." United States v. Hamilton, 413 F.3d 1138, 1141 n.2 (10th Cir. 2005).

19. When a wireless router is used to connect to the internet, it is the router itself that is assigned an IP address, and all the devices connected to the router share that address. Chris Hoffman, *How and Why All Devices in Your Home Share One IP Address*, How-To Geek (Apr. 15, 2013), www.howtogeek.com/148664/how-and-why-all-devices-in-your-home-share-one-ip-address/. Thus, when criminal activity is linked to an IP address but the IP address is assigned to an unsecured wireless router, a defendant may argue that there is no way to know whether the criminal activity was conducted by an occupant of the residence where the router is located or by someone else using the network. As noted in the text, courts have generally rejected this argument. *See, e.g.*, United States v. Schesso, 730 F.3d 1040 (9th Cir. 2013) (a warrant was supported by probable cause where it was based on an affidavit indicating that defendant's IP address had shared a child pornography video over a peer-to-peer network for a four-hour time period); United States v. Vosburgh, 602 F.3d 512, 526 (3d Cir. 2010) ("[E]vidence that the user of a computer employing a particular IP address possessed or transmitted child pornography can support a search warrant for the physical premises linked to that IP address."); United States v. Perez,

III. Particularity

The Fourth Amendment requires that search warrants "particularly describ[e] the place to be searched, and the persons or things to be seized."[20] The North Carolina Constitution contains similar language.[21] The particularity requirement can be broken into two aspects: particularity concerning the place to be searched and particularity concerning the items to be seized. The following sections will consider each aspect.

A. Describing the Place to Be Searched

A search warrant must specifically describe the place to be searched. This prevents a search warrant from becoming a general warrant.[22] The description must be such that "the executing officer [can] locate and identify the [place to be searched] with reasonable effort" and there is no realistic likelihood of a mistaken search of the wrong place.[23]

In cases involving digital devices, the "place to be searched" may be a single item of personal property, such as a suspect's computer or cellular phone. This is especially true when the device has already been seized. In such a

---

484 F.3d 735, 740 (5th Cir. 2007) (though use of an unsecured wireless connection would make it possible for a transmission of child pornography to have originated from outside of defendant's residence, the court rejected defendant's argument that "the association of an IP address with a physical address does not give rise to probable cause to search that [physical] address"); United States v. Thomas, No. 5:12-cr-37, 2012 WL 4892850, at *4 (D. Vt. Oct. 15, 2012) (unpublished) ("[C]ourts have generally concluded that the mere possibility that an IP address may be associated with an unsecure wireless network does not affect the probable cause determination."). *See generally* SEARCHING & SEIZING COMPUTERS, supra note 16, at 65 (discussing this issue and collecting cases).

20. U.S. CONST. amend. IV.

21. "General warrants, whereby any officer or other person may be commanded to search suspected places without evidence of the act committed, or to seize any person or persons not named, whose offense is not particularly described and supported by evidence, are dangerous to liberty and shall not be granted." N.C. CONST. art. I, § 20.

22. Maryland v. Garrison, 480 U.S. 79, 84 (1987) ("The manifest purpose of this particularity requirement was to prevent general searches. By limiting the authorization to search to the specific areas and things for which there is probable cause to search, the requirement ensures that the search will be carefully tailored to its justifications, and will not take on the character of the wide-ranging exploratory searches the Framers intended to prohibit.").

23. United States v. Gitcho, 601 F.2d 369, 371 (8th Cir. 1979). *See also* United States v. Howard, 621 F.3d 433 (6th Cir. 2010) (providing an almost identical formulation); United States v. Johnson, 437 F.3d 69 (D.C. Cir. 2006) (same, and collecting cases).

case, law enforcement usually may identify the item by its serial number or a similar descriptor, which is plainly sufficient to satisfy the particularity requirement.

Often, however, law enforcement may have reason to believe that a suspect will have evidence on his or her digital devices but will not know what specific devices the suspect possesses. As noted above, because data are easily transferred among digital devices, when there is probable cause to search any of a suspect's devices, there often will be probable cause to search all of them.[24] Therefore, courts generally have upheld descriptions of devices by ownership, e.g., "all computers and digital media in the possession of Frank Smith."

The most commonly litigated issue regarding the description of the place to be searched is whether a description of a physical location, such as a suspect's home or office, is sufficient to authorize a search of digital devices located therein even without a specific reference to digital devices in the application. Several courts have ruled that such a warrant is adequate when the evidence in question might be stored on a digital device, because a warrant authorizing the search of a particular location for a particular item generally authorizes the search of any container at the location that might reasonably house the evidence sought, and digital devices are containers for information.[25] So, for example, a warrant authorizing the search of a home for records of drug sales, lists of drug customers, and the like would allow the search of any drawer or box within the home in which the records could reasonably be found *and* the search of any computer or cell phone that could contain such records.[26]

---

24. See *supra* note 13 and accompanying text.

25. 2 Wayne R. LaFave, Search and Seizure § 4.10(b) (5th ed. 2012). *Cf.* United States v. Ross, 456 U.S. 798 (1982) (expressing a similar rule as to warrantless vehicle searches).

26. *See, e.g.*, State v. Gurule, 303 P.3d 838 (N.M. 2013) (because a digital camera was a potential "container" for child pornography images, a search warrant authorizing the search of a suspect's home for such images supported the seizure and search of the camera; there was no need for an officer to seek a second search warrant); United States v. Giberson, 527 F.3d 882 (9th Cir. 2008) (holding that a search warrant authorizing a search for "documents," without mentioning computers or electronic storage, allowed police to search a computer, as documents may be found in computers and there was "ample evidence" suggesting that the target documents could be found on the particular computer).

However, a few courts have suggested that digital devices are different and normally may be searched only if specifically permitted by the warrant.[27] This view may have been bolstered somewhat by the U.S. Supreme Court's statement in *Riley v. California*[28] that "[t]reating a cell phone as a container whose contents may be searched incident to an arrest is a bit strained as an initial matter." The Court did not spell out exactly how it viewed the data stored on digital devices, but the brief reference in *Riley* is at least reason to question the validity of the view that digital devices are information containers. Therefore, a cautious officer who anticipates needing to examine digital devices may wish to note that fact in the application and to provide for it in the proposed warrant. If the officer does not include computer-specific language in the application and warrant but encounters digital devices while executing the warrant, it may in some instances make sense to secure the devices but obtain an additional warrant before searching them.

Finally, officers frequently will want to search deleted files, slack space, metadata, and other nooks and crannies of an electronic device. While perhaps not legally necessary, it may be advisable to explain in the application that relevant data may be located in such spaces and to have the warrant expressly authorize the examination of those areas.

Case Summaries on Describing the Place to Be Searched

DESCRIPTION SUFFICIENT

State v. Gurule, 303 P.3d 838 (N.M. 2013) (because a digital camera was a potential "container" for child pornography images, a search warrant authorizing the search of a suspect's home for such images supported the seizure and search of the camera; there was no need for an officer to seek a second search warrant).

United States v. Brobst, 558 F.3d 982, 994 (9th Cir. 2009) (a warrant authorizing the seizure of "computers, compact disks, floppy disks, hard drives, memory cards, printers, and other portable digital devices, DVDs, and video tapes" described the items to be seized in sufficiently narrow terms, where investigators had been informed by a third party that the third party had discovered, in the defendant's home, a printed photograph depicting child pornography which appeared to have origi-

---

27. United States v. Payton, 573 F.3d 859 (9th Cir. 2009) (suggesting that computer-specific language normally is required before digital devices may be searched pursuant to a warrant; distinguishing *Giberson* and noting that "bare capability" of computers to hold documents is normally insufficient standing alone to justify search of computer absent explicit authorization).

28. ___ U.S. ___, ___, 134 S. Ct. 2473, 2491 (2014).

nated from the internet, because the investigator "could not have known what storage media [the defendant] used"; although the court describes the issue as concerning the description of the items to be seized, the devices themselves were to be further inspected and so might equally be described as places to be searched).

United States v. Giberson, 527 F.3d 882 (9th Cir. 2008) (holding that a search warrant authorizing a search for "documents," without mentioning computers or electronic storage, allowed police to search computers, as documents may be found in computers).

United States v. Summage, 481 F.3d 1075, 1079 (8th Cir. 2007) (a warrant was sufficiently particular where it authorized "the search and seizure of all video tapes and DVDs, pornographic pictures, video and digital recording devices and equipment, all equipment that is used to develop, upload, or download photographs and movies, computers, and any indicia of occupancy"; because officers did not know the "particular format" in which the images depicting criminal conduct were being kept, "it was necessary to search a broad array of items").

United States v. Hudspeth, 459 F.3d 922, 927 (8th Cir. 2006) (upholding a computer search conducted pursuant to a warrant allowing the search of any and all "records or documents regarding sales, payables, inventory, customer lists, financial statements, and personnel files" but not specifically mentioning computers: "While the inclusion of the word 'computer' would have specified one location among several where the officers might look for those items, its omission did not prevent the officers from searching [a] computer for such records."), *rev'd in part on other grounds*, 518 F.3d 954 (8th Cir. 2008) (en banc).

United States v. Hay, 231 F.3d 630, 637 (9th Cir. 2000) (a warrant authorizing the search and seizure of the defendant's "entire computer system" did not lack particularity because the government knew that illegal images had been sent to the defendant's computer but "had no way of knowing where the images were stored," the affidavit explained why it was necessary to seize the entire system, and there was sufficient language in the application to focus the search of the system on child pornography).

United States v. Upham, 168 F.3d 532, 535 (1st Cir. 1999) (a warrant authorizing the seizure and off-site search of "[a]ny and all computer software and hardware . . . computer disks [and] disk drives" was sufficiently particular; it precisely described a category of items—computer equipment—and the warrant established probable cause to search all such equipment; a seizure and search of all computer equipment could be likened to "the physical search of an entire house for a weapon or drugs").

DESCRIPTION INSUFFICIENT

State v. Russo, 336 P.3d 232 (Idaho 2014) (a victim reported that she was raped by a man who used his cell phone to record the rape; a search warrant that authorized the search of the suspect's home for evidence and that specifically authorized the seizure of his cell phones did not implicitly authorize the search of the cell phones; the court ruled that a separate warrant was needed to search the phones, as different interests are implicated in a search and in a seizure).

United States v. Payton, 573 F.3d 859 (9th Cir. 2009) (suggesting that computer-specific language normally is required before digital devices may be searched pursuant to a warrant).

United States v. Riccardi, 405 F.3d 852, 858, 863 (10th Cir. 2005) (a warrant which authorized the " 'seizure' of [the defendant's] computer and the search of 'all electronic and magnetic media stored within such devices' . . . did not specify the nature of the materials" to be examined and therefore "lacked the specificity required" by law).

B. Describing the Items to Be Seized

The second aspect of the particularity requirement is that a search warrant must describe the property to be seized, i.e., what the applicant is hoping to find.[29] When dealing with computer search warrants, the ultimate objects of the search usually are files or data, rather than physical objects such as computers and cell phones.[30] When this is the case, a computer search warrant should describe the files or data as specifically as possible.[31] Of course, in order to extract the data, the devices themselves may need to be

29. Marron v. United States, 275 U.S. 192, 196 (1927) ("As to what is to be taken, nothing is left to the discretion of the officer executing the warrant.").

30. There are exceptions to this rule. For example, if a suspect is believed to have stolen a particular computer during a break-in and the police obtain a search warrant for the suspect's home, the computer itself would be an object of the search, regardless of what files or data it might contain.

31. Searching & Seizing Computers, *supra* note 16, at 70 ("If computer hardware is contraband, evidence, fruits, or instrumentalities of crime, the warrant should describe the hardware itself. If the probable cause relates only to information, however, the warrant should describe the information to be seized,

seized, taken off-site, and examined—but the ultimate objective remains the seizure of the data.

Courts have recognized that it is often impossible to know in advance exactly what information will be uncovered during a search of a computer, just as it may be impossible to know in advance exactly what evidence of fraud will be uncovered during a search of a business's paper files. Thus, courts generally have upheld flexible descriptions that limited the items to be seized by reference to the crime under investigation, such as "files containing customer lists and drug transaction records," "still images or video footage of child pornography," or "evidence or information related to Medicaid fraud." Sometimes these limitations on the scope of a warrant can be strengthened by limiting the warrant to files created on or after a certain date or to files created by or referring to certain individuals.

Search warrants that do not restrict the items to be seized in any way but merely provide for a general rummaging through a suspect's digital devices likely will be deemed unlawful. The use of sweeping terms such as "all information" or "violation of any criminal law" may run afoul of the particularity requirement.

Many cases that address the description of the items to be seized also address the question of whether the warrant should include a search protocol that describes how an officer should go about looking for the items. The subject of search protocols is discussed in section III.C, below.

Finally, when describing items to be seized, officers may wish to include certain peripherals specifically in the application and warrant. For example, officers may wish to seize manuals, power cables, and passwords associated with digital devices, as seizing those items may be important to enabling a later forensic search.

Case Summaries on Describing the Items to Be Seized

DESCRIPTION SUFFICIENT

United States v. Christie, 717 F.3d 1156, 1164, 1165 (10th Cir. 2013) (noting that application of the "Fourth Amendment's particularity requirement to computer searches [was] still relatively new" but identifying as a "recognizable line" the notion that warrants lacking a "limiting principle" tend to be invalid, while warrants which are limited in their scope to either evidence of a specific crime or evidence of a particular type of material tend to be valid; in this case, the court

---

and then request the authority to seize the information in whatever form it may be stored (whether electronic or not).").

ruled that the warrant limited the search to information relevant to a homicide investigation, at least well enough for the federal good faith exception to the exclusionary rule to apply).

United States v. Farlow, 681 F.3d 15, 17 (1st Cir. 2012) (a warrant authorizing the search of nearly any digital device for almost any type of file was not overbroad where the object of the search was "evidence of the crimes of dissemination of indecent materials to minors or endangering the welfare of a child").

United States v. Triplett, 684 F.3d 500, 502, 505 (5th Cir. 2012) (a warrant authorizing the search of "electronic devices, electronic memory devices, [and] cell phones" was sufficiently particular because, when read in context with the rest of the warrant, there was a "nexus between the facts and circumstances [in that the underlying facts tied the warrant to an investigation for a missing person] and the items to be seized").

United States v. Evers, 669 F.3d 645, 653 (6th Cir. 2012) (a warrant was not unconstitutional due to its "failure to describe with particularity the computer files to be searched or to require the use of a search protocol" because the warrant "confined the search to evidence of child pornography on the computer, camera, and media described by the victim").

United States v. Burke, 633 F.3d 984, 992 (10th Cir. 2011) (search warrant authorizing officers to seize "computers" "hard drives" and "media storage" was sufficiently particular because the warrant stated that the defendant was suspected of the sexual exploitation of children; that brought "to officers' attention the purpose of the search" and effectively limited its object).

United States v. Burgess, 576 F.3d 1078, 1091 (10th Cir. 2009) (in a drug trafficking case, where a warrant that authorized a search for "computer records" was read in context to mean computer records pertaining to drug trafficking, the authorization to search "as it relate[d] to the computer, was limited to the kind of drug and drug trafficking information likely to be found on a computer, [such as] 'pay-owe sheets, address books, rolodexes [and] personal property which would tend to show a conspiracy to sell drugs' "; though the warrant itself did not explicitly authorize a search for image files, it did authorize a search for personal property which the court found "could reasonably include 'trophy photos'" because the affidavit attached to the warrant spoke to photographs of drug activity).

United States v. Wong, 334 F.3d 831, 834, 838 (9th Cir. 2003) (officers obtained a search warrant based on suspicion that the defendant murdered his girlfriend, then found child pornography in plain view on the defendant's computer; the search warrant was sufficiently particular where it limited the search to "data as it relates to this [homicide] case," a concept that was illustrated by a list of specific information sought; the items were described "with as much specificity as possible").

United States v. Hunter, 13 F. Supp. 2d 574 (D. Vt. 1998) (upholding a warrant authorizing a search of a suspect's office and computer for documents related to money laundering; the warrant was sufficiently specific because it identified a particular offense and included an illustrative list of types of documents that would be relevant; although officers would have to make some judgments about which documents met the description, and would necessarily scan many irrelevant documents, no greater specificity was possible in advance).

DESCRIPTION INSUFFICIENT

United States v. Shah, No. 5:13-CR-328-FL, 2015 WL 72118, at *13, *14, *11 (E.D.N.C. Jan. 6, 2015) (officers, investigating an intrusion against the computer system of the defendant's former employer, obtained a search warrant requiring Google to disclose "all e-mails stored in" an account associated with the defendant, and "[a]ll records or other information stored by an individual using the account"; the warrant authorized the government to seize or retain any information "that constitutes fruits, evidence, and instrumentalities of Title 18, United States Code, Section[] 1030 (Fraud and Related Activity in Connection with Computers)"; the defendant moved to suppress emails and other evidence seized under the warrant; the court ruled that because the cited statute "prohibits a wide array of activities" and is "expansive," and because the warrant "provide[d] no other details to clarify the crime at issue," the warrant "failed to provide the necessary particularity because [it] failed to state the particular crime for which the evidence was being sought"; however, the court nonetheless admitted the evidence under a good faith exception to the exclusionary rule).

State v. Henderson, 854 N.W.2d 616, 633 (Neb. 2014) (officers obtained a search warrant for a cell phone that was taken from a murder suspect upon arrest; the warrant authorized a search for "[a]ny and all information" on the phone; this description did not satisfy the particularity requirement; the court stated that "a warrant for the search of the contents of a cell phone must be sufficiently limited in scope to allow a search of only that content that is related to the probable cause that justifies the search," but it did not provide guidance on how that should be accomplished and took no position on the need for, or propriety of, a search protocol).

United States v. Galpin, 720 F.3d 436, 446 (2d Cir. 2013) (officers suspected a registered sex offender of failing to disclose his online identifiers as required by law and of luring young boys to his home; they obtained a search warrant that authorized the seizure and search of the offender's computers and other digital devices for evidence of violations of "NYS Penal Law and or Federal Statutes"; this was insufficiently particular as it did not limit the items to be seized to those connected to any specific crime; the court stated that the "particularity requirement assumes even greater importance" with digital searches as "advances in technology . . . have rendered the computer hard drive akin to a residence in terms of the scope and quantity of private information it may contain").

Mink v. Knox, 613 F.3d 995, 1011 (10th Cir. 2010) (warrant that authorized "the search and seizure of all computer and non-computer equipment and written materials in Mr. Mink's house, without any mention of any particular crime to which they might be related" lacked particularity).

United States v. Tracey, 597 F.3d 140 (3d Cir. 2010) (finding that a warrant lacked particularity with respect to the items to be seized, a problem that was not cured by the affidavit accompanying the search warrant application because the affidavit was not expressly incorporated into the warrant).

United States v. Rosa, 626 F.3d 56, 62 (2d Cir. 2010) (a warrant that "directed officers to seize and search certain electronic devices, but provided them with no guidance as to the type of evidence sought" failed the particularity requirement on two fronts as it "failed to describe with particularity the evidence sought and, more specifically, to link that evidence to the criminal activity supported by probable cause").

United States v. Otero, 563 F.3d 1127 (10th Cir. 2009) (a warrant which delineated "items to be seized" and "computer items to be seized" in two separate sections was invalid with respect to the computer items because the description of such items was wide-ranging and did not contain sufficient language limiting the items to be seized to those which were connected to the crime under investigation).

United States v. Riccardi, 405 F.3d 852, 862, 863 (10th Cir. 2005) (warrant in child pornography investigation authorized officers to search defendant's computer "and all electronic and magnetic media stored therein"; the warrant did not specifically state that the search was limited to evidence of child pornography offenses, and "thus permitted the officers to search for anything from child pornography to tax returns to private correspondence"; it was therefore lacking in particularity and was invalid, though the court declined to suppress the resulting evidence under the federal good faith exception).

United States v. Cioffi, 668 F. Supp. 2d 385 (E.D.N.Y. 2009) (search warrant allowing search of a suspect's Gmail account insufficiently particular as it did not limit the emails to be seized to those relevant to the specific charged securities crimes; although the application detailed what was sought, the application was not incorporated into the warrant).

C. Inclusion of a Search Protocol

An issue that is closely related to particularity is whether a search warrant for digital devices should include a search protocol or search strategy that prescribes how officers may examine the devices. A few courts have suggested that a search warrant for digital devices should include a search protocol to ensure that officers will effectively target evidence of criminal activity while minimizing their contact with personal information that is unrelated to the investigation.[32] A search protocol might specify, for example, that a search

32. *See, e.g.*, United States v. Comprehensive Drug Testing, Inc., 621 F.3d 1162, 1179 (9th Cir. 2010) (en banc) (Kozinski, J., concurring) (suggesting that, for computer searches, "the warrant application should normally include, or the issuing judicial officer should insert, a [search] protocol," which should be designed to "prevent[] agents involved in the investigation from examining or retaining any data other than that for which probable cause is shown"). *Cf.* State v. Fuller, 332 P.3d 937, 950 (Utah 2014) (ruling that a search warrant for computers satisfied the particularity requirement in part because (1) it limited the search to devices that contained evidence related to the criminal activity, namely, the possession and distribution of child pornography, and (2) it "set forth a specific 'search procedure' to prevent the officers from searching unrelated files"; the court stated that "[a]s computers, smartphones, and other devices can now be used to store millions of

for evidence of drug trafficking will begin with a review of the directory structure of the suspect's computer, continue with an examination of any files and folders with file names suggesting relevance, move on to keyword searching, and then conclude with a review of image files for trophy photos and the like.[33]

However, most courts have ruled that search warrants for digital devices need not include such search protocols.[34] As one court stated, "[i]t is unrealistic to expect a warrant to prospectively restrict the scope of a search by directory, filename or extension or to attempt to structure search methods—that process must remain dynamic."[35] Although "[r]espect for legitimate rights to privacy in papers and effects requires an officer executing a search warrant to first look in the most obvious places and as it becomes necessary to progressively move from the obvious to the obscure . . . in the end, there may be no practical substitute for actually looking in many (perhaps all) folders and sometimes at the documents contained within those folders, and that is true whether the search is of computer files or physical files."[36]

Even when an officer includes a search protocol in a search warrant, the protocol is, of necessity, often sufficiently broad and flexible that it provides little real privacy protection to the suspect.[37] If a judicial official insists on

---

files and other data—both personal and business-related—law enforcement must be increasingly cautious with respect to the particularity requirement because access to 'a huge array of one's personal papers in a single place increases law enforcement's ability to conduct a wide-ranging search into a person's private affairs.'"); *In re* Search Warrant, 71 A.3d 1158 (Vt. 2012) (ruling that issuing official could limit search techniques that could be used in executing a computer search warrant and could require the search to be conducted by personnel separated from investigators by a firewall).

33. A sample search protocol is reproduced in *United States v. Potts*, 586 F.3d 823, 827 (10th Cir. 2009).

34. United States v. Evers, 669 F.3d 645, 653 (6th Cir. 2012) (a warrant was not unconstitutional due to its "failure to describe with particularity the computer files to be searched or to require the use of a search protocol" because the warrant "confined the search to evidence of child pornography on the computer, camera, and media described by the victim"); United States v. Cartier, 543 F.3d 442, 447 (8th Cir. 2008) (a search warrant was not invalid per se due to its lack of search protocol); United States v. Khanani, 502 F.3d 1281 (11th Cir. 2007) (search protocol not required); United States v. Brooks, 427 F.3d 1246, 1251 (10th Cir. 2005) ("[W]e disagree with [the defendant] that the government was required to describe its specific search methodology. This court has never required warrants to contain a particularized computer search strategy.").

35. United States v. Burgess, 576 F.3d 1078, 1093 (10th Cir. 2009).

36. *Id.* at 1094.

37. See, for example, the protocol set forth in the *Potts* case, cited in full *supra* note 33.

including a search protocol in a computer search warrant, the officer seeking the warrant may wish to consult with his or her agency legal advisor or with a prosecutor to determine whether to accept the protocol requirement or to challenge the authority of the judicial official to impose it.[38]

Because the inclusion of a search protocol is often a response to a judicial official's concern about the expansive sweep of the plain view doctrine in computer search cases, readers interested in the search protocol issue should also review the discussion of plain view in section V.D, below.

IV. Selecting a Judicial Official

Any judicial official empowered to issue search warrants may issue search warrants for digital devices. However, there are circumstances under which a cautious officer handling a serious case may prefer to submit a search warrant application concerning a digital device to a superior court judge. First, a warrant from a superior court judge is valid throughout the state.[39] Where the officer plans to submit the device to a laboratory in another part of the state, such as the state crime laboratory, obtaining a warrant that is valid statewide may avoid any question about whether the warrant properly authorizes the laboratory search. (Of course, the state crime laboratory routinely performs chemical analyses in drug cases from across the state, regardless of whether the drugs were seized pursuant to a warrant issued by a superior court judge, so this issue may be unlikely to arise.) Second, if the officer is seeking a warrant for a new type of device or a new type of digitally stored information, a judge may be better suited than a magistrate to identify possible legal problems with the warrant. Finally, federal prosecutors generally prefer cases in which search warrants have been signed by a superior court judge,[40] so if the case may be referred for federal prosecution, the officer may prefer to present the warrant to a judge.

---

38. The United States Department of Justice advises federal officers and prosecutors to resist "[l]imitations on search methodologies." Searching & Seizing Computers, *supra* note 16, at 79.

39. Section 15A-243 of the North Carolina General Statutes (hereinafter G.S.). Search warrants issued by district court judges are valid throughout the district, and search warrants issued by magistrates are valid throughout the county. *Id.*

40. The reason for this preference seems to be a concern that search warrants issued by other judicial officials may be vulnerable to challenge in federal court. If an investigation is determined to be federal in character, the investigation must be conducted in compliance with the Federal Rules of Criminal Procedure. United States v. Smith, 914 F.2d 565, 569 (4th Cir. 1990) (holding that a warrant

V. Execution of the Warrant

A. On Site

When an officer obtains a search warrant that authorizes the search of a computer, the officer may conduct the search on site, that is, where he or she initially locates the computer. In fact, on-site search is the historical norm, as it is the manner in which searches of physical locations such as homes, offices, and storage units typically are conducted. On-site computer searches are not uncommon, but they are often preliminary in nature,[41] intended mainly to assist officers in determining which computers and other devices should be seized for further analysis.

As discussed in detail below, courts generally have rejected the idea that an on-site search is required. Where an on-site search can be done quickly, is likely to be effective, and can prevent the seizure of large amounts of legitimate data, it may be required by the Fourth Amendment's command of reasonableness. However, because it is rare for all of those circumstances to obtain in computer search cases, officers frequently will have the authority to seize digital devices for off-site examination without a preliminary search.

B. Off-Site Forensic Analysis

Off-site forensic analysis by specialized personnel is common in computer search cases. Courts generally have found this practice to be appropriate. As one federal court put it, "[t]he federal courts are in agreement that a warrant authorizing the seizure of a defendant's home computer equipment and digital media for a subsequent off-site electronic search is not unreasonable or overbroad."[42] Off-site analysis often is in everyone's interest, as a complete

---

must be obtained in compliance with Federal Rule of Criminal Procedure 41 if the warrant application was made "at the direction or urging of a federal officer"). Rule 41 allows a search warrant to be obtained from a federal "magistrate judge with authority in the district—or if none is reasonably available, a judge of a state court of record in the district." FED. R. CRIM. P. 41(b)(1). Because superior court is a court of record, a search warrant obtained from a superior court judge is in compliance with Rule 41 if no federal magistrate judge was available at the time of issuance.

41. *See, e.g.*, United States v. Cameron, 699 F.3d 621 (1st Cir. 2012) (officers conducted "preliminary" search of a computer at a suspect's home, then seized it for further analysis); State v. Lyons, 9 A.3d 596 (N.J. Super. Ct. App. Div. 2010) (officers conducted a "forensic preview" on site before seizing suspect's computer).

42. United States v. Evers, 669 F.3d 645, 652 (6th Cir. 2012). *See also* United States v. Hill, 459 F.3d 966, 975 (9th Cir. 2006) (a warrant was not "fatally defective in failing to require an onsite search and isolation of child pornography before removing storage media wholesale"); United States v. Hay, 231 F.3d 630,

forensic analysis of a computer can take weeks, and it would be burdensome to the police and intrusive to the computer's owner to insist that the police remain on site for the entire time. Furthermore, off-site analysis may be more secure than on-site work.[43]

Although perhaps not legally required, the best practice is to specify in the application and in the warrant itself the extent to which law enforcement is authorized to conduct off-site analysis.[44] Describing the amount of time that off-site analysis typically involves may help alleviate any concern about compliance with the statutory rule that a search warrant must be executed within forty-eight hours, discussed in section V.C, immediately below.[45]

Off-site analysis often involves the use of specialized forensic software. Courts generally have allowed the use of such software. While perhaps not legally required, an officer may wish to explain in the application that the use of forensic software is often necessary and may wish to seek express authorization for the use of such software.[46]

Removing a computer from a home or business can create a substantial hardship. If a suspect can show a legitimate need for access to a portion of

---

637 (9th Cir. 2000) (a warrant authorizing the search and seizure of the defendant's "entire computer system" was not overbroad and was not lacking particularity because the government knew that illegal images had been sent to the defendant's computer but "had no way of knowing where the images were stored," the affidavit explained why it was necessary to seize the entire system, and there was sufficient language in the application to focus the search of the system to child pornography; in addition, the affidavit "justified taking the entire system off site because of the time, expertise, and controlled environment required for a proper analysis"). *But cf.* United States v. Comprehensive Drug Testing, Inc., 621 F.3d 1162, 1168 (9th Cir. 2010) (en banc) (noting with approval that "[t]he magistrate judge . . . wisely made such broad seizure subject to certain procedural safeguards . . . . [T]he government was first required to examine the computer equipment and storage devices [on site] to determine whether [relevant] information . . . 'c[ould] be searched on-site in a reasonable amount of time and without jeopardizing the ability to preserve the data.' ").

43. Searching & Seizing Computers, *supra* note 16, at 77 (suggesting that "attempting to search storage media on-site may even risk damaging the evidence itself in some cases" because it may change metadata or leave a computer vulnerable to remote wiping or other manipulation).

44. *See* United States v. Grimmett, 439 F.3d 1263, 1269 (10th Cir. 2006) (upholding warrant where the "affidavit also made clear that the search of the computer would be off-site in a laboratory setting" because only careful laboratory analysis allows all relevant evidence to be exploited); United States v. Mutschelknaus, 592 F.3d 826 (8th Cir. 2010) (warrant allowing officers sixty days to conduct off-site examination of seized computer was reasonable, given the complexity of computer searches).

45. G.S. 15A-248.

46. *See generally* Searching & Seizing Computers, *supra* note 16, at 89.

the seized data, arrangements should be made to provide access. Typically, this is done through providing the suspect a copy of the needed data.[47]

C. The Forty-Eight-Hour Rule

Under Section 15A-248 of the North Carolina General Statutes (hereinafter G.S.), "[a] search warrant must be executed within 48 hours from the time of issuance." Cases from other jurisdictions suggest that it is sufficient if the initial seizure of the digital devices is completed within this time period, even if the subsequent off-site forensic analysis takes longer.[48] Indeed, any rule that all analysis must be completed within forty-eight hours would have severe implications for drug cases and for other cases requiring laboratory work. Any remaining concerns about the forty-eight-hour rule may be reduced

---

47. United States v. Hill, 459 F.3d 966 (9th Cir. 2006) (officers obtained a search warrant to search the defendant's computer and storage media for child pornography; they seized all his disks, etc., for off-site analysis; he argued that they should have been required to search the storage media on-site and release anything that didn't contain child pornography; both the district court and the reviewing court held otherwise, concluding that it was reasonable, given the difficult, time-consuming nature of computer searches, to take the computers off site; the district court ruled that the defendant was entitled to copies of his data, which would ameliorate the hardship of the seizure).

48. *See, e.g.*, Mastrogiovanni v. State, 751 S.E.2d 536, 539 (Ga. Ct. App. 2013) (defendant acknowledged that the initial search of his home, resulting in the seizure of his computer, was conducted within ten days as required by state law, but he contended that the off-site forensic analysis was not completed with ten days, rendering the search unlawful; the appellate court found "no authority for the proposition that the analysis of items seized during the execution of a valid search warrant requires a second search warrant"); United States v. Burgess, 576 F.3d 1078, 1097 (10th Cir. 2009) (forty-four-day delay in conducting forensic analysis did not render it an unlawful search; officers were diligent in their work, probable cause did not dissipate, and the defendant was not prejudiced by the delay; further, "any delay was due to [law enforcement's] efforts to make sure the job was done right"); United States v. Cameron, 652 F. Supp. 2d 74, 82 (D. Me. 2009) ("[T]he Court concludes that so long as the search warrant was timely executed and the computer and the discs were seized within the period the warrant stipulated, the continued forensic inspection of the computer and the discs did not violate the Fourth Amendment, [the criminal procedure rules], or the conditions of the search warrant itself."). In the federal courts, this issue has been addressed by a 2009 amendment to Federal Rule of Criminal Procedure 41, which now states that, "Unless otherwise specified, [a search] warrant authorizes a later review of [seized] media or information consistent with the warrant. The [ten-day] time [limit] for executing the warrant . . . refers to the seizure or on-site copying of the media or information, and not to any later off-site copying or review." FED. R. CRIM. P. 41(e)(2)(B)). For a lengthy discussion of this issue, see SEARCHING & SEIZING COMPUTERS, *supra* note 16, at 91.

by obtaining explicit authorization in the warrant for a laboratory forensic analysis, as discussed above.

Even if the initial seizure satisfies the forty-eight-hour rule, forensic analysis should still be completed reasonably promptly. Some courts have criticized extremely long delays in examining digital evidence on Fourth Amendment or other grounds.[49]

D. Plain View

Generally, courts have held that when a warrant authorizes the search of a computer, it authorizes at least a cursory review of every file on the computer. This is because of the ease with which files can be camouflaged or disguised through misleading file names or extensions.[50] Several commentators have

---

49. *See, e.g.*, United States v. Ganias, 755 F.3d 125, 137 (2d Cir. 2014) (finding a Fourth Amendment violation and reversing the defendant's conviction where the government did not examine the defendant's computers until eight months after seizing them and ultimately retained them for more than two years; "[t]he Government's retention of copies of [the defendant's] personal computer records for two-and-a-half years deprived him of exclusive control over those files for an unreasonable amount of time"); United States v. Cote, 72 M.J. 41, 43 (C.A.A.F. 2013) (computer search warrant provided that the initial search was to be executed within ten days and that any forensic analysis of a seized device was to be completed within ninety days, but officers conducted a forensic examination of a seized hard drive more than a year after the warrant issued; court concluded that "the Government's violation of the warrant's time limits for conducting an off-site search of the seized electronic device constituted more than a 'de minimis' violation of the warrant and resulted in an unreasonable search" and suggested in a footnote that even absent the explicit time limit in the warrant, the Fourth Amendment's reasonableness requirement may be implicated by such a long delay). *Cf.* United States v. Christi, 717 F.3d 1156, 1164, 1162 (10th Cir. 2013) (holding that a five-month delay in searching a seized computer was reasonable under the Fourth Amendment, "if not by a very great margin"; the court relied in part on the defendant's lack of contemporaneous objection to the delay and stated that in light of the amount of personal information that a user may store on a computer, it did "not doubt that an unreasonable delay in obtaining a search warrant can sometimes violate the Fourth Amendment").

50. *See, e.g.*, United States v. Stabile, 633 F.3d 219, 239, 240–41 (3d Cir. 2011) (searching video files pursuant to search warrant for financial crimes was ruled "objectively reasonable because criminals can easily alter file names and file extensions to conceal contraband," and court found that "the plain view doctrine applies to seizures of evidence during searches of computer files, [though] the exact confines of the doctrine will vary from case to case in a common-sense, fact-intensive manner"); United States v. Williams, 592 F.3d 511, 522 (4th Cir. 2010) (stating that a computer search requires "at least a cursory review of each file on the computer"). *Cf. Burgess*, 576 F.3d at 1094 ("[I]n the end, there may be no practical substitute for actually looking in many (perhaps all) folders and sometimes at the documents contained within those folders," though officers should

noted that computer searches, more than other types of searches, require officers to sift through large amounts of information unrelated to the crime under investigation.[51] As a result, officers executing computer search warrants often encounter evidence of crimes other than those based on which the warrants were issued.

When an officer searches a physical location pursuant to a search warrant and stumbles upon evidence of a crime other than the one that motivated the search, the evidence is said to be in "plain view," and it typically may be seized by the officer and used to support a criminal prosecution. Many courts have held that the same is true when an officer encounters unexpected evidence when searching a computer—for example, when an officer searching a computer for evidence related to a homicide encounters child pornography. These courts have concluded that the plain view doctrine applies and that the officer may continue searching the computer under the original warrant, even though the officer may now subjectively expect to find additional child pornography.[52]

"first look in the most obvious places and as it becomes necessary to progressively move from the obvious to the obscure."). A few cases have held, based on the particular facts involved, that it was unreasonable to believe that the objects of the search would be found in certain files on a computer. *See, e.g.*, United States v. Kim, 677 F. Supp. 2d 930 (S.D. Tex. 2009) (search of encrypted JPEG files with names suggestive of child pornography not authorized by warrant permitting a computer to be searched for evidence of computer intrusion; in light of various facts, not reasonable to believe that the encrypted files would contain evidence of computer intrusion; thus, child pornography that was actually found was not in plain view).

51. *See, e.g.*, Orin S. Kerr, *Searches and Seizures in a Digital World*, 119 HARV. L. REV. 531, 565 (2005) (stating that "computer technologies may allow warrants that are particular on their face to become general warrants in practice"); Paul Ohm, *Massive Hard Drives, General Warrants, and the Power of Magistrate Judges*, 97 VA. L. REV. IN BRIEF 1, 11 (2011) ("Computer search warrants are the closest things to general warrants we have confronted in the history of the Republic.").

52. *See, e.g.*, *Williams*, 592 F.3d at 515, 522 (defendant sent anonymous emails to a church expressing a sexual interest in some boys who attended school there; police obtained a search warrant for "computer systems and digital storage media" indicative of computer harassment or communicating threats; during the search, police found child pornography; child pornography was an "instrumentality" of the computer harassment charge and so was properly seized under the warrant; alternatively, because a computer search requires "at least a cursory review of each file on the computer," the child pornography was in plain view; the court applied the plain view doctrine as traditionally understood, notwithstanding the large amount of data that may be stored on a computer); United States v. Mann, 592 F.3d 779 (7th Cir. 2010) (officer obtained search warrant to search defendant's computer for evidence of voyeurism; he properly searched image files

Other courts have concluded that because computer searches bring so much information to officers' attention, the plain view doctrine must be limited in order to prevent computer search warrants from amounting to general warrants, allowing officers to rummage through a suspect's computer for evidence of any wrongdoing. The cases reflect two main strategies for limiting the effect of the plain view doctrine. One is to require, as a condition of issuing the warrant, that the prosecution forswear reliance on the plain view doctrine. The second is to order that the warrant be executed by a search team behind a "firewall" and that the search team report out to investigators only evidence related to the crime in connection with which the warrant was obtained.[53]

Finally, a few courts have attempted to chart a middle ground, holding that the plain view doctrine applies to the initial discovery of unexpected evidence, but that if the officer wishes to continue looking for additional evidence in the same vein, a second warrant is required.[54] Because North

---

on computer systematically, even though he thereby uncovered child pornography; however, court found it "troubling" that he did not stop and seek a second warrant for child pornography). *Cf.* United States v. Crespo Rios, 645 F.3d 37 (1st Cir. 2011) (officer obtained a search warrant for evidence of the defendant's attempts to lure minors into sexual activity; officer searched the defendant's digital media for child pornography; the court ruled that the inevitable discovery doctrine applied to the child pornography because a search pertaining to the solicitation offenses would have revealed the child pornography).

53. *In re* Search Warrant, 71 A.3d 1158 (Vt. 2012) (holding that a judicial official who issued a computer search warrant lacked the authority to prohibit law enforcement from relying on the plain view doctrine but had the authority to accomplish the same result by requiring that the search be conducted by third parties behind a "firewall" and that the search team provide to investigators only information relevant to the offense that gave rise to the search warrant); United States v. Comprehensive Drug Testing, Inc., 621 F.3d 1162, 1177 (9th Cir. 2010) (en banc) (noting that "over-seizing is an inherent part of the electronic search process" and suggesting that magistrate judges issuing search warrants should take steps to limit the government's access to data for which it has no probable cause, such as by requiring an on-site assessment of the feasibility of seizing only responsive data; by requiring data segregation to be done by someone other than the case agent; and perhaps by limiting the government's plain view rights; Judge Kozinski's concurrence provides more detailed suggestions); *In re* United States of America's Application for a Search Warrant to Seize and Search Electronic Devices from Edward Cunnius, 770 F. Supp. 2d 1138, 1139 (W.D. Wash. 2011) ("Because the government, in this application, refuses to conduct its search of the digital devices utilizing a filter team and foreswearing reliance on the plain view doctrine, the Court DENIES the application as seeking an overbroad or general warrant in violation of the Fourth Amendment and the law of this Circuit.").

54. United States v. Carey, 172 F.3d 1268, 1273 (10th Cir. 1999) (officer obtained search warrant for "evidence pertaining to the sale and distribution of

Carolina's appellate courts have yet to rule on the application of the plain view doctrine as it relates to computer searches, a cautious officer may wish to seek a second warrant whenever the focus of his or her search moves away from the crime that gave rise to the warrant.[55]

E. Return and Inventory

Under G.S. 15A-257, an officer who executes a search warrant must return the warrant to the clerk of the issuing court without unnecessary delay. The return normally is indicated on the warrant itself.[56] The officer must also provide the clerk with "a written inventory of items seized,"[57] and a list of the items seized must also be provided to the person from whom they were taken.[58] Form AOC-CR-206 may be used for creating an inventory.[59]

With computer searches, a timing issue frequently arises. Suppose that a warrant authorizes officers to search a defendant's home and computer for evidence of a crime and further allows the officers to conduct the computer search off site. The search of the home and the seizure of the computer typically take place shortly after the issuance of the warrant, but the search of the computer may not take place until days or weeks later. Should the warrant be returned after the search of the home, or should it wait until the

---

controlled substances"; officer opened a JPEG file with sexually suggestive name, apparently because the file could contain a photograph related to drug activity; it contained child pornography; officer continued viewing other .jpg files with sexually suggestive names, finding more child pornography; although the first image was in plain view, by "the officer's own admission . . . each time he opened a subsequent [image] file, he expected to find child pornography and not material related to drugs," so the plain view doctrine did not apply). *But see* United States v. Brooks, 427 F.3d 1246, 1251 (10th Cir. 2005) (noting that "we have not required a specific prior authorization along the lines suggested in *Carey* in every computer search"). This approach may be consistent with G.S. 15A-253, which provides for the seizure of evidence "inadvertently" uncovered by an officer in the course of executing a search warrant for an unrelated crime. The statutory requirement of inadvertence may limit the plain view doctrine as applied in North Carolina.

55. Searching & Seizing Computers, *supra* note 16, at 91 (concluding that "it remains prudent to seek a second warrant upon discovering evidence of an additional crime not identified in the initial warrant").

56. See form AOC-CR-119, "Search Warrant," available on the North Carolina Court System website at www.nccourts.org/Forms/Documents/19.pdf.

57. G.S. 15A-257.

58. *Id.* § 15A-254.

59. This form, "Inventory of Items Seized Pursuant to Search," is available on the North Carolina Court System website at www.nccourts.org/Forms/Documents/1031.pdf.

search of the computer is complete? A related issue is whether the inventory should list the computer itself or the files and data within the computer.

No North Carolina cases answer these questions. The prevailing practice appears to be to return the warrant after the initial search, even if the computer has not yet been subjected to an off-site examination. One justification for this practice is that it provides evidence of compliance with the requirement that a warrant be executed within forty-eight hours of issuance.[60] An inventory is normally provided at the same time, simply listing the computer as an item seized and making no reference to specific data or files within the computer. This is probably sufficient, notwithstanding the fact that, as noted above, the items to be seized under most computer search warrants are files and data rather than hardware.[61] A cautious officer might file a supplemental inventory listing the data or files seized after the off-site search of the computer. In any event, however, imperfect compliance with the return and inventory requirements is unlikely to require the suppression of evidence.[62]

F. Handling Digital Devices

Although this book is focused on the law, officers should be aware that certain technical procedures are recommended when handling digital devices when executing search warrants. The *North Carolina State Crime Laboratory Evidence Guide*[63] provides guidelines on handling digital devices properly during a search. It addresses issues such as whether to leave devices on or

---

60. G.S. 15A-248. This issue is discussed in detail in section V.C, above.

61. *See* Commonwealth v. Kaupp, 899 N.E.2d 809 (Mass. 2009) (sufficient to return warrant shortly after initial search and prior to forensic examination "listing the devices" seized); United States v. Hernandez, 183 F. Supp. 2d 468, 481 (D.P.R. 2002) (citation, internal quotation marks omitted) ("[B]ecause off-site computer searches are reasonable, it may be necessary . . . for the return of the warrant to be filed with the court before such off-site searching can be completed."); Searching & Seizing Computers, *supra* note 16, at 95 (suggesting that an inventory may simply list seized hardware without referring to specific data).

62. State v. Nadeau, 1 A.3d 445 (Me. 2010) (computer search warrant provided that the search was to be conducted, and an inventory returned, within ten days; no inventory was ever prepared, but this was a "ministerial" failure that did not warrant suppression of evidence); State v. Fruitt, 35 N.C. App. 177 (1978) (officer's failure to comply strictly with inventory requirement did not require suppression of evidence).

63. N.C State Crime Lab., North Carolina State Crime Laboratory Evidence Guide (Sept. 2013), *available at* www.ncdoj.gov/getdoc/0d2d2d94-2519-46a8-88f1-2989ef651433/Evidence-Guide-10-16-2013-(1).aspx.

turn them off and whether to shut devices down normally or simply unplug them. Officers who are unfamiliar with searching digital devices should review the guide. They may also contact the local State Bureau of Investigation district office and ask to speak to a member of the computer crimes unit for advice or consult with their own computer expert.

Digital devices, especially cellular phones, may be password protected. In some cases, officers with training in digital forensics may be able to bypass the password. In other cases, the manufacturer of the operating system may be able to extract some information from the device despite the password. The latter approach may require obtaining an additional search warrant to be served on the manufacturer. For example, Apple can extract "SMS . . . photos, videos, contacts, audio recording, and call history" from locked iPhones running certain versions of Apple's mobile operating system, but will do so only pursuant to a search warrant containing the specific language contained in Apple's law enforcement guidelines.[64] Because password protection may make it more difficult, or even impossible, to access the information on a digital device, officers should, with proper authorization in the search warrant, seize any papers near the devices that may contain passwords and attempt to prevent active devices from shutting down or "sleeping" such that entry of a password is required to activate the devices.

Finally, it is worth noting that even when the recommended practices are followed, technical limitations may exist. While enormous amounts of information may be extracted from many digital devices, digital evidence technicians warn that some will bear more fruit than others, depending on storage capacity, operating system, security features, and other factors.

VI. Special Cases

In certain cases, digital device searches may involve information that is privileged or otherwise entitled to special treatment. These issues are not unique to searches of digital devices, and this book is not a comprehensive

---

64. Apple, Inc., *Legal Process Guidelines: U.S. Law Enforcement*, APPLE.COM (Sept. 17, 2014), https://www.apple.com/jp/privacy/docs/legal-process-guidelines-us.pdf. Apple cannot obtain this information from iPhones running iOS 8 or later as a result of changes in Apple's encryption process. Jeff Welty, *Is Apple Intentionally Crippling Law Enforcement Access to Digital Evidence?* N.C. CRIM. L., UNC SCH. OF GOV'T BLOG (Oct. 1, 2014), http://nccriminallaw.sog.unc.edu/is-apple-intentionally-crippling-law-enforcement-access-to-digital-evidence/.

resource on these issues. However, two of the more prominent issues are addressed briefly below.

A. Devices That May Contain Privileged Material

Special care must be taken when searching computers that may contain privileged material, such as a computer at an attorney's office or in a medical practice. Courts have approved solutions such as having a special master conduct the search;[65] having the search performed by a "taint team" working for the prosecution;[66] and having the search conducted pursuant to a court-approved protocol designed to avoid review of privileged documents.[67] When an officer expects to encounter privileged material while executing a search,

---

65. United States v. Hunter, 13 F. Supp. 2d 574 (D. Vt. 1998) (suggesting this procedure, though approving as a less satisfactory alternative having the search done by officers not involved in the investigation at issue). *Cf. In re* Grand Jury Subpoenas, 454 F.3d 511, 522 (6th Cir. 2006) (use of a special master rather than a "taint team" or appellant's own attorneys was the more appropriate method by which to filter potentially privileged documents that were not already in the hands of the government; note that this is not a digital evidence case).

66. United States v. Triumph Capital Group, Inc., 211 F.R.D. 31 (D. Conn. 2002). *Cf.* United States v. Taylor, 764 F. Supp. 2d 230, 235, 234 (D. Me. 2011) (while the case law on the problem of how to handle seized email communications potentially subject to lawyer-client privilege did not "yield clear answers," the court found that "the government behaved reasonably here by immediately seeking judicial instructions once its agent noticed that e-mail headers reflected communications between lawyer and client" and rejected the defendant's argument that "the filter agent approach '[was] per se inadequate as a matter of law'"). For a summary and defense critique of the taint team approach, see Sara Kropf, *Protecting the Attorney-Client Privilege When the Government Executes a Search Warrant*, THE CHAMPION (National Association of Criminal Defense Lawyers, Sept. 2014): 18.

67. Preventive Med. Assocs., Inc. v. Commonwealth, 992 N.E.2d 257, 268 (Mass. 2013) ("Given the constitutional command of reasonableness and in light of the risk involved to the integrity of a defendant's attorney-client privilege, we conclude that in the future, when the Commonwealth seizes pursuant to a search warrant the e-mails of a defendant under indictment, before any search of those e-mails may take place, the Commonwealth must present to a Superior Court judge and obtain the judge's approval of the search protocol to be used and specifically the procedures proposed to protect against searches of privileged communications between the defendant and his attorneys. . . . Further, unless the Commonwealth can demonstrate a compelling contrary reason, the defendant must have an opportunity to be heard before the judge approves a particular search method.")

the issue should be raised and the solution specified in the application and warrant.[68]

B. Devices That Belong to the News Media

Under most circumstances, the federal Privacy Protection Act[69] precludes law enforcement officers from using search warrants to obtain material that a person or entity possesses in connection with "a purpose to disseminate to the public a newspaper, book, broadcast, or other similar form of public communication."[70] The Act was intended to provide the news media with greater protection from law enforcement intrusion than required by the Fourth Amendment.[71] However, the rise of blogging and social media arguably have brought a much wider range of persons under the protection of the Act, as many individuals might claim a "purpose to disseminate" information to one extent or another.[72]

Violations of the Act do not result in exclusion of evidence.[73] However, they may result in civil liability, as the Act provides for a civil cause of action.[74] As a result, any officer who wishes to seize evidence from individuals or organizations engaged in First Amendment activities should consult his or her agency's legal advisor. The Act contains a number of exceptions, and there may be options other than a search warrant through which the relevant information may be obtained.

---

68. For a good general discussion of this issue, see SEARCHING & SEIZING COMPUTERS, *supra* note 16, at 109.

69. 42 U.S.C. §§ 2000aa *et seq.*

70. *Id.* § 2000aa(a).

71. SEARCHING & SEIZING COMPUTERS, *supra* note 16, at 100 *et seq.*

72. *See, e.g.*, Sennett v. United States, 667 F.3d 531, 532, 533 (4th Cir. 2012) (addressing civil suit brought under the Act by a "photojournalist who claims a special interest in covering protests, political demonstrations, and 'grassroots activism'" and who published her photographs both in traditional news outlets and "on her website, her personal blog and the Internet in general").

73. 42 U.S.C. § 2000aa-6(e).

74. *Id.* § 2000aa-6(a).

Chapter 2: Warrantless Searches of Digital Devices

This chapter addresses warrantless searches of digital devices. It begins by considering situations in which digital devices may not be subject to a reasonable expectation of privacy, in which case inspection of such a device by a law enforcement officer might not be a search at all. Then it considers several recognized exceptions to the warrant requirement, including consent, search incident to arrest, the automobile exception, and exigent circumstances.

I. Reasonable Expectation of Privacy

Generally, a Fourth Amendment search takes place only when an officer's actions intrude upon a person's reasonable expectation of privacy.[1] Individuals normally have a reasonable expectation of privacy in the contents of their own electronic devices.[2] However, there are some circumstances under which a person may have no reasonable expectation of privacy in an electronic device with which he or she is associated. This section explores those circumstances.

---

1. Under *United States v. Jones*, 565 U.S. ___, 132 S. Ct. 945, 949, an officer also conducts a search when he or she "physically occupie[s] private property for the purpose of obtaining information." It is not clear how, if at all, this so-called trespass theory of the Fourth Amendment applies to computer searches. *See also* Florida v. Jardines, 569 U.S. ___, 133 S. Ct. 1409 (2013) (citing and quoting *Jones*).

2. Digital devices are "effects" within the meaning of the Fourth Amendment. In *Riley v. California*, 573 U.S. ___, 134 S. Ct. 2473 (2014), the U.S. Supreme Court ruled that a search warrant was necessary to search the cell phone of an arrestee, a ruling that makes sense only if there is a reasonable expectation of privacy in digital devices. Although *Riley* involved cell phones, the Court's reasoning clearly applies to other types of digital devices. Indeed, the Court once referred to cell phones as "minicomputers that also happen to have the capacity to be used as a telephone." *Id.* at ___, 134 S. Ct. at 2489. *See also* United States v. Heckencamp, 482 F.3d 1142, 1146 (9th Cir. 2007) (holding that the defendant "had a legitimate, objectively reasonable expectation of privacy in his personal computer"); United States v. Lifshitz, 369 F.3d 173 (2d Cir. 2004); Guest v. Leis, 255 F.3d 325 (6th Cir. 2001); Smallwood v. State, 113 So. 3d 724, 730, n.3 (Fla. 2013) (stating that the defendant "possessed a 'legitimate expectation of privacy' in his person and his personal electronic equipment," namely, his cellular phone); State v. Barajas, 817 N.W.2d 204, 216–17 (Minn. Ct. App. 2012) ("[W]e conclude that a person has the same reasonable expectation of privacy in the concealed digital contents of a cellular telephone as a person has in the concealed physical contents of a container.").

A. Workplace and School Devices

Individuals often use computers and other electronic devices in the course of their work or their education. Sometimes these devices are owned by the employer or the educational institution and are assigned to the individual. In other cases, individuals may use their own devices to connect to a network provided by the institution.

Different courts have reached different results regarding whether individuals retain an expectation of privacy in these settings. Among the factors that courts consider are the following:

- Whether the institution or the individual owns the device
- Whether the device is used by, or is assigned to, one individual exclusively
- Whether the device is used in a private location such as an individual office
- Whether the device is protected by an individual password
- The institution's policies regarding use of the device or network and the institution's right to monitor usage
- Whether authorities are interested in the contents stored locally on the device or only with the information sent from the device to the institution's network

Case Summaries on Workplace and School Devices

FINDING OR ASSUMING A REASONABLE EXPECTATION OF PRIVACY

City of Ontario v. Quon, 560 U.S. 746, 760 (2010) (assuming *arguendo* that police officers had a reasonable expectation of privacy in department-issued pagers, but noting that "employer policies concerning communications will of course shape the reasonable expectations of their employees, especially to the extent that such policies are clearly communicated").

United States v. Heckenkamp, 482 F.3d 1142, 1147 (9th Cir. 2007) (student retained a reasonable expectation of privacy in a computer despite the fact that he connected it to the school's network where there was no announced policy of monitoring, and instead, users were told that there would be only "limited instances in which university administrators may access [a user's] computer in order to protect the university's systems").

United States v. Finley, 477 F.3d 250 (5th Cir. 2007) (defendant had a reasonable expectation of privacy in a cell phone that his employer provided for him).

United States v. Ziegler, 474 F.3d 1184 (9th Cir. 2007) (defendant had a reasonable expectation of privacy in his work computer because it was located in an individual office, despite company policy allowing monitoring of the computer).

Leventhal v. Knapek, 266 F.3d 64 (2d Cir. 2001) (employee had a reasonable expectation of privacy in his workplace computer where he had a private office and exclusive use of his computer and his employer had no computer use policy that diminished his expectation of privacy).

FINDING NO REASONABLE EXPECTATION OF PRIVACY

State v. Robinson, 270 P.3d 1183, 1192 (Kan. 2012) (defendant lacked a reasonable expectation of privacy in Internet searches conducted on a computer he "used at the workplace of his mentor"; although the defendant had a password-protected account on the computer that may have established some privacy interest in password-protected files, the defendant's search history could be viewed by network administrators without using the password, and the defendant knew that his internet activity could be monitored).

United States v. Hamilton, 778 F. Supp. 2d 651, 653 (E.D. Va. 2011) (school employee had no reasonable expectation of privacy in email messages stored on his work computer; the school's computer use policy stated that "[a]ll data stored or transmitted over this system may be monitored"; that destroyed any expectation of privacy as to the emails, even though they were created prior to the promulgation of the policy).

Miller v. State, 335 S.W.3d 847 (Tex. App. 2011) (defendant lacked a reasonable expectation of privacy in a thumb drive that he brought to work, connected to work computers, used for work purposes, and did not password protect).

United States v. Barrows, 481 F.3d 1246 (10th Cir. 2007) (employee had no reasonable expectation of privacy in his personal computer after he brought it to work, connected it at least to some degree to the workplace network, used it in an exposed area, and left it on, with no password protection, when he was away from his desk).

United States v. Angevine, 281 F.3d 1130, 1134 (10th Cir. 2002) (university professor had no reasonable expectation of privacy in computer owned by the university but issued to him, where the university's policy "explicitly cautions computer users that information flowing through the [u]niversity network is not confidential either in transit or in storage on a [u]niversity computer").

United States v. Simons, 206 F.3d 392, 398 (4th Cir. 2000) (employee had no reasonable expectation of privacy in work computer where employer's policy indicated that Internet use would be monitored and therefore "placed employees on notice that they could not reasonably expect that their Internet activity would be private").

B. Use of File-Sharing Software

Peer-to-peer (P2P) file-sharing software allows computer users to share music, movies, photographs, and other material with one another. It allows "computers [to] communicate directly with each other, not through central servers."[3] Thus, a user may retrieve files from other users' computers and may make his or her files available to other users. Examples of peer-to-peer software products include BitTorrent, Kazaa, and LimeWire.

Users of such software are able to choose which files on their computers to make available to other members of the network and which to keep private. Some programs also allow users to make files available only to select network users or "friends."

Courts consistently hold that when a user makes a file available to all users of a peer-to-peer network, the user has relinquished his or her reasonable expectation of privacy in that file. For example, when a collector of child pornography makes images or video recordings available to an entire network, and a law enforcement officer who is a member of the network obtains the images or recordings from the collector, the officer has not invaded the collector's reasonable expectation of privacy. This is so even if the officer uses software that is not available to the general public in order to seek out files containing child pornography.[4]

Even when a user makes a file available only to select "friends," some courts have ruled that the user has relinquished his or her reasonable expectation

3. Metro-Goldwyn-Mayer Studios Inc. v. Grokster, Ltd., 545 U.S. 913 (2005).

4. State v. Daigle, 93 So. 3d 657, 665 (La. Ct. App. 2012) (a defendant who uses peer-to-peer software has no reasonable expectation of privacy in shared files even "if the investigating law enforcement officer uses software specially modified to screen for child pornography, such as ShareazaLE or the Wyoming Tool Kit, provided that the software has no greater access to the defendants' computer files than that available to any other Gnutella client").

of privacy in the file. This is based on the so-called third-party doctrine, the United States Supreme Court's holding that "a person has no legitimate expectation of privacy in information he voluntarily turns over to third parties."[5] The reasoning of these cases would appear to apply to files shared with other users through services not normally considered peer-to-peer networks, such as Dropbox or Google Docs.

At least one court has ruled that even though a user relinquishes his or her reasonable expectation of privacy in a file by allowing others to access it using peer-to-peer software, the user may still have a reasonable expectation of privacy in the file if it is obtained by other means, such as an officer's search of the user's computer.[6]

Case Summaries on Use of File-Sharing Software

United States v. Hill, 750 F.3d 982 (8th Cir. 2014) (following Eighth Circuit precedent and concluding that defendant did not have a reasonable expectation of privacy in publicly shared computer files that he made accessible to others through the use of LimeWire peer-to-peer file sharing software).

United States v. Conner, 521 F. App'x 493, 497 (6th Cir. 2013) (unpublished) ("Public exposure of information [via file-sharing software] defeats an objectively reasonable expectation of privacy under the Fourth Amendment.").

United States v. Brooks, No. 12-CR-166 (RRM), 2012 WL 6562947, at *2 (E.D.N.Y. Dec. 17, 2012) (unpublished) ("[C]ourts have uniformly held that a user of a private or 'closed' peer-to-peer network such as GigaTribe who makes available files to his 'friends' does not have an objectively reasonable expectation of privacy in those files he shared.").

United States v. Sawyer, 786 F. Supp. 2d 1352, 1356 (N.D. Ohio 2011) (defendant had no reasonable expectation of privacy in files he shared using GigaTribe; although GigaTribe is a "closed" peer-to-peer sharing system, which allows only approved "friends" to access selected files on one's computer, "the rationale of the decisions analyzing open file sharing programs is still persuasive" because once the defendant "granted his 'friends' access to his files, he had no control over the manner in which his friends used that access").

---

5. Smith v. Maryland, 442 U.S. 735, 743–44 (1979).
6. State v. Bailey, 989 A.2d 716 (Me. 2010).

State v. Bailey, 989 A.2d 716 (Me. 2010) (although defendant used P2P file-sharing software, he maintained a reasonable expectation of privacy in shared files on his computer against access by means other than a file-sharing network—specifically, against a police officer who accessed the files by searching the defendant's computer).

United States v. Borowy, 595 F.3d 1045, 1048 (9th Cir. 2010) (defendant had no reasonable expectation of privacy even though he had tried to adjust the settings on file-sharing software to limit others' access to his computer; "[d]espite his efforts, [the defendant's] files were still entirely exposed to public view . . . [, and his] subjective intention not to share his files did not create an objectively reasonable expectation of privacy in the face of such widespread public access").

United States v. Stults, 575 F.3d 834 (8th Cir. 2009) (defendant had no reasonable expectation of privacy in computer on which he had installed peer-to-peer file-sharing software, and agents' use of such software to examine the contents of the defendant's computer and to copy images of child pornography from the computer was not a search).

United States v. Ganoe, 538 F.3d 1117, 1127 (9th Cir. 2008) (defendant had no reasonable expectation of privacy in the contents of a computer on which he had installed file-sharing software: "Although as a general matter an individual has an objectively reasonable expectation of privacy in his personal computer . . . we fail to see how this expectation can survive Ganoe's decision to install and use file-sharing software, thereby opening his computer to anyone else with the same freely available program.").

United States v. King, 509 F.3d 1338 (11th Cir. 2007) (similar to *Ganoe* and *Stults*).

C. Lack of Ownership or Other Interest

Generally, "a defendant may not object to the search and seizure of the property of another."[7] In order to contest a search, therefore, a defendant must show that the property that was searched belonged to, or was in the legitimate possession of, the defendant.[8]

7. State v. Boyd, 169 N.C. App. 204 (2005).

8. State v. Stitt, 201 N.C. App. 233, 241 (2009) (stating that a defendant must have an "ownership or a possessory interest" in the property in question in order to challenge a search).

Thus, a person who steals a car has no reasonable expectation of privacy in its contents.[9] Similarly, courts consistently have ruled that a person who is in possession of a stolen computer, cellular phone, or other electronic device generally does not have a reasonable expectation of privacy in the data stored on the device. A somewhat similar situation may arise when a defendant is living in a place, such as a halfway house, where cellular phones are not permitted. A defendant who possesses a digital device in violation of residential rules may be deemed to lack a reasonable expectation of privacy in the device.[10]

Case Summaries on Lack of Ownership or Other Interest

United States v. Clinton, No. CR 12-40018, 2012 WL 5185746, at *3 (D.S.D. Oct 17, 2012) (defendant lacked a reasonable expectation of privacy in a cell phone which belonged and was registered to another despite the fact that the phone was found on the defendant's person upon his arrest because "mere possession of the cell phone, without more, is insufficient to establish a Fourth Amendment right to privacy in [the phone's] contents").

State v. Oliveras, 65 So. 3d 1162, 1167 (Fla. Dist. Ct. App. 2011) (stating that a thief "lacked any reasonable expectation of privacy with respect to any communication he transmitted to, through, or from the stolen computer").

Casella v. Borders, 404 F. App'x 800, 803 (4th Cir. 2010) (unpublished) (in a civil case brought under 42 U.S.C. § 1983, the court ruled that an arrestee's girlfriend lacked a legitimate expectation of privacy in a cellular phone lent to the arrestee containing nude pictures of the girlfriend because the girlfriend "allege[d] no facts indicating she exercised a right to control the cell phone or its contents after giving phone" to the arrestee).

State v. Thunder, 777 N.W.2d 373 (S.D. 2010) (defendant lacked a reasonable expectation of privacy in a cell phone he used as an alarm clock

---

9. *See* State v. Mlo, 335 N.C. 353 (1994) (defendant had no reasonable expectation of privacy in a car he was using without authorization); State v. Greenwood, 301 N.C. 705, 709 (1981) ("No thief has any reasonable expectations of privacy in his use of the property he has stolen.").

10. United States v. Huart, 735 F.3d 972 (7th Cir. 2013) (defendant was not permitted to have a cell phone at his halfway house, and house rules provided that any resident who did have a cell phone was required to permit staff to search the phone at any time; accordingly, he had no reasonable expectation of privacy in his phone).

which contained evidence suggesting that the defendant raped a young girl, because the defendant's possession of the phone was wrongful as the phone was purchased for another family member, the defendant did not ask permission to use the phone, and the phone had been activated in another family member's name).

State v. Stitt, 201 N.C. App. 233, 241 (2009) (defendant moved to suppress cellular telephone records obtained by the State; the motion was properly denied as the defendant failed to establish "an ownership interest in the cellular telephones or [that he] had been given a possessory interest by the legal owner," and in fact it appeared that the defendant stole the telephones from a man he had murdered; courts "will not assume ownership or a possessory interest in property based on mere possession").

United States v. Mercado-Nava, 486 F. Supp. 2d 1271 (D. Kan. 2007) (defendant lacked standing to challenge a search of two cellular phones found on his person at the time of his arrest because he failed to assert ownership of either during trial and did not testify as to having an expectation of privacy in either at suppression hearing).

Hicks v. State, 929 So. 2d 13 (Fla. Dist. Ct. App. 2006) (defendant had no reasonable expectation of privacy in a stolen computer, so officers' search thereof did not violate the Fourth Amendment).

United States v. Caymen, 404 F.3d 1196, 1200 (9th Cir. 2005) (defendant had no reasonable expectation of privacy in a computer that he obtained by fraud because "[t]he Fourth Amendment does not protect a defendant from a warrantless search of property that he stole").

D. Lost and Abandoned Property

When a person voluntarily discards property or renounces any claim to it, the person is deemed to have abandoned the property and to have relinquished any expectation of privacy in the property.[11] Similarly, a person loses any expectation of privacy in an item when he or she places the item in a location in which the person has no reasonable expectation of privacy.[12]

---

11. *See, e.g.*, State v. Joe, 222 N.C. App. 206 (2012) (noting both the rule and an exception to it when the person relinquishes the property as a result of unlawful police activity); State v. Eaton, 210 N.C. App. 142 (2011) (holding that the defendant abandoned a plastic baggie when he discarded it on a public road).

12. Such as in an "abandoned shack," United States v. Jackson, 585 F.2d. 653 (4th Cir. 1978) (cited in State v. Hemphill, 210 N.C. App. 759 (2011) (unpublished)),

Even when a person merely loses or inadvertently misplaces property, his or her expectation of privacy in the property is diminished. However, it is reduced only to the extent necessary to enable "law enforcement officials [to] identify[] and return[] such property to the owner."[13]

These principles apply to electronic devices as well as to other types of property and have formed the basis for some interesting court opinions.

Case Summaries on Lost and Abandoned Property

FINDING OR ASSUMING A REASONABLE EXPECTATION OF PRIVACY

United State v. Lopez-Cruz, 730 F.3d 803, 809 (9th Cir. 2013) (holding that the defendant did not abandon two cell phones that were in his car when he told an officer that they belonged to a friend; he did not "disclaim use of them or otherwise dissociate himself from them," but merely disclaimed ownership of them).

People v. Schutter, 249 P.3d 1123, 1125 (Colo. 2011) (defendant who accidentally locked his iPhone in a gas station restroom, leading a gas station employee to turn it over to police, did not abandon the phone; and even if "an otherwise reasonable expectation of privacy . . . is diminished when that property is lost or mislaid because it is only reasonable to expect that an officer . . . will examine it to learn how it can be returned to its owner," there was no need for an officer to examine the phone in this case, because the defendant knew where he had left it, but had not yet returned to retrieve it).

United States v. Crist, 627 F. Supp. 2d 575 (M.D. Pa. 2008) (defendant owned a computer which he kept in a house he rented; he did not stay current on the rent and allowed the house to fall into squalor, leading the landlord to hire a crew to move the defendant's property, including the computer, out of the house, though the landlord did not commence formal eviction proceedings; the defendant's actions did not constitute abandonment of the computer).

FINDING NO REASONABLE EXPECTATION OF PRIVACY

State v. Gould, 963 N.E.2d 136 (Ohio 2012) (defendant lacked a reasonable expectation of privacy in a hard drive containing child pornography that he left at his mother's house because defendant "had not

---

or buried in the ground on property that belongs to another, State v. Teltser, 61 N.C. App. 290 (1983).

13. Gudema v. Nassau Cnty., 163 F.3d 717, 722 (2d Cir. 1998).

made any inquiry about the hard drive or asserted control over it for almost four months" and therefore had abandoned the drive).

Miller v. State, 335 S.W.3d 847 (Tex. App. 2011) (defendant lacked a reasonable expectation of privacy in a thumb drive he accidentally left at work; he often left the drive unattended, had mislaid the drive before, had not password protected it, and had not even labeled it with his name).

United States v. Soto, 779 F. Supp. 2d 208, 219 (D. Mass. 2011) ("[B]y leaving his computer in a stolen car given over to the possession of a [compatriot], [the defendant] forfeited any legitimate expectation of privacy that he may have had in its hard drive.").

United States v. Larson, No. 10-00328-01-CR-W-DW, 2011 WL 6012927, at *4 (W.D. Mo. Nov. 18, 2011) (unpublished) (defendant who left thirty-one disks containing child pornography in the chimney of a foreclosed home failed to "in any way indicate an intent to maintain ownership" of the disks and therefore abandoned them), *report and recommendation adopted,* 2011 WL 6012593 (W.D. Mo. Dec. 1, 2011) (unpublished).

State v. Dailey, No. 8-10-01, 2010 WL 3836204, at *3 (Ohio Ct. App. Oct. 4, 2010) (defendant "voluntarily abandoned his cell phone when he slipped out of his coat and left it and its contents [including the phone] behind in order to escape being detained" for shoplifting by a loss prevention employee of a retail store).

E. Relinquishing Control Temporarily

A number of cases address the extent to which a person may lose a reasonable expectation of privacy in an electronic device by relinquishing control of the device temporarily. Most of the reported cases involve an individual giving a device to a repair person, who then discovers child pornography on the device and calls law enforcement. Some courts have addressed this fact pattern under the private search doctrine, discussed in the next section, while others have considered whether the owner relinquished his or her expectation of privacy in the device by allowing a repair person unfettered access to the device.

The idea that a person loses his or her expectation of privacy in the contents of a digital device by entrusting the device to another finds some support in the idea, discussed in detail in chapter 4, that a person has no expectation of privacy in the numbers he or she dials on a telephone because those numbers are shared with the telephone company. However, the parallel is not exact, and courts may be reluctant to endorse completely the relinquishment of privacy rationale. If a person loses his or her expectation of privacy in a device by bringing it to a repair person, it would seem that law enforcement could thoroughly search every device in any repair shop without violating the Fourth Amendment, whether or not a repair person had found anything on the device, or indeed, whether or not a repair person had even looked at the device. For this reason, the private search rationale may be a better way to analyze these cases.

Case Summaries on Relinquishing Control Temporarily

United States v. Tosti, 733 F.3d 816, 822 (9th Cir. 2013) (defendant gave his computer to a technician for repair; the technician viewed images on the computer, including thumbnail images of child pornography, and contacted police; the police subsequently viewed the same images without a warrant; the court upheld this under the private search doctrine but also stated that "[s]ince [the repair person]—a private individual to whom [the defendant] had voluntarily delivered his computer with the explicit understanding that he would inspect the system to complete the repairs—could discern the content of the photos, any expectation of privacy [the defendant] had in those pictures was extinguished").

State v. Ballard, 276 P.3d 976, 980 (N.M. Ct. App. 2012) (defendant who had given, for repair purposes, his laptop and two external hard drives containing child pornography to a co-worker who subsequently discovered the illicit content "lost any expectation of privacy he may have had once he gave the computer and external hard drives" to his co-worker), *rev'd on other grounds sub nom.* State v. Olsson, 324 P.3d 1230 (N.M. 2014).

Melton v. State, 69 So. 3d 916 (Ala. Crim. App. 2010) (defendant "relinquished any reasonable expectation of privacy in the files containing child pornography when he exposed the [repair personnel] to those files [by asking them to repair his computer without first removing or password-protecting the files]"; "[b]ecause he did not retain a privacy interest in those files, the officers did not violate Fourth Amendment principles when they viewed the contents of any of those files, regardless of whether the officers exceeded the scope of the search conducted by" the repair personnel).

Commonwealth v. Sodomsky, 939 A.2d 363, 369 (Pa. Super. Ct. 2007) (defendant lacked a reasonable expectation of privacy in the files on a computer he brought in for repairs; "[i]f a person is aware of, or freely grants to a third party, potential access to his computer contents, he has knowingly exposed the contents of his computer to the public and has lost any reasonable expectation of privacy in those contents").

State v. Horton, 962 So. 2d 459, 464, 465 (La. Ct. App. 2007) (Best Buy employees who were installing a new hard drive on the defendant's computer discovered child pornography on the device; this was "solely a 'private search'"; furthermore, "because he had voluntarily relinquished control of the computer to the repair store and failed to secure the images [in question]," the defendant lacked a reasonable expectation of privacy).

Rogers v. State, 113 S.W.3d 452, 458 (Tex. App. 2003) (defendant lost any reasonable expectation of privacy in the images on his computer when he "voluntarily relinquished control to [a] computer repair store" and expressly requested that the store back up his image files).

United States v. Barth, 26 F. Supp. 2d 929, 937 (W.D. Tex. 1998) ("Defendant did not lose his reasonable expectation of privacy in his closed, individual files when he gave [his computer] hard drive to [a repairman]. . . . Defendant gave the hard drive to [the repairman] for the limited purpose of repairing a problem unrelated to specific files and also expected that he would have the unit back the following morning to continue his business. Defendant, therefore, retained his reasonable expectation of privacy in the files.").

F. Call Logs

Most cellular phones can display a list of phone numbers from which calls recently have been received and to which calls recently have been made. These lists are sometimes called "call logs," "call histories," or "recent calls." It is possible to argue that such call logs consist solely of routing information that has already been disclosed to the service provider, and that the owner or possessor of the cellular phone therefore has no reasonable expectation of privacy in the information.[14] As reflected in the case summaries below,

14. *See generally* Smith v. Maryland, 442 U.S. 735, 744 (1979) (no expectation of privacy in numbers dialed from landline telephone because "[w]hen he used his phone, petitioner voluntarily conveyed numerical information to the telephone company and 'exposed' that information to its equipment in the ordinary course

a few courts have accepted this argument. A majority have not, and the U.S. Supreme Court's emphasis on the private and personal nature of the information that may be contained in cell phones likely further undermines the argument.[15] The related issue of obtaining phone records from service providers is discussed in chapter 3.

A few courts have gone even further and have suggested that "phone book" or "address book" information stored on a phone may not be subject to a reasonable expectation of privacy. Such a suggestion is almost certainly mistaken, as that information may be stored locally and is not necessarily shared with the service provider.[16]

Case Summaries on Call Logs

United States v. Gomez, 807 F. Supp. 2d 1134, 1140 (S.D. Fla. 2011) ("[T]he weight of authority agrees that accessing a cell phone's call log or text message folder is considered a 'search' for Fourth Amendment purposes.").

United States v. Maldonado, No. 09-40031-01/02-SAC, 2009 WL 2760798, at *12 (D. Kan. Aug. 26, 2009) (unpublished) ("Just as there is no reasonable expectation of privacy in numbers called or numbers calling, because they are voluntarily turned over to third parties, *see Smith v. Maryland*, 442 U.S. 735 . . . (1979), there may be no reasonable expectation of privacy in a cell phone's recent call directory or phonebook directory.")

United States v. Fierros-Alavarez, 547 F. Supp. 2d 1206 (D. Kan. 2008) (defendant had no reasonable expectation of privacy in call log and address book, as dialed and received call information is shared with phone company and address book contained nothing more than names and phone numbers similar to that in call log).

United States v. Finley, 477 F.3d 250, 259 (5th Cir. 2007) ("[W]e conclude that [the defendant] had a reasonable expectation of privacy in the call records and text messages on [his] cell phone.")

---

of business. In so doing, petitioner assumed the risk that the company would reveal to police the numbers he dialed").

15. Riley v. California, 573 U.S. ___, ___, 134 S. Ct. 2473, 2488–89 (2014) (stating that cell phone searches "implicate privacy concerns far beyond those implicated by the search of a cigarette pack, a wallet, or a purse").

16. Address book information may be shared in some instances, depending on the extent to which it is maintained on the phone's subscriber identity module (SIM) card. *See generally Subscriber identity module*, Wikipedia, http://en.wikipedia.org/wiki/Subscriber_identity_module (last visited Dec. 29, 2014).

II. Private Searches

If a person's reasonable expectation of privacy in a computer or other electronic device is compromised by a private actor rather than by a government entity, there is no Fourth Amendment violation.[17] Even when a law enforcement officer repeats the private search, there is generally no Fourth Amendment issue unless the officer exceeds the scope of the original search.[18] So, for example, if one roommate picks up another's smartphone, scrolls through the photographs saved there, and sees pictures of the latter engaged in illegal conduct, there has been no Fourth Amendment search. Nor will there be one if the former shows the phone to a law enforcement officer.

Courts generally have applied the private search doctrine even when the search is unlawful, such as when "a burglar discover[s] evidence of his victim's criminality and sen[ds] it to the police."[19] Most courts have followed this principle with regard to evidence obtained during computer intrusions by a hacker.

Fact patterns that raise private search issues often involve several related doctrines as well. For example, if A stores his laptop at B's house, B looks through the files on the laptop and finds evidence of criminality, and B notifies police, there are several possible justifications for a subsequent search of the laptop by the police:

- A may have relinquished his reasonable expectation of privacy in the laptop by storing it at B's house
- B may have had actual or apparent authority to allow the police to search the laptop
- B may have conducted a private search that was merely replicated by the police

Case Summaries on Private Searches

SEARCH JUSTIFIED UNDER PRIVATE SEARCH DOCTRINE

United States v. Tosti, 733 F.3d 816 (9th Cir. 2013) (defendant gave his computer to a technician for repair; the technician viewed images on the computer, including thumbnail images of child pornography, and contacted police; the police subsequently viewed the same images

---

17. *See generally* Burdeau v. McDowell, 256 U.S. 465, 475 (1921) (holding that the Fourth Amendment "applies to governmental action," not private action).

18. United States v. Jacobsen, 466 U.S. 109 (1984) (law enforcement officer examined damaged package already inspected by an employee of the freight carrier).

19. 1 Wayne R. LaFave, Search and Seizure § 1.8(a) (5th ed. 2012) (citing cases).

without a warrant; this did not violate the Fourth Amendment because the police did not exceed the scope of the technician's search—even though the police viewed some of the images in a larger format—and so there was no government intrusion on the defendant's privacy).

Rann v. Atchison, 689 F.3d 832, 838 (7th Cir. 2012) (police did not exceed the scope of a previously conducted private search by opening digital storage devices and viewing images, despite the fact that there was no evidence that the victim or her mother had opened and viewed the images as part of their private search; the victim and her mother "knew the contents of the digital media devices when they delivered them to the police, the police were 'substantially certain' the devices contained child pornography," and therefore the scope of the private search was not expanded).

United States v. Goodale, No. CR12-3011, 2012 WL 1376996, at *7 (N.D. Iowa Apr. 19, 2012) (unpublished) (investigators did not violate the Fourth Amendment by viewing the internet search history of the defendant's computer during an interview with a child victim because the victim brought the computer to the interview and demonstrated how he had previously discovered illicit internet searches and, therefore, the "governmental intrusion went 'no further than the private search'"), *aff'd*, 738 F.3d 917 (8th Cir. 2013).

People v. Clendenin, 939 N.E.2d 310 (Ill. 2010) (police did not exceed the scope of a private search by viewing files on a disk provided by a private searcher who had previously discovered child pornography on the disk).

United States v. Jarrett, 338 F.3d 339 (4th Cir. 2003) (applying the private search doctrine to child pornography obtained by hacker).

United States v. Steiger, 318 F.3d 1039 (11th Cir. 2003) (a hacker accessed the defendant's computer and found child pornography, which the hacker provided to the police; this was a private search that did not implicate the Fourth Amendment).

United States v. Grimes, 244 F.3d 375, 383 (5th Cir. 2001) (a computer repair technician searched the defendant's computer and found child pornography; the search "being private in nature, is not subject to Fourth Amendment analysis").

SEARCH NOT JUSTIFIED UNDER PRIVATE SEARCH DOCTRINE

People v. Michael E., 178 Cal. Rptr. 3d 467 (Cal. Ct. App. 2014) (defendant gave his computer to a technician for repair; the technician viewed images of minors that were sexually suggestive but not pornographic and contacted police; at the behest of an officer, the technician looked for additional files, eventually locating video files of child pornography; the court ruled that the officer exceeded the scope of the private search when he instructed the technician to look for additional files; the officer's actions could not be justified as simply a more thorough search of the same "container" the technician searched, because a computer hard drive contains too much information to be treated as a single container).

United States v. D'Andrea, 648 F.3d 1, 8 (1st Cir. 2011) (suggesting that the private search doctrine did not apply where a private individual obtained access to the defendant's online account by "piec[ing] together the password by surreptitiously taking scraps of paper on which [the defendant] had jotted down various letters and numbers" because in such circumstances, the defendant did not "assume[] the risk" of disclosing the data to another).

United States v. Runyan, 275 F.3d 449, 464, 465 (5th Cir. 2001) (police exceeded the scope of a private search "when they examined disks that the private searchers did not examine" but "did not exceed the scope of the private search if they examined more files on the privately-searched disks" than the private searchers had).

III. Consent Searches

Assuming that a defendant has a reasonable expectation of privacy in a computer or other electronic device, a law enforcement officer may search the device only with a warrant, discussed in chapter 1, unless one of the several exceptions to the warrant requirement applies. The remainder of this chapter discusses the exceptions, starting with consent.

Fourth Amendment rights, like other rights, may be waived. Thus, "[c]onsent, when given voluntarily, is an exception to the warrant requirement."[20] The issues that most often arise with consent searches are

20. State v. Boyd, 207 N.C. App. 632, 637 (2010). *See also* Schneckloth v. Bustamonte, 412 U.S. 218 (1973).

(1) whether the person who consented had the actual or apparent[21] authority to consent to the search of the item in question, (2) whether consent was obtained voluntarily, and (3) whether the search exceeded the scope of the consent.

A. Authority to Consent

A search may be based on consent only if consent is given by a person with the actual or apparent authority to consent. The issue of authority to consent is frequently litigated outside the context of digital devices, and that body of law will not be discussed here.[22] Factors that courts have considered when deciding whether a person has the authority to consent specifically to the search of an electronic device include where the device is located, i.e., in a common area of a residence or in a bedroom used by a single occupant; whether the device is password protected, and if so, whether the person giving consent knows the password; whether the person giving consent regularly uses the device; and whether the person giving consent owns the device or has been entrusted with it by its owner.

Case Summaries on Authority to Consent

AUTHORITY PRESENT

United States v. Watkins, 760 F.3d 1271 (11th Cir. 2014) (defendant's wife's consent to a full search of the family computer was not limited by the defendant's prior consent to a limited search of the computer where the defendant was present at the time of his wife's consent and did not object).

State v. Sobczak, 833 N.W.2d 59 (Wis. 2013) (girlfriend was spending the weekend with defendant boyfriend at boyfriend's parents' home while they were away; when boyfriend went to work, she asked for and received boyfriend's consent to use his laptop; she saw child pornography on the computer and contacted law enforcement; she allowed an officer into the house and permitted him to see the pornography; defendant argued that she had permission to do neither, but the court

21. The U.S. Supreme Court has recognized that police may act on consent from a person who reasonably appears to have authority over a location or an item, even if it subsequently turns out that the person lacked authority. Illinois v. Rodriguez, 497 U.S. 177 (1990). *See also* Section 15A-222(3) of the North Carolina General Statutes (hereinafter G.S.) (allowing searches based on the consent of "a person who . . . is reasonably apparently entitled" to give it).

22. A full discussion may be found in Robert L. Farb, Arrest, Search, and Investigation in North Carolina 199–202 (4th ed. 2011).

ruled that she had the run of the house as the defendant's girlfriend and as a person allowed to remain in the house by herself; she also had full use of the laptop).

United States v. Clutter, 674 F.3d 980, 982, 985 (8th Cir. 2012) (police determined that the defendant had committed several burglaries, including stealing computer equipment; the defendant's father "gave [the officers] permission to search the entire residence" he shared with his son; this was sufficient to support seizure of two computers from a common area of the home and one computer from an area controlled by the defendant's father; officers subsequently obtained search warrants for the computers and discovered child pornography on them; among other justifications for the seizure, officers reasonably relied on the father's "actual or apparent authority to consent to a temporary seizure.").

United States v. Stabile, 633 F.3d 219, 232, 234 (3d Cir. 2011) (consent of a woman who was living with, and who thought that she was married to, the defendant was sufficient to allow officers to seize and search the defendant's computers; factors relevant to determining common authority include "the identity of the user(s), whether password protection is used, and the location of the computer in the house"; although the defendant arrived as the officers were leaving and stated "I take it [her consent] back," this had no legal effect).

United States v. King, 604 F.3d 125 (3d Cir. 2010) (defendant sexually abused his girlfriend's 2-year-old daughter with his girlfriend's consent; when officers learned of the situation and came to the defendant's home, the defendant's girlfriend agreed to allow the officers to seize her computer; the defendant stated that the computer contained his hard drive and objected to the seizure of the hard drive; the court ruled that the girlfriend's consent to the seizure of the computer also supported the seizure of the drive because the defendant assumed the risk that the girlfriend would so consent; the court distinguished *Georgia v. Randolph*, 547 U.S. 103 (2006), as applying only to residences, not to personal property).

United States v. Jackson, 598 F.3d 340 (7th Cir. 2010) (defendant's mother had apparent authority to consent to a search of a computer case belonging to the defendant where officers saw the defendant give his mother the case and she stated that he gave it to her so that she could download pictures of her grandchild).

United States v. Hudspeth, 518 F.3d 954 (8th Cir. 2008) (wife's consent to a search of a shared computer was valid even though (1) her husband, who was not present, had previously refused consent and (2) officers did not tell the wife of her husband's refusal).

United States v. Meador, No. 1:06 CR 134 CDP DDN, 2008 WL 4922001 (E.D. Mo. Jan. 7, 2008) (unpublished) (murder suspect's mother had apparent authority to consent to a search of a vehicle owned by her husband but driven by her son; however, she did not have any authority to consent to the search of a cellular phone registered to her husband's account but used by her son).

United States v. Andrus, 483 F.3d 711 (10th Cir. 2007) (defendant's father had apparent authority to consent to a search of a password-protected computer located in his 51-year-old son's bedroom; the bedroom was characterized as not a "true common area" because the father signed a computer search consent form, led officers to the bedroom, and remained silent as to his lack of authority over the device; officers were also unaware of password protection prior to search), *decision clarified on denial of reh'g*, 499 F.3d 1162 (10th Cir. 2007).

United States v. Buckner, 473 F.3d 551 (4th Cir. 2007) (wife had apparent authority to consent to a search of a computer that she leased and that was located in a common area of the home she and her husband shared; although husband had password-protected files, the officer who conducted the search did not know that they were password protected because no one told him so and because, by creating a forensic image of the hard drive, he bypassed any passwords).

United States v. Morgan, 435 F.3d 660 (6th Cir. 2006) (defendant's wife had apparent authority to consent to a search of a computer located in the basement of the family home, a common area to which wife had access; wife represented to detective that she occasionally used the computer and that she and defendant did not maintain unique user accounts, though she failed to indicate that she more frequently used a personal laptop).

AUTHORITY ABSENT

United States v. James, 353 F.3d 606 (8th Cir. 2003) (friend's consent was not sufficient to support a search of computer disks represented by the defendant to the friend as backup disks for defendant's computer; the friend had no actual authority to consent because the defendant had not given the friend permission to "exercise control" over disks simply by asking the friend to store them; and the friend had no apparent authority to consent because officers knew that the defendant wished to keep the disks private based on an intercepted jail letter and the fact that the disks were labeled "confidential", "personal", and "private"; the defendant had not abandoned the disks because he claimed ownership of them by labeling the envelope, and the defendant's instructions to destroy the disks did not constitute abandonment).

Trulock v. Freeh, 275 F.3d 391 (4th Cir. 2001) (one user of a shared computer has no authority to consent to a search of password-protected files belonging to another user).

B. Voluntariness of Consent

Consent is voluntary if it is "the product of an essentially free and unconstrained choice by its maker."[23] Voluntariness "is a question of fact to be determined from the totality of all the circumstances."[24] The same factors that are relevant to the voluntariness of a suspect's consent to a police search of his or her home or car are relevant to the voluntariness of a suspect's consent to a police search of his or her laptop or cell phone. Appropriate considerations include the setting in which consent is sought; the personal characteristics of the suspect, such as his or her age, education, and intelligence; any threats, promises, or intimidation by law enforcement; and other relevant matters.

One issue that seems to arise with particular frequency in cases involving digital devices is the extent to which an officer's misrepresentation of the purpose of a search may undermine the voluntariness of consent. For example, an officer may ask for consent to search a suspect's computer for evidence of hacker intrusions, identity theft, or other matters, when in fact, the officer believes that the computer contains child pornography. As the cases summarized below show, such misrepresentations are not always fatal to the voluntariness of a suspect's consent, but they may cause some courts to examine more closely both the voluntariness of the consent and its intended scope.

23. *Schneckloth*, 412 U.S. at 225.
24. *Id.* at 223.

Case Summaries on Voluntariness of Consent

CONSENT VOLUNTARY

United States v. Rounds, 749 F.3d 326, 338 (5th Cir. 2014) (rejecting the defendant's argument that his consent to a search of his phone was involuntary because his discussion with officers was "directed to the issue of narcotics" but the officers were actually investigating a sex crime, and finding no support for the theory that the defendant's consent was involuntary "because police officers did not inform him for what purpose they wished to search his phone").

United States v. Williams, 760 F.3d 811, 816 (8th Cir. 2014) (after determining that a defendant was not in custody for *Miranda* purposes when, in the course of a warrant search of his home, he gave consent to search his car and seize the laptop located therein, the court further concluded that the defendant's consent was voluntary despite the "'police dominated' atmosphere arising from the execution of [the] search warrant").

United States v. Muhlenbruch, 634 F.3d 987, 999 (8th Cir. 2011) (child pornography suspect consented to a search of his computer during an interview at a police station; applying standard factors such as the defendant's age, lack of intoxication, experience with law enforcement, and the like, the court found that the consent was voluntary; even though the defendant "initially refused consent and requested to speak to an attorney," whereupon "the officers explained that they would need [him] to remain at the police station until they could obtain a search warrant," this did not undermine the voluntariness of the consent, as it "was not a threat but merely a truthful explanation of the process the officers would take to protect evidence").

United States v. Farley, 607 F.3d 1294, 1307 (11th Cir. 2010) (defendant who had been corresponding online with undercover officer about having sex with the officer's imaginary 11-year-old daughter was approached by officers who "initially attempted to disguise the purpose of [their] questioning by telling [the defendant] it was a national security matter" based on an "FBI program that picks up certain words online like terrorist, threats and things of that nature"; this deception did not render the defendant's subsequent consent to search his computer involuntary because by the time the defendant consented, the officers had made clear the true focus of their investigation).

State v. Bailey, 989 A.2d 716 (Me. 2010) (officer who suspected a defendant of possessing child pornography asked for permission to search the defendant's computer for evidence of hacker intrusions; the defendant consented; the officer then searched all video files on the computer, finding child pornography; the consent was voluntary notwithstanding the officer's deception, but the officer's search exceeded the scope of consent because a search for evidence of intrusions would not naturally include an examination of video files).

People v. Prinzing, 907 N.E.2d 87 (Ill. App. Ct. 2009) (officers suspected the defendant of possessing child pornography; they told the defendant that they believed that he may have been the victim of fraudulent credit card charges and asked to search his computer for evidence of the fraud, including computer viruses; the defendant agreed and the officers searched the computer, finding child pornography; the defendant moved to suppress, arguing that his consent was based on the officers' misrepresentations and was therefore involuntary; the court disagreed, ruling that the officers had genuine concerns about an irregular credit card transaction and so had a "twofold purpose" and that, in any event, trickery is just one factor in the voluntariness analysis; the defendant also argued that he gave the officers consent to search for viruses and evidence of credit card fraud and that the scope of his consent did not include image files, which would not be likely to contain such information, and the court agreed on this point).

CONSENT INVOLUNTARY

State v. Barajas, 817 N.W.2d 204, 218 (Minn. Ct. App. 2012) (defendant's consent to a search of his cell phone was involuntary where, among other things, he "was in a vulnerable position because of his citizenship status, his lack of proficiency in English, and the absence of a neutral interpreter," and it was unclear whether his consent was obtained in Spanish).

United States v. Parson, 599 F. Supp. 2d 592, 598 (W.D. Pa. 2009) (officers determined that the elderly defendant's credit card had been used to make payments to a child pornography website; they went to the defendant's home and told him that he "could be a victim of identity theft"; the defendant "thought that the [officers] were there to help him with his identity theft problems, so he turned on [his] computer" and allowed the officers to search it; they found child pornography; based principally on the officers' misrepresentation regarding the supposed identity theft investigation, the court ruled that the defendant's consent was involuntary).

C. Scope of Consent

An officer conducting a search based on consent may search only to the extent allowed by the person who gave consent. So, for example, if an officer asks a suspect for consent to search the suspect's cell phone, and the suspect replies, "you may search my text messages but not my pictures," the officer generally must abide by that limitation. Sometimes the scope of consent is expressed in a way that permits multiple interpretations. In such cases, it is important to remember that "[t]he standard for measuring the scope of a suspect's consent under the Fourth Amendment is that of 'objective' reasonableness what would the typical reasonable person have understood by the exchange between the officer and the suspect?"[25]

Scope-of-consent issues that frequently arise in digital device cases include:

- Whether a general consent to search a home, office, or vehicle includes consent to search a computer or electronic device located therein
- Whether consent to search a home, office, or vehicle for a specified offense includes consent to search a computer or electronic device located therein
- How exhaustively a search may be conducted based on consent to "look at," "seize," "examine," or "search" an electronic device—for example, may an officer use forensic software to analyze the device?
- Whether consent to search a computer includes consent to search associated storage devices and peripherals
- How long an officer may retain a device pursuant to consent to search it

Of course, officers can eliminate most of these issues by being clear about the scope of the searches they wish to conduct. For example, an officer could ask for consent to search a suspect's home, specifying that the search would include the suspect's digital devices.

Case Summaries on Scope of Consent

SEARCHES WITHIN SCOPE OF CONSENT

United States v. Suing, 712 F.3d 1209, 1211, 1212 (8th Cir. 2013) (the defendant's general consent to a search of his vehicle, "to include luggage, containers, and contents," supported an officer's search of "an

25. Florida v. Jimeno, 500 U.S. 248, 251 (1991) (holding that "a suspect's general consent to a search of his car . . . include[s] consent to examine a paper bag lying on the floor of the car," *id.*).

external computer hard drive in a bag on the front passenger seat" that contained child pornography; the court noted with approval that when the officer first discovered the pornography, he "stopped the search, called a prosecutor for advice, and obtained a new warrant authorizing the search for child pornography").

United States v. Lucas, 640 F.3d 168, 178 (6th Cir. 2011) (officers obtained consent to search the defendant's home for drugs and "other material or records pertaining to narcotics," found marijuana plants, then searched his laptop computer, finding child pornography; the court held that the computer search was within the scope of consent, given that marijuana growers often keep records on their computers and that the defendant, although present, did not object to the search of the computer; the court emphasized that its decision was "based on the facts of this case").

United States v. Emanuel, 440 F. App'x 881, 885 (11th Cir. 2011) (unpublished) (defendant voluntarily consented to the seizure and search of his computer; the defendant's possessory interest in the computer was not unreasonably interfered with despite the fact that thirty-four days elapsed between seizure and procurement of a search warrant; original consent "was not limitless," but in the absence of a "specific time limit or a revocation" searching the computer ten months after obtaining the warrant was within the scope of the original consent).

United States v. Chappell, No. 1:10-cr-531-WSD-ECS-1, 2011 WL 5352947, at *6 (N.D. Ga. Nov. 4, 2011) (unpublished) (defendant's "general consent" to search of hotel room encompassed "the hotel room and all containers, including electronic data storage materials and devices"; seizure of various electronic devices including computers, cell phones, CDs, floppy disks, and a thumb drive was reasonable because agents lacked appropriate on-site equipment to perform a search pursuant to consent).

United States v. Gilbert, No. 10-03093-01-CR-S-RED, 2011 WL 5119122, at *2 (W.D. Mo. Sept. 30, 2011) (the defendant's general consent to a search of his truck "extended to the search and seizure of the cell phone" found therein; the investigating officer did not exceed the scope of the defendant's consent by opening the phone and reading text messages; even if the officer exceeded the scope of consent, the search was justified under the automobile exception, discussed later in this chapter), *report and recommendation adopted*, 2011 WL 5118976 (W.D. Mo. Oct. 27, 2011).

United States v. Coates, 685 F. Supp. 2d 551 (M.D. Pa. 2010) (defendant implicitly consented to an officer's search of his phone when he handed it to the officer and stated that he wanted the officer to see a threatening text message; the defendant did not limit the scope of the officer's examination of the phone and assumed the risk that in the course of attempting to find the text message, the officer would see other material—such as child pornography—on the phone), *aff'd*, 462 F. App'x 199 (3d Cir. 2012) (unpublished).

State v. Nadeau, 1 A.3d 445, 456 (Me. 2010) (search of the contents of a flash drive was within the scope of a defendant's consent to the seizure of the drive because when defendant gave the drive to investigating officers, he knew they were looking for child pornography and defendant expressed "no limitations on what [officers] might do with it" and "voluntarily handing the flash drive to the police was tantamount to handing over the child pornography itself").

United States v. Luken, 560 F.3d 741 (8th Cir. 2009) (officers suspected the defendant of possessing child pornography and asked for consent to search his computer; he agreed in writing, authorizing the officers to "seize and view" his computer; the officers seized the computer, and one of them later examined its contents using special forensic software, finding child pornography; the defendant moved to suppress, arguing that the comprehensive forensic examination conducted by the officer went beyond "view[ing]" the computer, but neither the trial court nor the appellate court agreed, in part because the officers told the defendant prior to the search that they had access to forensic tools that allowed them to recover deleted files, etc.).

Lemons v. State, 298 S.W.3d 658 (Tex. App. 2009) (officers asked the defendant if he had been talking to a minor on his cell phone; shortly thereafter, an officer asked to see the defendant's cell phone and the defendant handed it to him; after looking at the call log, the officer accessed the phone's camera feature and saw a nude picture of the minor; the appellate court rejected the defendant's argument that by looking at the picture, the officer exceeded the scope of the defendant's consent).

Blake v. Knieper, No. 03-74097, 2009 WL 1689308, at *8 (E.D. Mich. June 16, 2009) (unpublished) (holding that it was "objectively reasonable" for law enforcement officers to interpret a defendant's consent to seize his computer as including consent to seize two "CD-ROMs sitting next to it," citing *Miller*, below).

United States v. Herndon, 501 F.3d 683, 690 (6th Cir. 2007) (holding that a probation condition requiring the defendant to consent to an officer's search of his computer included a search of external drives; "the term 'computer' is commonly understood to include the collection of components involved in a computer's operation").

United States v. Miller, 450 F. Supp. 2d 1321 (M.D. Fla. 2006) (defendant's consent to search his "computer" properly "included his consent for officers to remove the computer and attached hard drive," given that the hard drive was clearly intended for use with the computer).

Guy v. State, 913 A.2d 558 (Del. 2006) (defendant consented to a "complete and thorough search" of his apartment and stood silently by as officers searched his pager; the search was within the scope of the defendant's consent).

United States v. Brooks, 427 F.3d 1246 (10th Cir. 2005) (officers told the defendant that they were investigating him for possession of child pornography; he signed a consent to a "complete search" of his computer; although the officers told the defendant that they would use a "pre-search" disk, they ended up doing a manual search instead; although the method used for searching was different than the one explained to the defendant, the search was still permitted under the defendant's broad consent).

United States v. Long, 425 F.3d 482 (7th Cir. 2005) (defendant consented to a search of his office and computer; the fact that officers used forensic software to search the computer did not cause the search to be beyond the scope of his consent).

United States v. Rossby, 81 F. App'x 109, 110 (9th Cir. 2003) (unpublished) (holding that a search of a defendant's non-password-protected laptop computers was within the scope of his consent, which authorized officers to conduct a "complete search" of his office and to take "from my premises any letters, papers, materials, or other property which they may desire").

United States v. Al-Marri, 230 F. Supp. 2d 535 (S.D.N.Y. 2002) (defendant's consent to a search of his home inherently included consent to search containers, including a computer, within the home; the scope of consent was particularly clear here, where defendant, upon request, unplugged the computer and handed it to the officers).

United States v. Greene, 56 M.J. 817 (N-M. Ct. Crim. App. 2002) (officers did not exceed the scope of consent, which allowed them to search a defendant's residence and to remove and retain items therefrom, simply by keeping a seized computer for three months to conduct a detailed examination of it).

People v. Berry, 731 N.E.2d 853, 864 (Ill. App. Ct. 2000) (officer asked the defendant, in the course of discussing the ownership of the defendant's cellular phone, "mind if I take a look at [your phone]," and the defendant said, "[g]o right ahead"; this was sufficient to allow the officer to turn the phone on, at which point, the officer immediately noted incriminating data).

SEARCHES OUTSIDE SCOPE OF CONSENT

United States v. Lopez-Cruz, 730 F.3d 803 (9th Cir. 2013) (defendant agreed that an officer could "look at" and "search" cell phones, but such consent did not include consent for the officer to answer the phones when they rang and to impersonate the defendant).

State v. Bailey, 989 A.2d 716 (Me. 2010) (officer who suspected defendant of possessing child pornography asked for permission to search his computer for evidence of hacker intrusions; defendant consented; officer then searched all video files on the computer, finding child pornography; the consent was voluntary notwithstanding the officer's deception, but the officer's search exceeded the scope of the consent because a search for evidence of intrusions would not naturally include an examination of video files).

People v. Prinzing, 907 N.E.2d 87 (Ill. App. Ct. 2009) (officers suspected the defendant of possessing child pornography; they told the defendant that they believed that he may have been the victim of fraudulent credit card charges and asked to search his computer for evidence of the fraud, including computer viruses; the defendant agreed and the officers searched the computer, finding child pornography; the defendant moved to suppress, arguing that his consent was based on the officers' misrepresentations and was therefore involuntary; the court disagreed, ruling that the officers had genuine concerns about an irregular credit card transaction and so had a "twofold purpose" and that, in any event, trickery is just one factor in the voluntariness analysis; the defendant also argued that he gave the officers consent to search for viruses and evidence of credit card fraud and that the scope of his consent did not include image files, which would not be likely to contain such information, and the court agreed on this point).

United States v. Osorio, 66 M.J. 632 (A.F. Ct. Crim. App. 2008) (defendant consented to a search of an external hard drive when officers indicated that they wanted to see pictures he had taken at a party at which a sexual assault took place; officers later searched for, and found, child pornography; appellate court ruled that the search exceeded the scope of the defendant's consent).

United States v. Zavala, 541 F.3d 562 (5th Cir. 2008) (officers suspected a defendant of drug trafficking, executed a *Terry* stop of his car, placed the defendant's cell phone on the roof of the car, and obtained the defendant's consent to search the car; this consent did not extend to the defendant's cell phone).

United States v. Richardson, 583 F. Supp. 2d 694 (W.D. Pa. 2008) (holding that a search of the defendant's hard drive for child pornography exceeded the scope of the defendant's consent, which was given in the context of a discussion of possible illegal use of the defendant's credit card, i.e., of the defendant being a victim of some type of fraud).

United States v. Stierhoff, 477 F. Supp. 2d 423 (D.R.I. 2007) (officers asked to search the defendant's computer, indicating that they were interested in poems he wrote in connection with his stalking of a young woman; the defendant consented, indicating that the poems were in a particular folder; officers also searched another folder, labeled "offshore," and found evidence of tax evasion; search of the "offshore" folder exceeded the scope of the defendant's consent, which was limited by the expressed object of the search), *aff'd*, 549 F.3d 19 (1st Cir. 2008).

United States v. Carey, 172 F.3d 1268, 1270 (10th Cir. 1999) (officers suspected the defendant of drug activity and obtained his consent to a "complete search of the premises and property" where he lived; the officers seized and searched a computer, finding evidence of child pornography; the defendant's general consent to the search of his apartment did not authorize a search of the computer).

United States v. Turner, 169 F.3d 84 (1st Cir. 1999) (defendant called the police to report seeing an intruder in a neighbor's apartment; the neighbor reported a sexual assault; after officers noticed that the defendant's window screen was ajar, they asked to search his apartment for evidence that the intruder had been in his apartment as well; the defendant gave consent; during the search, the officers began to suspect that the defendant was the assailant; after noticing a screen saver of a sexual nature on the defendant's computer, one officer began to search it, locating child pornography; the defendant later moved to suppress, and the appellate court ruled that the search exceeded the scope of the defendant's consent, which was limited to a search for evidence that an intruder had been in his apartment).

Smith v. State, 713 N.E.2d 338 (Ind. Ct. App. 1999) (officers asked for and received consent to search the defendant's vehicle for guns, drugs, money, or illegal contraband; they seized two cellular phones, and by partially disassembling them determined that they were "cloned," i.e., modified so that the charges would be billed to someone other than the user; trial and appellate courts ruled that the search exceeded the scope of the defendant's consent because guns, drugs, etc. were not likely to be found in the phones).

IV. Searches Incident to Arrest

When a suspect is arrested, the police may conduct a "full search of [his or her] person" as a means of ensuring officer safety and preventing the destruction of evidence.[26] The police may search the arrestee's pockets, wallet, and the like as part of the search. The authority to search the arrestee does not depend on the specific circumstances of the particular arrest. Rather, it is categorical. Does this authority extend to cell phones and other digital devices carried by the arrestee?

The issue percolated through the lower courts for years, with most, including North Carolina's appellate courts, answering yes,[27] but some answering

26. United States v. Robinson, 414 U.S. 218 (1973).

27. *See, e.g.,* United States v. Flores-Lopez, 670 F.3d 803 (7th Cir. 2012) (search of cell phone incident to arrest was proper where the search was limited to obtaining the phone number associated with the device; the court compared this limited search to a "frisk" rather than a "strip search" and reserved judgment on whether a "more extensive search" of a phone's contents would require a greater justification); United States v. Curtis, 635 F.3d 704 (5th Cir. 2011) (upholding search of cell phone incident to arrest, citing *United States v. Finley*, 477 F.3d 250 (5th Cir. 2007)); United States v. Murphy, 552 F.3d 405 (4th Cir. 2009) (upholding search of cell phone incident to arrest, in part because call logs and text messages are volatile, i.e., evidence may disappear as new calls and text messages are received); Hawkins v. State, 723 S.E.2d 924, 925, 926 (Ga. 2012) (upholding phone search incident to arrest as reasonable and describing cell phones as " 'roughly analogous' to a container that properly can be opened and searched for electronic data, similar to a traditional container"; the state high court quoted the appellate court's statement (704 S.E.2d 886, 892 (2010)) that a "search must be limited as much as is reasonably practicable by the object of the search," meaning that an

no.[28] In 2014, the U.S. Supreme Court ruled that cell phones may not be searched incident to arrest in the case of *Riley v. California*.[29] The Court stated that cell phone searches do not strongly implicate the traditional justifications for searches incident to arrest. Although "officers remain free to examine the physical aspects of a phone to ensure that it will not be used as a weapon," the data on the phone does not pose a risk of physical harm.[30] Similarly, there is little risk that the data on a phone will be destroyed by the arrestee. The Court indicated that an arrestee's phone may be seized while

---

officer may not conduct a "fishing expedition"); State v. Wilkerson, 363 N.C. 382, 434 (2009) (holding, with little discussion, that "the seizure and the search of the [defendant's] telephone were properly accomplished pursuant to a lawful arrest"; note that the evidence obtained during the search of the phone appears to have been "the serial number, located inside the cell phone," which may have been obtained by a search of the physical device as opposed to the data within it).

28. *See, e.g.*, United States v. Wurie, 728 F.3d 1, 8 (1st Cir. 2013) (defendant was arrested after officers saw him sell drugs; officers seized his phone and examined his call log, which revealed his home phone number; this led officers to his home, where they found drugs; defendant moved to suppress, arguing that the search of the home was the fruit of an unlawful search of the phone; the government replied that it was a valid search incident to arrest; the federal trial court ruled for the government, but the First Circuit disagreed, stating that phones now contain "immense" amounts of data, including the "kind of information one would previously have stored in one's home," and that allowing officers to examine the data on a phone does little to advance officer safety or the preservation of evidence; thus, categorically, the data on phones may not be examined under the search incident to arrest doctrine), *aff'd sub nom.* Riley v. California, 573 U.S. ___, 134 S. Ct. 2473 (2014); Smallwood v. State, 113 So. 3d 724, 735 (Fla. 2013) (citations omitted) (citing *Arizona v. Gant*, 556 U.S. 332 (2009), the court ruled that an officer "unquestionably was authorized to take physical possession of [the defendant's] electronic device used as a phone as part of the search incident to the [defendant's] arrest because the device was present on [the defendant's] body. . . . However, once the electronic, computer-like device was removed from [the defendant's] person, there was no possibility that [the defendant] could use the device as a weapon, nor could he have destroyed any evidence that may have existed on the phone. Accordingly, neither the officer protection nor the evidence preservation justification for the warrant exception applied. . . . Thus, pursuant to *Gant*, [the officer] was constitutionally required to obtain a warrant before searching the contents of, and the data in, [the defendant's] electronic device cell phone."); State v. Smith, 920 N.E.2d 949 (Ohio 2009) (searches incident to arrest are justified to preserve evidence and to ensure officer safety, but neither purpose is served by searching a cell phone that has been secured; cell phones are not like other "containers" because (1) they do not contain other physical objects and (2) they may store a "wealth" of personal information; therefore, without a warrant, officers may take steps to preserve data in a cell phone but may not search it absent an officer safety concern or an exigency).

29. 573 U.S. ___, 134 S. Ct. 2473 (2014).

30. *Id.* at ___, 134 S. Ct. at 2485.

officers seek a search warrant and that the risk of remote wiping during the interim was low and can be managed by using Faraday bags (which prevent radio waves from reaching the mobile device) and other tools.

On the other side of the ledger, the Court found a strong privacy interest militating against such searches. It noted that phones often contain vast quantities of data, making a search far more intrusive than traditional searches of pockets, wallets, and purses incident to arrest. Indeed, the Court observed that many phones can access data stored on remote servers, making a search extend far beyond the immediate area of the arrestee. Emphasizing the need to establish a clear and workable rule, the Court therefore categorically exempted cell phones, regardless of their capacity or sophistication, from the search incident to arrest doctrine.

Although the *Riley* case involved cell phones, the Court's reasoning appears to apply to digital devices more broadly. The Court referred to cell phones as "minicomputers," and tablets and laptops are likely to contain just as much personal information as cell phones, if not more.[31] Thus, offi-

---

31. *Id.* at ___, 134 S. Ct. at 2489. Even before *Riley*, the few cases on point suggested that courts were skeptical of allowing laptops to be searched incident to arrest. *See, e.g.*, United States v. Urbina, No. 06-CR-336, 2007 WL 4895782 at *14 (E.D. Wis. Nov. 6, 2007) (unpublished) (upholding search of cell phone incident to arrest but stating in dicta that "[i]n the case before this court, it is clear that [the officer] limited his search to the phone's address book and call history. If the evidence in a future case were to show that the warrantless search conducted by law enforcement was essentially equivalent to a search of a personal computer, without sufficient exigencies to justify such a search, the court's reaction may be different, because of the substantial invasion of privacy."); United States v. Park, No. CR-05-375 SI, 2007 WL 1521573, at *8 (N.D. Cal. May 23, 2007) (unpublished) (invalidating search of an arrestee's cell phone ninety minutes after arrest and noting in disapproving dicta that "the government asserted that, although the officers here limited their searches to the phones' address books, the officers could have searched any information—such as emails or messages—stored in the cell phones. In addition, in recognition of the fact that the line between cell phones and personal computers has grown increasingly blurry, the government also asserted that officers could lawfully seize and search an arrestee's laptop computer as a warrantless search incident to arrest."); State v. Washington, 110 Wash. App. 1012 (2002) (unpublished) (holding, with little analysis, that officers lacked authority to search a laptop incident to arrest, even where they had probable cause to believe that the laptop was stolen). *Cf.* Schlossberg v. Solesbee, 844 F. Supp. 2d 1165, 1169 (D. Or. 2012) (holding that the search of a digital camera incident to the owner's arrest was unjustified, and rejecting the comparison between electronic devices and containers because "[e]lectronic devices do not store physical objects which are in plain view once the containers are opened" and "the storage capability of an electronic device is not limited by physical size as a container is"). *But see* People v. Reese, No. C065511, 2011 WL 4347024 (Cal. Ct. App. Sept. 19, 2011) (unpublished) (officers searched

cers generally should not search digital devices incident to arrest, beyond examining them physically to ensure that they do not conceal a weapon. If there is reason to believe that the devices may contain relevant evidence, officers may seize them and seek a search warrant.

Because *Riley* is a recent decision, questions may arise about whether it applies retroactively. As explained elsewhere in detail, the answer almost certainly is no. *Riley* applies to all pending cases, i.e., all cases in which convictions are not yet final, including cases on direct appeal, even if the search took place before the decision was issued. But it is extremely unlikely to apply retroactively to closed cases.[32]

V. Automobile Exception

Because automobiles are highly mobile and because drivers have reduced expectations of privacy in automobiles as opposed to residences, automobiles in public places may be searched based on probable cause without a warrant. A search pursuant to the automobile exception to the warrant requirement may extend to any location in the vehicle, including closed containers, where the object of the search may reasonably be found.[33] Historically, a majority of courts have ruled that where there is probable cause to believe that evidence of a crime may be found in a particular vehicle, any electronic devices in the car are "containers" and may be searched to the extent that the search reasonably might uncover evidence of the crime in question.

The Supreme Court's decision in *Riley v. California*, discussed above in section IV, calls this reasoning into question. Although *Riley* does not directly

---

the defendant's laptop incident to arrest because the laptop was in the defendant's vehicle, which the officers searched incident to arrest under then-prevailing law; the search was proper because the laptop was simply a container within the vehicle, similar to a briefcase).

32. Jessica Smith, *Riley and Retroactivity*, N.C. CRIM. L., UNC SCH. OF GOV'T BLOG (July 29, 2014), http://nccriminallaw.sog.unc.edu/riley-and-retroactivity/. Although *Riley* applies in pending cases, it does not automatically follow that all evidence found in searches of cell phones incident to arrest prior to *Riley* will be suppressed. The State may be able to argue for a good faith exception to the exclusionary rule, as discussed in detail in Jeff Welty, *Riley and Good Faith*, N.C. CRIM. L., UNC SCH. OF GOV'T BLOG (July 30, 2014), http://nccriminallaw.sog.unc.edu/riley-and-good-faith/.

33. California v. Acevedo, 500 U.S. 565, 580 (1991) ("The police may search an automobile and the containers within it where they have probable cause to believe contraband or evidence is contained."); United States v. Ross, 456 U.S. 798 (1982).

concern the automobile exception, the Court there stated that "[t]reating a cell phone as a container whose contents may be searched incident to an arrest is a bit strained," in part because a phone may access data not contained on the phone itself through network connections.[34] If phones, and by extension other digital devices, are treated differently than traditional containers for purposes of the search incident to arrest doctrine, they may also need to be treated differently under the automobile exception. Two post-*Riley* cases have so ruled, though it is too early to tell how courts generally will resolve the matter.[35]

Case Summaries on the Automobile Exception

CELL PHONES: SEARCH PERMITTED

Note that each of the following cases was decided pre-*Riley* and thus should be viewed with caution for the reasons discussed above.

> **United States v. Stringer, No. 10-05038-01-CR-SW-GAF, 2011 WL 3847026 (W.D. Mo. July 20, 2011)** (unpublished) (conducting an "extensive review of case law" and finding a split of authority on the point but following what the court describes as the majority view that cellular telephones in vehicles should be treated like any other container for purposes of the vehicle exception).
>
> **United States v. Cole, No. 1:09-CR-0412-ODE-RGV, 2010 WL 3210963 (N.D. Ga. Aug. 11, 2010)** (unpublished) (search of defendant's cell phone found inside vehicle subsequent to defendant's arrest was justified under the automobile exception where officer conducting lawful roadblock checkpoint observed handgun magazine and bag of marijuana in center console of defendant's vehicle).
>
> **United States v. Garcia-Aleman, No. 1:10-CR-29, 2010 WL 2635071 (E.D. Tex. June 9, 2010)** (search of automobile and its contents, including cell phone for evidence of drug crimes, was justified based on the automobile exception and the existence of probable cause to believe cell phone contained evidence of crime being investigated), *report and recommendation adopted*, 2010 WL 2635073 (E.D. Tex. June 30, 2010) (unpublished).

---

34. 573 U.S. at ___, 134 S. Ct. at 2491.

35. United States v. Camou, 773 F.3d 932 (9th Cir. 2014) (summarized below); Chung v. State, ___ S.W.3d ___, No. 10-13-00307-CR, 2014 WL 5408439 (Tex. App. Oct. 23, 2014) (same).

State v. Boyd, 992 A.2d 1071 (Conn. 2010) (applying automobile exception to uphold search of cell phone taken from passenger seat of car defendant had been driving).

People v. Chho, No. H034693, 2010 WL 1952659 (Cal. Ct. App. May 17, 2010) (unpublished) (officers obtained consent to search the defendant's car and found 6 ounces of marijuana; his cell phone was in the car and rang frequently; the combination of the drugs and the frequently ringing phone provided probable cause to believe that the phone would contain evidence of drug activity, and the officers properly opened it and reviewed two text messages on it under the automobile exception).

United States v. Fierros-Alavarez, 547 F. Supp. 2d 1206 (D. Kan. 2008) (search of cell phone that was located inside vehicle of suspected drug trafficker was justified based on vehicle exception plus probable cause to believe that the phone would contain evidence of drug trafficking).

United States v. Rocha, No. 06-40057-01-RDR, 2008 WL 4498950, at *6 (D. Kan. Oct. 2, 2008) (unpublished) (holding, as to cell phones found in RV in which drugs were being transported, "[b]ecause probable cause existed to believe that evidence of a crime would be found in the cell phone information, the automobile exception allows the search of the cell phones just as it allows a search of other closed containers found in vehicles").

United States v. James, No. 1:06CR134 CDP, 2008 WL 1925032, at *4 (E.D. Mo. Apr. 29, 2008) (search of cell phone that was inside vehicle was justified: "Because probable cause existed to believe that evidence of a crime would be found in the cell phone call records and address book, the automobile exception allows the search of the cell phone just as it allows a search of other closed containers found in vehicles.").

State v. Novicky, No. A07-0170, 2008 WL 1747805 (Minn. Ct. App. Apr. 15, 2008) (unpublished) (search of cell phone on front seat of vehicle was justified under automobile exception; evidence of ownership of cell phone was likely to be relevant evidence in establishing ownership of gun that was next to it).

United States v. Meador, No. 1:06 CR 134 CDP DDN, 2008 WL 4922001, at *13 (E.D. Mo. Jan. 7, 2008) (unpublished) (pagers and cell phones "may be considered closed containers," and here, there was probable cause to search a cell phone that was found in a vehicle).

United States v. Woodley, No. 04-80335, 2005 WL 3132205 (E.D. Mich. Nov. 22, 2005) (unpublished) (search of pager authorized by automobile exception).

CELL PHONES: SEARCH NOT PERMITTED

United States v. Camou, 773 F.3d 932, 942 (9th Cir. 2014) (relying in part on *Riley*, the court held that "cell phones are not containers for purposes of the vehicle exception" because they are so unlike physical containers such as boxes, bags, and lunch buckets).

Chung v. State, ___ S.W.3d ___, No. 10-13-00307-CR, 2014 WL 5408439, at *6 (Tex. App. Oct. 23, 2014) (defendant was stopped for a traffic infraction; a drug dog alerted on his car, and further investigation revealed drugs in the vehicle; later, an officer searched the defendant's cell phone on the theory that it had once been inside the car and so fell within the automobile exception; the court ruled that the exception did not apply because the defendant's "cell phone was not in his car when the officers searched the vehicle after the drug dog alert" but instead was with the defendant; more generally, based on *Riley*, the court expressed "grave doubts that a cell phone is a 'container' that could be searched pursuant to the automobile exception").

United States v. Lujan, No. 2:11CR11-SA, 2012 WL 2861546, at *11 (N.D. Miss. July 11, 2012) (unpublished) (during a traffic stop, an officer developed probable cause to believe that a vehicle was being used for narcotics trafficking; although a warrantless search of the vehicle was therefore permissible, a warrantless search of a cell phone in the vehicle was not permitted under the automobile exception because there was no probable cause to believe that the phone contained evidence of any crime; given the volume of personal data that may be contained in a phone, it was not enough that "cell phones have been recognized as tools of the narcotics trade").

COMPUTERS AND OTHER DEVICES

Burch v. City of Florence, 913 F. Supp. 2d 1221 (N.D. Ala. 2012) (collecting, and following, cases on cell phones to conclude that a digital camera inside a vehicle is a "container" that may be searched under the vehicle exception to the warrant requirement).

State v. Newman, 237 P.3d 1222 (Idaho Ct. App. 2010) (a laptop was properly *seized* under the vehicle exception where police had probable cause to believe that the suspect was using the computer for criminal activity; note, however, that the computer was only *searched* after search warrants were obtained).

United States v. Burgess, 576 F.3d 1078 (10th Cir. 2009) (officers developed probable cause to believe that a vehicle contained evidence of drug crimes; it was proper to *seize* the computer and hard drive found therein; court declined to decide whether it was proper to *search* the devices under the automobile exception, instead finding that the searches were proper under a search warrant).

VI. Exigent Circumstances

The exigent circumstances exception to the warrant requirement applies when there is probable cause to conduct a search but obtaining a search warrant would be too time-consuming in light of a risk of danger, a risk of destruction of evidence, or some other concern. The cases collected below consider the application of the exception to digital devices.

Although the exigent circumstances exception is often thought of as allowing a warrantless search, there may be cases in which it supports only a warrantless seizure. For example, an officer may need to seize an electronic device from a suspect to prevent the destruction of evidence, yet there may be no urgency in extracting the evidence from the device. In such a case, the exigent circumstances would not support an immediate search of the device, and the officer would need to obtain a search warrant. Under these circumstances, the officer should not unreasonably delay seeking a warrant, though there is no fixed rule for how long a delay must be before it becomes unreasonable.[36]

Case Summaries on Exigent Circumstances

CELL PHONES: SEARCH PERMITTED

United States v. Gomez, 807 F. Supp. 2d 1134 (S.D. Fla. 2011) (exigent circumstances justified examining and answering a defendant's cellular telephone; the defendant appeared to be a drug courier, was observed using his phone, and when apprehended, his phone rang repeatedly

36. *United States v. Burgard*, 675 F.3d 1029 (7th Cir. 2012), contains a good summary of the law on this issue. The *Burgard* court ruled that a six-day delay in obtaining a search warrant for a seized cell phone was not unreasonable under the facts of that case.

with calls from a single caller; an officer reasonably believed that the calls would contain evidence of drug activity).

United States v. Santillan, 571 F. Supp. 2d 1093 (D. Ariz. 2008) (exigent circumstances justified the seizure of a cell phone that a defendant, a suspected "spotter" for drug traffickers, appeared to be using to help coordinate the movements of vehicles smuggling drugs; a search of the phone was also justified in order to preserve information in call log).

United States v. Zamora, No. 1:05 CR 250 WSD, 2006 WL 418390 (N.D. Ga. Feb. 21, 2006) (unpublished) (finding warrantless searches of cellular phones to be justified by exigent circumstances; similar to *Parada,* below).

United States v. Parada, 289 F. Supp. 2d 1291, 1303–04 (D. Kan. 2003) ("Because a cell phone has a limited memory to store numbers, the agent recorded the numbers in the event that subsequent incoming calls effected the deletion or overwriting of the earlier stored numbers. This can occur whether the phone is turned on or off, so it is irrelevant whether the defendant or the officers turned on the phone. . . . [U]nder these circumstances, the agent had the authority to immediately search or retrieve, as a matter of exigency, the cell phone's memory of stored numbers of incoming phone calls, in order to prevent the destruction of this evidence.").

CELL PHONES: SEARCH NOT PERMITTED

United States v. Davis, 787 F. Supp. 2d 1165 (D. Or. 2011) (collecting cases and holding that exigent circumstances did not justify the search of the defendant's cellular telephone; the telephone was found in the defendant's vehicle, which had crashed during a high-speed chase; the defendant had fled on foot but had already been apprehended, removing any exigency).

United States v. Sams, No. CR209-49, 2010 WL 2892711, at *5 (S.D. Ga. June 29, 2010) (unpublished) (a cell phone was confiscated from a drug suspect's hand during a traffic stop; an officer searched the phone at the time of arrest and later at the police station; the search was not supported by any warrant exception, including exigent circumstances; although "cell phones are commonly used communications devices, particularly in situations involving criminal activity," the government failed to show that evidence would be destroyed if the phone were not searched without a warrant; however, evidence found on the phone was not suppressed due to the subsequent issuance of a valid warrant), *report and recommendation adopted*, 2010 WL 2892713 (S.D. Ga. July 21, 2010) (unpublished).

United States v. Morales-Ortiz, 376 F. Supp. 2d 1131 (D.N.M. 2004) (stating in *dicta* that a search of a cell phone's address book, unlike a search of its call log, cannot be justified on the basis of an exigent need to preserve evidence, since the address book is not subject to being overwritten by incoming calls).

COMPUTERS AND OTHER DEVICES

***In re* J.C.L., 325 P.3d 740 (Or. Ct. App. 2014)** (an officer suspected a juvenile of having child pornography on his computer; the officer determined that the juvenile had given his computer to an acquaintance for repairs; the officer contacted the acquaintance, who said that the juvenile had recently instructed him to delete everything on the computer; the court ruled that the officer's decision to seize the computer without a warrant at that time was supported by exigent circumstances, even though the acquaintance was cooperative with the officer).

United States v. Brown, 701 F.3d 120, 127 (4th Cir. 2012) (officers learned that child pornography was being downloaded through the internet connection at an ambulance business; their suspicions focused on two employees; they obtained a search warrant for the business and executed it, finding nothing; the two employees then arrived, returning from an ambulance call; officers asked them if they had computers in the ambulance, and when they said that they did, officers seized them; the officers did not search the computers until they obtained a warrant; the court ruled that the seizure at issue here of one employee's laptop was supported by exigent circumstances, specifically, "to prevent either it or its contents from being damaged or destroyed").

United States v. Bradley, 488 F. App'x 99 (6th Cir. 2012) (unpublished) (seizure of a defendant's laptop computer suspected of being used to download child pornography at a local fire station was justified by exigent circumstances because the officer had an objectively reasonable fear that evidence would be destroyed absent the seizure and because any possessory interference was brief, while the government's interest in "curbing the spread of child pornography" was significant; a twenty-six-hour delay in procuring a search warrant was not excessive).

United States v. Bradley, 644 F.3d 1213, 1261 (11th Cir. 2011) (in a Medicaid fraud investigation, an officer "seized" a business's computer servers by shutting them down, based on his knowledge that the servers were connected to an external network and a concern "that the data stored on the hard drives might be corrupted or erased before he could copy them"; this action was justified by the exigent circumstances doctrine, given employees' "ability and incentive" to remove incriminating data remotely).

United States v. Mitchell, 565 F.3d 1347 (11th Cir. 2009) (warrantless seizure of a computer was justified after a defendant admitted during a consensual interview in his home that it contained child pornography; because the defendant did not consent to a search of the computer, however, a warrant was necessary for the search, and a twenty-one-day delay in obtaining the warrant was excessive).

State v. Maxwell, 275 P.3d 220 (Utah 2011) (seizure of a defendant's computer was justified by exigent circumstances because the defendant had an incentive to destroy the computer, said "maybe I ought to just destroy my computer" when officers asked if they could seize and search it, and officers reasonably believed the defendant was capable of destroying the hard drive; officers did not impermissibly create the exigency by stating a "need" to take the computer; and officers were not required to use a means less intrusive than seizure when preserving evidence pursuant to exigency).

United States v. Trowbridge, No. 3:07-CR-0196-b-B, 2007 WL 4226385, at *1 (N.D. Tex. Nov. 29, 2007) (unpublished) (exigency justified the seizure of computers to prevent the destruction of evidence of "swatting," i.e., obtaining others' personal information and then "making false 911 calls to elicit response by police, fire and ambulance to residences"; police then sought a warrant to search the computers).

State v. Rupnick, 125 P.3d 541 (Kan. 2005) (the seizure—but not search—of a laptop was justified by exigent circumstances when officers had probable cause to believe that the computer contained data that the defendant had stolen from a former employer and the defendant knew of the officers' suspicions; he could have destroyed the data quickly and easily).

VII. Other Exceptions to the Warrant Requirement

There are several other possible justifications for a warrantless search of a computer or other electronic device. These possible justifications appear to come up less frequently in practice, so they are treated only briefly below.

A. Border Searches

Generally, officers may search people and items coming into the United States, without a warrant or even individualized suspicion, under the border search doctrine. North Carolina has international seaports and airports to which this doctrine applies. Several cases have upheld searches of digital devices under the border search doctrine.[37] However, the Ninth Circuit recently ruled that a full forensic analysis of a computer is so intrusive that, even at the border, it must be supported by reasonable suspicion.[38] The U.S. Supreme Court's emphasis in *Riley* on the unique nature of digital storage may lend support to the Ninth Circuit's reasoning, though it is too early to tell whether *Riley* will have a significant impact on border search cases or whether other courts will follow the Ninth Circuit's lead.

After complaints by international travelers concerned about the security of private information and important business data, the Department of Homeland Security promulgated standards for border searches of electronic devices, including laptops.[39]

---

37. *See, e.g.*, United States v. Stewart, 729 F.3d 517 (6th Cir. 2013) (upholding search of defendant's computers under the doctrine; defendant had just arrived at an international airport on a flight from Japan; the airport was the functional equivalent of the border; the fact that the defendant's computers were taken off-site for analysis did not convert the search into an "extended border search" requiring reasonable suspicion); United States v. Arnold, 523 F.3d 941 (9th Cir. 2008); United States v. Romm, 455 F.3d 990 (9th Cir. 2006); United States v. Ickes, 393 F.3d 501 (4th Cir. 2005); United States v. Roberts, 274 F.3d 1007 (5th Cir. 2001) (diskettes).

38. United States v. Cotterman, 709 F.3d 952 (9th Cir. 2013) (the defendant and his wife were returning to the United States from Mexico when agents learned that the defendant was a sex offender and was suspected of involvement in sex tourism; they seized two laptops and conducted an initial on-site search that revealed no contraband but several password-protected files; they retained the computers and found child pornography in a subsequent forensic analysis; the court ruled that computers may store such a large quantity of personal information, and a forensic analysis is so intrusive, that even at the border, a forensic analysis requires reasonable suspicion, but it concluded that reasonable suspicion was present in this case).

39. U.S. Customs & Border Protection, CBP Directive No. 3340-049 (Aug. 20, 2009), www.dhs.gov/xlibrary/assets/cbp_directive_3340-049.pdf; U.S. Immigration & Customs Enforcement, Directive No. 7-6.1, Border

B. Probation Searches

At a minimum, warrantless searches of a probationer's computers and other electronic devices are permissible if (1) they are based upon reasonable suspicion and (2) submission to such searches is a condition of the defendant's probation.[40] Some courts have gone further, ruling that reasonable suspicion supports a search of a probationer's devices even absent a probation condition, given the reduced expectation of privacy associated with probation.[41]

Because the existence of a probation condition requiring submission to warrantless searches may be legally significant, it is important to note that virtually all North Carolina probationers are subject to the warrantless search condition in Section 15A-1343(b)(13) of the North Carolina General Statutes (hereinafter G.S.). That standard condition of probation provides that a probationer must submit to warrantless searches of his "person . . . vehicle and premises" by a probation officer, at least "for purposes directly related to the probation supervision." The condition applies only to searches conducted "while the probationer is present," and so may not support, for example, seizing digital devices and sending them off for forensic analysis.[42] A probationer also must submit to certain searches by law enforcement officers, as specified in G.S. 15A-1343(b)(14).[43]

The probation officer search provision is expansive in that it appears to authorize search requests that are not based on particularized suspicion of wrongdoing.[44] However, the reach of the provision is not completely clear.

Searches of Electronic Devices (Aug. 18, 2009), www.dhs.gov/xlibrary/assets/ice_border_search_electronic_devices.pdf.

40. United States v. Knights, 534 U.S. 112 (2001) (warrantless search of probationer's apartment did not violate the Fourth Amendment where it was supported by reasonable suspicion and where submitting to warrantless searches was a condition of the defendant's probation).

41. *See, e.g.*, United States v. Yuknavich, 419 F.3d 1302 (11th Cir. 2005) (despite absence of warrantless search condition, warrantless search of probationer's computer was permissible, given reasonable suspicion that probationer was using the computer to access the internet, in violation of the terms of his probation); State v. Purtell, 851 N.W.2d 417 (Wis. 2014) (probation officer could search probationer's computer with reasonable suspicion).

42. G.S. 15A-1343(b)(13).

43. This search provision differs from the probation officer search provision in that (1) it requires reasonable suspicion that the probationer is engaged in criminal activity and (2) it does not include the probationer's "premises."

44. The statute provides that a probationer must consent to searches at "reasonable times." An earlier version of the statute, which contained similar language, was interpreted as allowing suspicionless searches in *United States v. Midgette*, 478 F.3d 616 (4th Cir. 2007).

Unlike the special provision applicable to certain sex offenders, discussed below, the standard condition does not expressly state that it includes digital devices, leaving it open for argument whether the condition encompasses a probationer's electronic devices that are in his residence, in his vehicle, or on his person.[45]

Some probationers are subject to conditions that clearly require consent to warrantless searches of their digital devices. The catchall provision in G.S. 15A-1343(b1)(10) allows a judge to impose "any other conditions determined by the court to be reasonably related to [the defendant's] rehabilitation." Under this authority, a judge might add language expressly mandating that a defendant must submit to searches of his or her computers or electronic devices. A judge might also authorize searches of such devices even if they are not in the defendant's residence, in his or her vehicle, or on his or her person. If the condition fashioned by the court has some connection to the defendant's crime or personal history, it will likely be upheld. Courts in other jurisdictions have upheld conditions such as suspicionless searches[46] and the installation of software to enable continuous monitoring of the probationer's computer usage.[47]

Finally, defendants placed on probation as a result of certain sex offenses are subject to the provisions of G.S. 15A-1343(b2)(9); that statute requires submission to warrantless searches by a probation officer and clarifies that "warrantless searches of the probationer's computer or other electronic [devices] . . . shall be considered reasonably related to the probation supervision."

---

45. This issue is similar in some respects to the matter of whether a search warrant authorizing the search of, for example, a residence, includes authorization to search digital devices contained therein. That question is discussed in chapter 1.

46. *See, e.g.*, United States v. Holm, 326 F.3d 872, 879 (7th Cir. 2003) (finding "entirely reasonable" a condition authorizing "random searches of [a child pornography defendant's] computer").

47. *Compare* United States v. Goddard, 537 F.3d 1087 (9th Cir. 2008) (upholding monitoring condition for child pornography defendant), *with* United States v. Sales, 476 F.3d 732, 737 (9th Cir. 2007) (rejecting broad monitoring provision for counterfeiting defendant and stating that "[a] computer monitoring condition in some form may be reasonable. However, to comply with the Fourth Amendment, it must be narrowly tailored—producing no greater deprivation of liberty than is reasonably necessary.").

C. Inventory Searches

Warrantless inventory searches may be conducted in order to protect the owner's property while it is in police custody, protect the police against claims of lost or stolen property, and protect the police from danger.[48] Inventory searches must be conducted pursuant to standardized procedures.[49] Thus, when a law enforcement officer impounds a car or arrests a defendant carrying a suitcase, the officer may examine and inventory the contents of the car or suitcase pursuant to an inventory policy. This may cause the officer to realize that, for example, there is a cell phone in the glove compartment of the car, or a laptop in the suitcase.

The inventory process should probably end at that point. The officer likely may not examine the contents of electronic devices without a warrant on the basis that the officer is conducting an inventory of the contents. So long as the devices themselves are identified, logged, and kept safe, virtually all of the purposes of a valid inventory search are achieved.[50] Furthermore, the U.S. Supreme Court's ruling in *Riley* suggests that digital devices should not be treated as mere physical containers for Fourth Amendment purposes.

D. Independent Source/Inevitable Discovery

Technically, the independent source and inevitable discovery doctrines are exceptions to the exclusionary rule, not exceptions to the warrant requirement. Nonetheless, they bear mentioning because they will serve to render the results of some warrantless searches admissible. For example, in *United*

---

48. Colorado v. Bertine, 479 U.S. 367 (1987).

49. Florida v. Wells, 495 U.S. 1 (1990).

50. *See, e.g.*, People v. Nottoli, 130 Cal. Rptr. 3d 884, 897 (Cal. Ct. App. 2011) (search of smartphone's contents was not justified as an inventory search; "there was no evidence that [turning the phone on and searching it] was [done] in accordance with any standardized policy or practice governing inventory searches"); United States v. Davis, 787 F. Supp. 2d 1165 (D. Or. 2011) (citing *Wall, infra* this note); United States v. Wall, No. 08-60016-CR, 2008 WL 5381412, at *4 (S.D. Fla. Dec. 22, 2008) (unpublished) ("[T]here is no need to document the phone numbers, photos, text messages, or other data stored in the memory of a cell phone to properly inventory the person's possessions because the threat of theft concerns the cell phone itself, not the electronic information stored on it."); United States v. Flores, 122 F. Supp. 2d 491, 494 (S.D.N.Y. 2000) ("[N]either a calendar book nor a cellular telephone is a 'container' that has 'contents' that need to be inventoried for safekeeping in the traditional sense of those terms."). *Cf.* State v. Granville, 423 S.W.3d 399 (Tex. Crim. App. 2013) (defendant who was arrested and jailed retained a reasonable expectation of privacy in the contents of his cell phone, even though it had been inventoried and was in the jail's property room).

States v. Hughes,[51] the First Circuit considered a consent search of the defendant's computers. The defendant claimed that his consent was coerced, but the court determined that even if it was, the contents of the computers would inevitably have been discovered by search warrant because the officers had probable cause, "had support staff on stand-by, ready to apply for a warrant, and the warrant issued the next day."[52] However, the inevitable discovery doctrine applies only when testimony supports the conclusion that discovery was inevitable; mere argument of counsel to that effect is insufficient.[53]

Similarly, in *United States v. Stabile*,[54] another federal appeals court considered the actions of an officer who began searching the defendant's hard disk, pursuant to a warrant, for evidence of financial crimes. The officer saw lurid file names, then viewed the files, which contained child pornography. The court applied the independent source doctrine to admit the child pornography, concluding that even if the officer exceeded the scope of the first search warrant by viewing the files, he would have sought a second warrant based on the file names, which he clearly had a right to view under the first warrant.

---

51. 640 F.3d 428 (1st Cir. 2011). *See also* United States v. Crespo-Rios, 645 F.3d 37, 42 (1st Cir. 2011) (regardless of whether there was probable cause to search the defendant's computer and digital media for child pornography specifically, it was inevitable that child pornography would have been discovered in the process of searching the defendant's media for evidence for which probable cause to search did exist).

52. *Hughes*, 640 F.3d at 440.

53. State v. Wells, ___ N.C. App. ___, 737 S.E.2d 179 (2013) (defendant attempted to solicit sexual activity with a child using his computer; officers obtained an arrest warrant for him and a search warrant for his house; the home searched revealed no evidence; the defendant turned himself in for arrest; officers coerced a statement from the defendant, who revealed that his laptop was at his workplace; officers then retrieved the laptop, which contained evidence; the court ruled that the laptop was the fruit of an unlawful interrogation and that while it was "entirely logical" that the police would have searched the workplace next, there was no evidence introduced that they would have done so).

54. 633 F.3d 219 (3d Cir. 2011).

Chapter 3: Electronic Communications

More than a million times per year, law enforcement officers turn to electronic communications service providers to obtain information about suspects' electronic communications, such as phone calls, emails, and text messages.[1] For example, an officer may seek a court order for information about the location of a suspect's cell phone, for a list of the phone numbers a suspect has called in the past thirty days, or for the contents of text messages sent by a suspect in the hours before a crime. Such requests are governed by a patchwork quilt of federal and state statutory and constitutional law. The law in this area is unsettled and is rapidly evolving, but this chapter provides a practical primer.

I. Important Distinctions

In order to understand the law in this area, it is necessary to understand several distinctions concerning the types of information that law enforcement officers may seek and the sources of law that may protect that information.

A. Content vs. Non-Content

Generally, law enforcement officers must make a stronger showing to be allowed to access the content of a suspect's communications than is required to access non-content information about the suspect's communications. For example, an officer must obtain a wiretap order to listen in on the content of a suspect's telephone conversations—the actual words spoken during the call. But the officer may obtain non-content information about the call, such as what time it began, what phone number initiated or received the call, and how long it lasted, with lesser process.

---

1. Eric Lichtblau, *Wireless Firms Are Flooded by Requests to Aid Surveillance*, N.Y. Times, July 8, 2012, www.nytimes.com/2012/07/09/us/cell-carriers-see-uptick-in-requests-to-aid-surveillance.html?_r=0 ("In the first public accounting of its kind, cellphone carriers reported that they responded to a startling 1.3 million demands for subscriber information last year from law enforcement agencies seeking text messages, caller locations and other information in the course of investigations.").

The distinction between content and non-content information exists for all types of electronic communications. The content of an email means the words, numbers, and other information in the body of the email. Non-content information about email includes the identity of the account from which it came, the identity of the account to which it was sent, the time it was sent, and other information contained in the email's electronic header. Similarly, the content of a social media post includes the words or pictures shared by the user, while non-content information about the post includes the time it was posted, the size of the post, and the like.

Among non-content information, officers are frequently interested in routing and addressing information, which reveals the recipient of the communication. This information is sometimes called "envelope" information in a nod to traditional mail, where the recipient's name and address are printed on the outside envelope and, as a result, are less protected than the contents of the letter inside.[2]

B. Real-Time vs. Historical

Generally, law enforcement officers must make a higher showing to access real-time, ongoing information about a suspect's electronic communications than is required to access historical information about a suspect's past communications. For example, as discussed in detail below, an officer needs a court order to employ a pen register or trap-and-trace device to obtain real-time information about calls dialed or received by a suspect. But a lesser process, such as a subpoena, may suffice to obtain the suspect's phone records, including a list of calls previously dialed or received by a suspect. As explained below, the distinction between real-time and historical information is particularly important in the context of location information.

---

2. *See, e.g.,* United States v. Osunegbu, 822 F.2d 472, 481 n. 23 (5th Cir. 1987) ("[A]n addresse or addressor generally has no expectation of privacy as to the outside of mail."); United States v. Choate, 576 F.2d 165 (9th Cir. 1978) (ruling that address information is not protected by a reasonable expectation of privacy because "the information would foreseeably be available to postal employees and others looking at the outside of the mail"). For a case applying similar reasoning in a digital context, see *United States v. Forrester,* 512 F.3d 500, 510 (9th Cir. 2007) ("Analogously, e-mail and Internet users have no expectation of privacy in the to/from addresses of their messages or the IP addresses of the websites they visit because they should know that this information is provided to and used by Internet service providers for the specific purpose of directing the routing of information.").

C. Constitutional vs. Statutory

The search and seizure of physical evidence is regulated principally by the Fourth Amendment. Although state and federal statutes are sometimes relevant, constitutional considerations are usually paramount. By contrast, state and federal statutory rules play a much larger role in regulating law enforcement access to digital evidence.

Some of the relevant statutes were enacted precisely because there is so little constitutional protection for certain information regarding electronic communications. For example, in *Smith v. Maryland*,[3] the United States Supreme Court ruled that the installation and use of a pen register to track the phone calls made by a robbery suspect was not a "search" under the Fourth Amendment. The Court reasoned that the suspect voluntarily disclosed the numbers he dialed to the phone company in the course of making the calls, and that he therefore had no reasonable expectation of privacy in the numbers. Congress subsequently enacted statutory limits on the use of pen registers, as did North Carolina.[4] As discussed in detail below, the Stored Communications Act also provides statutory protection for a great deal of information that is not protected by the Fourth Amendment.

In other instances, information is constitutionally protected but statutory law goes beyond what the Constitution requires. For example, wiretapping intrudes on a reasonable expectation of privacy, is a Fourth Amendment search, and so would normally require a warrant as a matter of constitutional law. But under both federal and state statutory law, wiretapping actually requires a so-called "super warrant," based not just on probable cause but also on a showing that other investigative techniques have failed or are impractical. Because the statutory standard is higher than the constitutional bar, litigation regarding wiretap orders has generally been under the statutes rather than under the Fourth Amendment.

The foregoing does not mean that the Fourth Amendment and other constitutional provisions are unimportant where digital evidence is concerned. Statutory law does not always offer more robust protection for information about electronic communications than does constitutional law. Specifically, as explained below, constitutional law has begun to play an important role in courts' decisions about the contents of electronic communications and about law enforcement access to cell site location information and other

---

3. 442 U.S. 735 (1979).

4. The relevant federal statutes, 18 U.S.C. §§ 3121 *et seq.*, were enacted in 1986. The relevant state statutes, Sections 15A-260 *et seq.* of the North Carolina General Statutes (hereinafter G.S.), were enacted in 1988.

digital evidence that can be used to track the location of a suspect. Therefore, this chapter will consider both constitutional and statutory protections that may apply to various types of information.

II. Historical Information

The remainder of this chapter analyzes in detail the different categories of information that law enforcement might seek. This section considers the law with respect to historical information regarding electronic communications. Many aspects of this area of the law are comparatively settled, though other aspects remain in flux.

A. Content

1. Constitutional Protection

Courts have disagreed about whether the contents of emails, text messages, and other forms of electronic communication are protected by the Fourth Amendment. The debate has centered on whether such communications are subject to a reasonable expectation of privacy. Courts have recognized that traditional methods of communication such as phone calls and letters are subject to such an expectation,[5] and it is easy to argue that contemporary modes of electronic communication should be treated the same way.

However, some courts have concluded or suggested that modern electronic communications normally are not subject to a reasonable expectation of privacy. Some of these courts have reasoned that once a communication is delivered to the intended recipient, the sender loses control of it and so has no expectation of privacy in it.[6] Others have found that the typical terms of service for electronic communications services destroy any expectation of

---

5. *See, e.g.*, United States v. Jacobsen, 466 U.S. 109, 114 (1984) (holding that "[l]etters and other sealed packages are in the general class of effects in which the public at large has a legitimate expectation of privacy").

6. *See, e.g.*, United States v. Lifshitz, 369 F.3d 173, 190 (2d Cir. 2004) (stating that a probationer "may not . . . enjoy . . . an expectation of privacy in transmissions over the Internet or e-mail that have already arrived at the recipient"); State v. Carle, 337 P.3d 904, 910 (Or. Ct. App. 2014) (stating that "the general notion that a person has a reasonable expectation of privacy in letters or text messages does not compel the conclusion that she has a reasonable expectation of privacy in a copy of a sent text message that is found on the recipient's phone," as the sender's ability to control the message terminates with delivery).

privacy in the contents of communications.[7] It is also possible to argue that when a person sends an email, text message, or similar communication, the person reveals the content of that message to his or her service provider and thereby loses any reasonable expectation of privacy.[8]

The U.S. Supreme Court has not yet addressed the issue. The closest it has come is to assume without deciding that users have a reasonable expectation of privacy in the contents of their pager messages.[9] Even without a Supreme Court decision on point, however, the debate seems to have turned decisively in favor of the view that electronic communications typically are subject to a reasonable expectation of privacy. The leading case is *United States v. Warshak*,[10] a decision by the U.S. Court of Appeals for the Sixth Circuit. In *Warshak*, the court considered the Fourth Amendment status of the contents of email. The court observed that email is the predominant contemporary form of communication, largely taking the place of traditional mail. In light of "the fundamental similarities between email and tradi-

---

7. *See, e.g.*, United States v. Bode, No. ELH-12-158, 2013 WL 4501303, at *16 (D. Md. Aug. 21, 2013) (unpublished) (reasoning that "whether a user has a reasonable expectation of privacy in . . . electronic communications stored or transmitted by a third-party service can be affected by the terms of service at issue" and ruling that the terms of service of an online chat room used by the defendant deprived the defendant of any reasonable expectation of privacy; among other things, the terms of service stated that all content was "logged and supervised" and could be "disclose[d] . . . to the authorities at [the service provider's] discretion"); United States v. Hart, No. 08-109-C, 2009 WL 2552347, at *2 (W.D. Ky. Aug. 17, 2009) (footnote omitted) (unpublished) ("The record indicates that the defendant had to agree to Yahoo! Terms of Service that . . . expressly notified Yahoo! users of the firm's policy of disclosing [account contents]. By his conduct, the defendant did not show that he sought to preserve his subscriber or account information and his [account contents] as private.").

8. *See, e.g.*, Orin S. Kerr, *A User's Guide to the Stored Communications Act, and a Legislator's Guide to Amending It*, 72 Geo. Wash. L. Rev. 1208, 1210 (2004) (collecting cases and stating that "[i]t is too early to tell" whether courts will apply this reasoning to the contents of communications). As discussed above in note 2, with respect to postal mail, courts distinguish between information printed on the outside of the envelope and information contained within it. There is no reasonable expectation of privacy in the former, as it is intentionally disclosed to the postal service to enable the mail to be delivered. There is a reasonable expectation of privacy in the latter, as the postal service generally does not open mail in the course of delivery. One could argue that electronic communications don't have envelopes—that both the routing/addressing information and the contents of the communication are disclosed in their entirety to the service provider.

9. City of Ontario v. Quon, 560 U.S. 746, 760 (2010) (assuming arguendo that a police officer "had a reasonable expectation of privacy in the text messages sent on the pager provided to him by [his employer]").

10. 631 F.3d 266 (6th Cir. 2010).

tional forms of communication," the court reasoned, "it would defy common sense to afford emails lesser Fourth Amendment protection" than letters and telephone calls.[11] Unless emails were given "strong protection under the Fourth Amendment," the court opined that "the Fourth Amendment would prove an ineffective guardian of private communication, an essential purpose it has long been recognized to serve."[12] Thus, the court ruled that the contents of emails are subject to a reasonable expectation of privacy and cannot be obtained without a search warrant or an exception to the warrant requirement.

Although *Warshak* concerned email, courts since have applied its reasoning to text messages and other forms of electronic communication. As one leading commentator has observed,

> Several courts have agreed with the Sixth Circuit since *Warshak*, including federal courts in Kansas and the District of Columbia, and the state of Washington Court of Appeals. Other courts have applied *Warshak* to find a reasonable expectation of privacy in stored Facebook messages, text messages, faxes, and password-protected websites. Moreover, multiple courts have presumed Fourth Amendment protection in emails. . . . In contrast, no court has reached the contrary result. *Warshak* has been adopted by every court that has squarely decided the question. The case law is not entirely settled, as only one federal court of appeals has squarely addressed the issue. But the trend in the case law is to recognize fairly broad Fourth Amendment protection, backed by a warrant requirement, for stored contents such as emails.[13]

The reasoning in *Warshak* may draw some further support from the recent U.S. Supreme Court decision in *Riley v. California*.[14] The Court in *Riley* considered whether an arrestee's cellular phone may be searched incident to his or her arrest. The Court concluded that a cellular phone may not be searched incident to arrest, in part because such a search would be exceptionally intrusive. As relevant here, the Court noted that "[e]ven the most basic phones" can store many different forms of information, including text

---

11. *Id.* at 285–86.

12. *Id.* at 286.

13. Orin S. Kerr, *The Next Generation Communications Privacy Act*, 162 U. Pa. L. Rev. 373 (2014) (footnotes omitted).

14. 573 U.S. ___, 134 S. Ct. 2473 (2014).

messages, and further observed that data stored on remote servers, presumably including email, may be accessed through a phone.[15] This reasoning suggests that the Court may view electronic communications as subject to an expectation of privacy.

The general rule established in *Warshak* is not without exceptions. For example, the *Warshak* court itself noted that unusually intrusive terms of service could destroy a reasonable expectation of privacy.[16] However, it is increasingly clear that the contents of electronic communications generally are protected by the Fourth Amendment and that officers therefore need a search warrant (or perhaps the functional equivalent, such as a court order supported by probable cause) to obtain the contents of suspects' electronic communications, unless exigent circumstances exist or one of the other recognized exceptions to the warrant requirement applies.[17]

Courts may be less likely to recognize a reasonable expectation of privacy in posts to social networking websites. Such posts are typically broadcast in a way that one-to-one emails and text messages are not. However, they may be available to only a limited roster of "friends" or "followers," so there may be an expectation of privacy from those who are not on the approved roster. Several cases have addressed the issue and have not agreed on the answer. The outcome may depend on the specific network in question and on the privacy settings selected by the user.[18]

---

15. *Id.* at ___, 134 S. Ct. at 2489.

16. 631 F.3d at 287 (emphasis in original) ("[W]e are unwilling to hold that a subscriber agreement will *never* be broad enough to snuff out a reasonable expectation of privacy. . . . [I]f the [service provider] expresses an intention to 'audit, inspect, and monitor' its subscriber's emails, that might be enough to render an expectation of privacy unreasonable.").

17. "The governing premise of the Fourth Amendment is that a governmental search and seizure of private property unaccompanied by prior judicial approval in the form of a warrant is *per se* unreasonable unless the search falls within a well-delineated exception to the warrant requirement . . . ." State v. Cooke, 306 N.C. 132, 135 (1982).

18. *See* Romano v. Steelcase Inc., 907 N.Y.S.2d 650 (Sup. Ct. 2010) (finding no reasonable expectation of privacy in Facebook and MySpace postings in light of terms of use and the fact that postings are "shared with others"); Ehling v. Monmouth-Ocean Hosp. Serv. Corp., 872 F. Supp. 2d 369, 374–75 (D.N.J. 2012) (emphasis in original) (citations omitted) ("There appears to be some consistency in the case law on the two ends of the privacy spectrum. On one end of the spectrum, there are cases holding that there is *no* reasonable expectation of privacy for material posted to an unprotected website that anyone can view. . . . On the other end of the spectrum, there are cases holding that there *is* a reasonable expectation of privacy for individual, password-protected online communications. . . . Courts, however, have not yet developed a coherent approach to

2. Statutory Protection

The key source of statutory protection for historical contents is the Stored Communications Act, or SCA.[19] The SCA was enacted in 1986. Electronic communications technology has evolved considerably since that time. The act therefore uses terms, and makes distinctions, that are archaic as applied to modern electronic communications services.

---

communications falling between these two extremes. Although most courts hold that a communication is not necessarily public just because it is accessible to a number of people, courts differ dramatically in how far they think this theory extends. . . . [The plaintiff in this civil case adequately stated a claim for invasion of privacy through the viewing of her Facebook posts because she alleged that] her comment was disclosed to a limited number of people who she had individually invited to view a restricted access webpage."); People v. Harris, 949 N.Y.S.2d 590, 593 (Crim. Ct. 2012) ("Tweets are not e-mails sent to a single party. At best, the defense may argue that this is more akin to an e-mail that is sent to a party and carbon copied to hundreds of others. There can be no reasonable expectation of privacy in a tweet sent around the world."); Roasio v. Clark Cnty. Sch. Dist., No. 2:13-CV-362 JCM, 2013 WL 3679375, at *6 (D. Nev. July 3, 2013) (unpublished) (suggesting that whether tweets are subject to a reasonable expectation of privacy may depend on the privacy settings applied by the user, but ruling in this case that because an approved recipient disclosed a student's tweets to school officials, there could be no Fourth Amendment violation; "it is well-established that when a person shares information with a third party, that person takes the risk that third person will share it with the government"); Pearce v. Whitenack, 440 S.W.3d 392, 402 (Ky. Ct. App. 2014) (regardless of privacy settings, a police officer had no reasonable expectation of privacy in a Facebook posting that was disclosed to his employer by a recipient; "as with all internet communications, [the officer] ran the risk that even a posting or communication he intended to remain private would be further disseminated by an authorized recipient"); United States v. Ulbricht, No. 14-cr-68, 2014 WL 5090039, at *13 (S.D.N.Y. Oct. 10, 2014) (footnote, citations omitted) (unpublished) ("There are, of course, many ways in which users may set up the privacy settings or password protection for their Facebook and Gmail accounts, as well as access to their laptops and these settings and protections are relevant to a [reasonable expectation of privacy] analysis. . . . It is also possible for more than one individual to have access to a single shared Facebook or Gmail account. It also seems likely that many of [the defendant's] emails were to individuals other than himself, which could defeat an expectation of privacy in them. . . . The Court has no idea whether [the defendant] had a reasonable subjective expectation that all aspects of his Facebook and Gmail accounts would be private, or none."); R.S. *ex rel.* S.S. v. Minnewaska Area Sch. Dist., 894 F. Supp. 2d 1128, 1142 (D. Minn. 2012) (holding "that one cannot distinguish a password-protected private Facebook message from other forms of private electronic correspondence," and thus, "based on established Fourth Amendment precedent, [a student] had a reasonable expectation of privacy to her private Facebook information and messages").

19. 18 U.S.C. §§ 2701 *et seq.*

The SCA generally prohibits electronic communications service providers from disclosing information to law enforcement,[20] then creates exceptions for various types of information with various types of legal process. In other words, it protects some content more than others, with some being available only with a search warrant, while other material is available with a court order that may be issued based on a showing akin to reasonable suspicion, and yet other information being available with a simple subpoena.

The level of protection offered by the SCA depends on factors such as whether the service provider is classified as a "remote computing service" or an "electronic communications service"; whether the communication is deemed to be in "electronic storage"; and the age of the communication. As noted above, these terms do not map neatly onto modern service providers. Furthermore, courts have disagreed about the proper interpretation of critical terms in the statute, especially the term "electronic storage."[21] The result is significant uncertainty about the scope and proper interpretation of the SCA.

Fortunately, because the emerging consensus under *Warshak* is that the contents of communications generally are protected by the Fourth Amendment, and because the warrant requirement of the Fourth Amendment is as demanding as even the highest level of protection offered by the SCA, it is not necessary to explore the intricacies of the SCA's content rules. Compliance with the Fourth Amendment's warrant requirement will also satisfy the SCA. Readers interested in the details of the SCA's regulations regarding contents are encouraged to consult the sources cited in the margin,[22] but as

---

20. 18 U.S.C. § 2702(a).

21. The SCA requires a search warrant to access the contents of electronic communications that have been "in electronic storage in an electronic communications system for one hundred and eighty days or less." 18 U.S.C. § 2703(a). The term "electronic storage" is defined in 18 U.S.C. § 2711, which adopts the definition in 18 U.S.C. § 2510(17), which states that it includes "any temporary, intermediate storage of a wire or electronic communication incidental to the electronic transmission thereof" and "any storage of such communication by an electronic communication service for purposes of backup protection of such communication." The controversy concerns whether an email that has been received and read—but not deleted—is in "electronic storage," and specifically, whether it remains in the recipient's email system "for purposes of backup protection." In *Theofel v. Farey-Jones*, 359 F.3d 1066 (9th Cir. 2003), the Ninth Circuit answered the question in the affirmative. The government strongly objected because the ruling resulted in many emails being available only by search warrant that would otherwise have been available with lesser process.

22. Kerr, *A User's Guide*, *supra* note 8; U.S. Dep't of Justice, Computer Crime & Intellectual Prop. Section, Searching & Seizing Computers & Obtaining Electronic Evidence in Criminal Investigations (3d ed. 2009), *available at* www.justice.gov/criminal/cybercrime/docs/ssmanual2009.pdf;

a practical matter, using a warrant to obtain historical content is the safest course.

3. Practice and Procedure

In North Carolina, it is usually law enforcement officers who apply for search warrants.[23] Nothing in the SCA requires a different procedure for search warrants for historical contents. The SCA permits any "governmental entity," broadly defined,[24] to seek access to such information.

North Carolina law allows many judicial officials to issue search warrants.[25] To be valid under the SCA, however, a search warrant may be issued only by a "court of competent jurisdiction."[26] Among state courts, that term includes only "a court of general criminal jurisdiction of a State authorized by the law of that State to issue search warrants."[27] Magistrates and clerks are excluded by that definition, and the status of district court judges is unclear.[28] Officers should therefore seek such search warrants from superior court judges.

Jeffrey B. Welty, *Prosecution and Law Enforcement Access to Information about Electronic Communications*, ADMIN. OF JUST. BULL. No. 2009/05 (UNC School of Government, 2009), http://sogpubs.unc.edu//electronicversions/pdfs/aojb0905.pdf?

23. G.S. 15A-244 does not limit who may apply for a search warrant, and it is possible that in some instances a prosecutor or an attorney for a law enforcement agency might be the applicant.

24. 18 U.S.C. § 2711(4) (defining the term to include "a department or agency of the United States or any State or political subdivision thereof").

25. G.S. 15A-243.

26. 18 U.S.C. §§ 2703(a), (b).

27. 18 U.S.C. § 2711(3)(b).

28. G.S. 7A-270 provides that "[g]eneral jurisdiction for the trial of criminal actions is vested in the superior court and the district court divisions of the General Court of Justice," which suggests that district courts are courts of general jurisdiction. But *State v. Spencer*, 7 N.C. App. 282, 286 (1970), contrasts district courts, having "jurisdiction over misdemeanors only," with "a court of general jurisdiction such as our superior court." The SCA's definition of "court of competent jurisdiction" is similar to the definition that has long been part of the federal wiretap statutes, which has been interpreted to include a fairly wide range of judicial officials. For example, in *United States v. Pacheco*, 489 F.2d 554, 563 (5th Cir. 1974), the federal appeals court held that a state supreme court justice had "general criminal jurisdiction," notwithstanding the defendant's argument that the justice's jurisdiction was limited to appeals. The court cited legislative history suggesting that the "general criminal jurisdiction" language was only intended to prevent officials with limited legal training, such as magistrates, from issuing wiretap orders. See also United States v. Feola, 651 F. Supp. 1068 (S.D.N.Y. 1987) (similar, as to a trial "justice" in New York); United States v. Pine, 473 F. Supp. 349 (D. Md. 1978) (similar, as to a Baltimore County Circuit Court judge). So there is a reasonable argument that district court judges can sign search warrants for historical content, but the issue is not settled.

Generally, search warrants for historical contents should be processed like other search warrants. The normal practice appears to be to serve such a warrant only on the service provider, not on the suspect.[29] However, the suspect might still learn of the warrant, either through a courtesy notification from the service provider or—less likely—by reviewing search warrants in the clerk's office. In some instances, typically involving ongoing investigations, the applicant may wish temporarily to prevent the subscriber from learning of the existence of the search warrant. There are two provisions of law relevant to such a situation. First, the warrant likely could be issued under seal if it meets the general standard for sealing search warrants under North Carolina law.[30] This would prevent the subscriber from accessing the warrant through the clerk's office. Second, the SCA allows the applicant to seek a court order requiring the service provider not to disclose the existence of the warrant if doing so would endanger any person, create a risk of flight, or jeopardize an investigation.[31]

Case Summaries on Historical Content

United States v. DiTomasso, ___ F. Supp. 3d ___, No. 14-cr-160, 2014 WL 5462467 (S.D.N.Y. Oct. 28, 2014) (concluding that the contents of electronic communications generally are subject to a reasonable expectation of privacy; rejecting the government's arguments to the contrary based on the fact that the defendant's emails and one-on-one chats were shared with their recipients and that the services used by the defendant had terms of service that allowed some monitoring of

---

29. Many cases describe this practice in passing. *See, e.g.*, United States v. Cameron, 699 F.3d 621, 630 (1st Cir. 2012) (noting that investigators "subsequently served search warrants on Yahoo! for information about the Yahoo! accounts that had been accessed from [the suspect's] computers. The data produced by Yahoo! in response to the search warrants included emails that had been sent to and from those accounts."); Commonwealth v. Gomolekoff, 910 A.2d 710, 712 (Pa. Super. Ct. 2006) (noting that "[a] search warrant for the email account of [a suspect], was served on America Online"). Given the emerging consensus that the subscriber has a reasonable expectation of privacy in the contents of his or her electronic communications, an argument could be made that the subscriber should be served when the warrant seeks the contents of communications, subject to the avenues for delay of service noted in the text.

30. *In re* Investigation into Death of Cooper, 200 N.C. App. 180 (2009) (allowing search warrants to be sealed when necessary to protect strong government interests and when sealing order is narrowly tailored).

31. 18 U.S.C. § 2705(b) (allowing a court to issue such an order "for such period as the court deems appropriate").

contents; and ruling that both the sender and the recipient of an email have a reasonable expectation of privacy in its contents).

State v. Hinton, 319 P.3d 9, 13, 14 (Wash. 2014) (holding, under the state constitution, that text messages are subject to a reasonable expectation of privacy and noting that "[t]ext messages can encompass the same intimate subjects as phone calls, sealed letters, and other traditional forms of communication"; the court also ruled that the expectation of privacy is not destroyed upon delivery, for "[j]ust as subjecting a letter to potential interception while in transit does not extinguish a sender's privacy interest in its contents, neither does subjecting a text communication to the possibility of exposure on someone else's phone").

State v. Clampitt, 364 S.W.3d 605 (Mo. Ct. App. 2012) (defendant was charged with manslaughter after a fatal automobile collision; the state used investigative subpoenas to obtain the contents of the defendant's text messages, both for the time around the accident and afterwards; the defendant moved to suppress, arguing that he had a reasonable expectation of privacy in the content of his text messages, and so the Fourth Amendment required the use of a search warrant; the trial court agreed and the state appealed; the lower court followed *Warshak* and rejected the application of the third-party doctrine, and the appellate court agreed).

United States v. Hamilton, 701 F.3d 404, 408 (4th Cir. 2012) (strongly suggesting "that one may generally have a reasonable expectation of privacy in email," though finding no such expectation where emails are stored on an employer's computer and the employer has a computer policy defeating an expectation of privacy).

United States v. Ali, 870 F. Supp. 2d 10 (D.D.C. 2012) (recognizing that individuals have a reasonable expectation of privacy in the content of emails sent or received through a commercial service provider).

City of Ontario v. Quon, 560 U.S. 746, 760 (2010) (assuming without deciding that the respondent "had a reasonable expectation of privacy in the text messages sent on the pager provided to him by [his government employer]" and observing in *dicta* that "[c]ell phone and text message communications are so pervasive that some persons may consider them to be essential means or necessary instruments for self-expression, even self-identification," which "might strengthen the case for an expectation of privacy").

United States v. Warshak, 631 F.3d 266 (6th Cir. 2010) (ruling that historical email contents are generally protected by the Fourth Amendment and may normally be obtained only with a search warrant).

Guest v. Leis, 255 F.3d 325 (6th Cir. 2001) (citations, internal quotation marks omitted) ("Users [of an online bulletin board] would logically lack a legitimate expectation of privacy in the materials intended for publication or public posting. . . . [Users] would lose a legitimate expectation of privacy in an e-mail that had already reached its recipient; at this moment, the e-mailer would be analogous to a letter-writer, whose expectation of privacy ordinarily terminates upon delivery of the letter.").

B. Non-Content

For the most part, the law regarding law enforcement access to historical non-content information about electronic communications is straightforward. There is an important exception, however, concerning information related to location.

1. Basic Subscriber Information

Most non-content information of interest to law enforcement is not protected by the Fourth Amendment. Under *Smith v. Maryland*,[32] information such as the name and address of a cell phone subscriber or the times and durations of telephone calls made by the subscriber are not subject to a reasonable expectation of privacy, as the subscriber voluntarily conveys this information to the service provider in the course of obtaining service.[33]

However, there is statutory protection for this information. The SCA contains a general rule that service providers "shall not knowingly divulge a record or other information pertaining to a subscriber to or customer of such service . . . to any governmental entity."[34] There are several exceptions

32. 442 U.S. 735 (1979).

33. *See, e.g.*, United States v. Wheelock, 772 F.3d 825 (8th Cir. 2014) (ruling that a defendant had no reasonable expectation of privacy in "subscriber data," including his name and address, because he had disclosed it to his internet service provider; collecting other circuit court cases reaching the same conclusion). Although Justice Sotomayor suggested in her concurrence in *United States v. Jones*, 565 U.S. ___, 132 S. Ct. 945, 957 (2012), that "it may be necessary to reconsider the premise that an individual has no reasonable expectation of privacy in information voluntarily disclosed to third parties," the Court as a whole has yet to revisit *Smith.*

34. 18 U.S.C. § 2702(a)(3).

to the rule. One of the exceptions is for a category of information that is set forth in 18 U.S.C. § 2703(c)(2) and generally known as basic subscriber information. That information includes the subscriber's name; address; "local and long distance telephone connection records, or records of session times and durations"; length and type of service; "telephone or instrument number or other subscriber number or identity, including any temporarily assigned network address"; and means of payment, including any credit card or bank account number.

Basic subscriber information is available with a subpoena, a court order, or a search warrant.[35] If a subpoena is used, it may be a trial subpoena, a grand jury subpoena, or, if authorized by statute, an administrative subpoena. A North Carolina statute grants the State Bureau of Investigation (SBI) the power to issue an administrative subpoena for "information concerning local or long-distance toll records or subscriber information" when such information is material to an active SBI investigation.[36] In some cases, the SBI may adopt other agencies' investigations to the extent necessary to enable the SBI to exercise this subpoena power.

If a court order is used to access basic subscriber information, it must be a court order that complies with 18 U.S.C. § 2703(d). Such orders are discussed in detail in the following section.

If a search warrant is used, it must be a search warrant that complies with the SCA's search warrant provisions, including limitations on which judicial officials may issue warrants. These provisions are discussed in detail above, in section II.A.3 of this chapter.

The SCA states that "[a] governmental entity receiving [non-content records] is not required to provide notice to a subscriber or customer."[37] Furthermore, the SCA allows an investigator to seek a court order requiring the service provider not to disclose the existence of a subpoena for records if doing so would endanger any person, create a risk of flight, or jeopardize an investigation.[38]

2. Other Non-Content

Although much of the non-content information of interest to law enforcement is basic subscriber information, discussed above, officers sometimes seek other non-content information. For example, officers may seek information

35. 18 U.S.C. § 2703(c).
36. G.S. 15A-298.
37. 18 U.S.C. § 2703(c)(3).
38. 18 U.S.C. § 2705(b) (allowing a court to issue such an order "for such period as the court deems appropriate").

about the email address associated with an account, the subscriber's date of birth, or routing and addressing information for communications other than phone calls, such as emails. As noted above, this non-content information generally is not subject to a reasonable expectation of privacy under *Smith* and so is not protected by the Fourth Amendment.

However, this information is protected under the SCA. It is subject to the general rule prohibiting disclosure to law enforcement set forth in 18 U.S.C. § 2702(a)(3). Officers may overcome this obstacle with a court order or a search warrant—a subpoena is not enough to obtain this information.[39]

If a search warrant is used, it must be a search warrant that complies with the SCA's search warrant provisions, including limitations on which judicial officials may issue warrants. These provisions are discussed in detail above, in section II.A.3 of this chapter.

A court may issue an order compelling production of non-content information only if the applicant "offers specific and articulable facts showing that there are reasonable grounds to believe that the contents of a wire or electronic communication, or the records or other information sought, are relevant and material to an ongoing criminal investigation."[40] This standard appears to be similar to reasonable suspicion and is less than the probable cause required for a search warrant.

Such orders must be sought from a court of competent jurisdiction, as that term is defined in the SCA. As discussed in connection with search warrants in section II.A.3 of this chapter, it is safest to have a superior court judge review applications for court orders of this kind. Such orders may be sought ex parte, without notifying the subscriber.[41] In fact, the SCA allows an investigator to seek a court order requiring the service provider not to disclose the existence of a court order for records if doing so would endanger any person, create a risk of flight, or jeopardize an investigation.[42] Such an

---

39. 18 U.S.C. § 2703(c)(1).

40. 18 U.S.C. § 2703(d).

41. 18 U.S.C. § 2703(c)(3). If the subscriber has been charged and is a party to a criminal case, it is possible to argue that while proceeding ex parte is permitted under federal law, it is prohibited by state law. *See generally* G.S. 15A-951(b) (requiring that motions be served on the opposing party).

42. 18 U.S.C. § 2705(b) (allowing a court to issue such an order "for such period as the court deems appropriate").

order presumably also could be sealed in an appropriate case.[43] All court orders should be filed with the clerk of court.[44]

3. Location Information

The most controversial legal issue regarding historical non-content information concerns records that may reveal a subscriber's physical location—typically, records that concern the location of the person's cellular phone. Many phones are equipped with GPS receivers, in which case a service provider may have very accurate information about the phone's location. All phones connect to cellular towers when they are powered on, even if no call is in progress, so at a minimum, a service provider may have records of which tower interfaced with a particular subscriber's telephone at a given time—information that may indicate the subscriber's general location.

From a statutory perspective, the status of historical GPS and cellular tower information is clear. This information is non-content information but is not basic subscriber information. Thus, it is available with a search warrant or a court order under the SCA as described in section II.B.2 of this chapter, immediately above.

The controversy concerns the constitutional status of this information. Some courts have ruled that there is no reasonable expectation of privacy in this information and that it is unprotected by the Fourth Amendment. These courts generally reason that location information is no different from other non-content information that is disclosed to the service provider in the course of obtaining service.

Other courts have ruled that location information is, by its nature, so personal that it must be protected by a reasonable expectation of privacy. This view gained some momentum as a result of the Supreme Court decision in *United States v. Jones*.[45] In *Jones*, the Court considered the warrantless installation and monitoring of a GPS tracking device on a vehicle used by a suspected drug dealer. A majority of the Court ruled that the installation of the device constituted a trespass to the vehicle for purposes of obtaining

---

43. A court would likely apply the standard applicable to sealing search warrants. *In re* Investigation into Death of Cooper, 200 N.C. App. 180 (2009) (allowing search warrants to be sealed when necessary to protect strong government interests and when sealing order is narrowly tailored).

44. G.S. 7A-109(a)(1) (requiring the clerk to follow record-keeping rules designed to record "every determinative legal action, proceeding, or event which may affect the person or property of any individual, firm, corporation, or association").

45. 565 U.S. ___, 132 S. Ct. 945 (2012).

information and so violated the Fourth Amendment, a holding with no application in the context of cell phone location information. However, it appeared that five Justices[46] also believed that at least long-term GPS tracking of a suspect would intrude upon a suspect's reasonable expectation of privacy and so would implicate the Fourth Amendment. One could argue that if long-term GPS tracking implicates the Fourth Amendment, so does long-term cell phone tracking.

The cases summarized below reflect the controversy. Given the uncertainty, the safest course for law enforcement officers is to procure a search warrant when seeking location information. Readers interested in historical location information may also be interested in section III.B.1 of this chapter, below, concerning real-time location information, and in chapter 4 of this book, concerning the use of tracking devices.

Case Summaries on Historical Location Information

United States v. Shah, No. 5:13-CR-328-FL, 2015 WL 72118, at *7, *8 (E.D.N.C. Jan. 6, 2015) (ruling that cell phone location information and Facebook user location information could properly be obtained under 18 U.S.C. § 2703(d) without a search warrant or a showing of probable cause; stating that "[a]lthough the Fourth Circuit has not directly addressed the issue raised here, most courts which have considered a Fourth Amendment challenge to collection of this data . . . have relied on the rules regarding third party/business records . . . to uphold the government's action," reasoning "that no expectation of privacy applies because cell phone users voluntarily convey the cell site location data to their providers"; finding "the reasoning underlying these cases persuasive in denying defendant's motion"; and rejecting the idea that there were five votes in *Jones* for a warrant requirement for location information, because "it is not clear how these five justices would rule on the circumstances at issue here, where a GPS device was not used, the tracking information is historical, rather than real-time, and a federal statute expressly provides for the method by which the location information was obtained").

United States v. Guerrero, 768 F.3d 351, 358 (5th Cir. 2014) (reaffirming the Fifth Circuit's prior ruling in *In re Application of the U.S. for Historical Cell Site Data*, 724 F.3d 600 (5th Cir. 2013), and ruling that cellular subscribers voluntarily disclose their location to

46. Justice Sotomayor, Justice Alito, and the three justices who joined Justice Alito's opinion.

service providers, rendering that information not subject to a reasonable expectation of privacy; the court also noted that the government violated the SCA by using a subpoena rather than a court order to obtain location information about the defendant but ruled that "suppression is not a remedy for a violation of the Stored Communications Act").

United States v. Davis, 754 F.3d 1205 (11th Cir. 2014) (relying in part on *Jones* and ruling that tracking the location of a suspect's cellular phone is a Fourth Amendment search that requires a warrant and cannot be done under the lower standard in 18 U.S.C. § 2703(d); and rejecting the applicability of the third-party doctrine because subscribers are unaware that they are sharing location information with service providers), *rehearing en banc granted and opinion vacated,* 573 F. App'x 925 (11th Cir. 2014).

Commonwealth v. Augustine, 4 N.E.3d 846, 862 (Mass. 2014) (holding that cellular site location information (CSLI) is protected by the state constitution's equivalent of the Fourth Amendment and can be obtained only with a search warrant based on probable cause; rejecting the applicability of the third-party doctrine because users do not actively and voluntarily disclose their location to service providers; "CSLI is purely a function and product of cellular telephone technology, created by the provider's system network at the time that a cellular telephone call connects to a cell site").

United States v. Graham, 846 F. Supp. 2d 384, 389 (D. Md. 2012) (collecting cases and stating that while the issue has not been decided by the Fourth Circuit, "[a] majority of courts . . . have concluded that the acquisition of historical cell site location data pursuant to the Stored Communications Act's specific and articulable facts standard does not implicate the Fourth Amendment, regardless of the time period involved"; the court adopts the majority view, reasoning that cell site location records are the business records of the provider, not private papers of the subscriber).

***In re* Application of the U.S. for an Order Authorizing the Release of Historical Cell-Site Info., 809 F. Supp. 2d 113, 126 (E.D.N.Y. 2011)** (holding that the disclosure of long-term, historical cell site information implicates the Fourth Amendment because of its intrusiveness; "[a]pplying the third-party-disclosure doctrine to cumulative cell-site-location records would permit governmental intrusion into information which is objectively recognized as highly private").

In re **Application of the U.S., 620 F.3d 304 (3d Cir. 2010)** (somewhat confusing opinion rules that historical location information is normally available with a court order under the 18 U.S.C. § 2703(d) standard but that a judicial official has the discretion to require a warrant under certain circumstances).

III. Real-Time Information

Law enforcement officers are increasingly interested in obtaining real-time access to information about suspects' electronic communications. For certain types of real-time monitoring, such as wiretapping, the legal requirements for obtaining access are well settled. For other aspects of real-time data collection, the legal requirements are less clear.

A. Content

The greatest intrusion on individual privacy takes place when law enforcement seeks to access the content of an individual's electronic communications in real time. Historically, the principal type of communication that law enforcement sought to intercept in real time was telephone calls. Of course, as modern communications technologies have proliferated, officers have become interested in real-time interception of emails, text messages, and other means of communication. Real-time interception remains relatively rare, however, with the federal and state courts together issuing 3,576 orders authorizing interception in 2013,[47] and North Carolina's state courts issuing just 22 such orders.[48]

At the constitutional level, in most instances, the contents of electronic communications are subject to a reasonable expectation of privacy, are protected by the Fourth Amendment, and may not be intercepted without a warrant. In *Katz v. United States*,[49] the U.S. Supreme Court ruled that a person who uses a telephone is "entitled to assume that the words he utters into the mouthpiece will not be broadcast to the world."[50] Section II.A of this chapter summarizes the debate about whether users have a reasonable

---

47. Admin. Office of the U.S. Courts, *Wiretap Report 2013*, USCOURTS.GOV, www.uscourts.gov/Statistics/WiretapReports/wiretap-report-2013.aspx (last visited Jan. 5, 2015).

48. *Id.* at Table 2.

49. 389 U.S. 347 (1967).

50. *Id.* at 352.

expectation of privacy in communications made using modern methods such as email and text messaging, and notes that courts have generally begun to find that such communications, like telephone calls, are subject to a reasonable expectation of privacy. Thus, as a general rule, the Fourth Amendment's protections apply, and real-time access to content normally may not be obtained without a warrant.

Real-time access to content is not usually addressed under the constitutional framework, however. Such access is regulated by federal and state statutes, and the statutory requirements go above and beyond the warrant requirement of the Fourth Amendment. Therefore, litigation typically takes place under the statutory rules.

At the federal level, the Wiretap Act[51] generally makes it a felony to "intentionally intercept[], endeavor[] to intercept[], or procure[] any other person to intercept or endeavor to intercept, any wire, oral, or electronic communication."[52] The use of the broad phrase "wire, oral, or electronic communication" makes clear that the prohibition applies to a range of communication technologies, not just to phone calls. Law enforcement may gain legal permission to engage in wiretapping only with a wiretap order. Such an order may be sought from a federal judge, in connection with the investigation of enumerated federal crimes, with the approval of a designated federal prosecutor.[53] A judge may issue such an order only upon finding probable cause and that "normal investigative procedures have been tried and have failed or reasonably appear to be unlikely to succeed if tried or to be too dangerous."[54] The requirement that normal investigative procedures be impractical distinguishes wiretap orders from search warrants, which may be issued based on probable cause alone. Because of this additional requirement, wiretap orders are sometimes called "super warrants."

The federal Wiretap Act also provides that a wiretap order may be sought from a state judge, in connection with the investigation of enumerated state crimes. Any such order must be issued "in conformity with [federal law] and with the applicable State statute."[55] In other words, the federal Wiretap Act allows state judges to issue wiretap orders on similar terms to federal judges, subject to any state laws that may be more restrictive than federal

51. 18 U.S.C. §§ 2510 *et seq.*
52. 18 U.S.C. § 2511(1)(a).
53. 18 U.S.C. § 2516(1).
54. 18 U.S.C. § 2518(3)(c).
55. 18 U.S.C. § 2516(2).

law. North Carolina has enacted its own laws regulating wiretapping,[56] which are somewhat more exacting than the federal Wiretap Act.[57]

Like its federal counterpart, North Carolina's statutory scheme makes the interception of a wire, oral, or electronic communication a felony, subject to certain exceptions.[58] It also creates a procedure for obtaining a court order authorizing such interception. The procedure is available in connection with the investigation of the types of crimes listed in G.S. 15A-290, including drug trafficking, many violent and sexual offenses, and certain crimes related to the obstruction of justice. Only the Attorney General or his or her designee may apply for such an order,[59] though of course the application may be prompted by a request from other law enforcement agencies.[60] The application is reviewed by a three-judge panel, constituted as described in the statutes.[61] As under the parallel federal statute, the panel may issue an order only upon finding probable cause and that normal investigative techniques are impractical.[62]

Because suspects may use multiple phones or addresses, sometimes in an effort to evade surveillance, under certain conditions a so-called roving wiretap order may be issued. Such an order allows investigators to intercept any line used by a suspect without returning to the court for specific authorization.[63]

---

56. *See generally* G.S. 15A-286 *et seq.*

57. G.S. 15A-297 states that "[i]t is the intent of [the state wiretapping laws] to conform the requirements of all interceptions of wire, oral, or electronic communications conducted by investigative or law enforcement officers in this State to provisions of [federal law], except where the context indicates a purpose to provide safeguards even more protective of individual privacy and constitutional rights."

58. G.S. 15A-287. Perhaps the most important exception is consent. North Carolina is a one-party consent state, meaning that the consent of a single party to the conversation removes it from the scope of the wiretapping laws. *Id.* For example, inmates who place telephone calls from jails or prisons typically are warned that their calls may be recorded, and by placing a call, implicitly consent to such recording. *See, e.g.,* State v. Troy, 198 N.C. App. 396 (2009). Some courts also uphold the recording of inmate phone calls under the federal and state statutory exceptions for interception in the ordinary course of a law enforcement officer's duties. *See* 18 U.S.C. § 2510(5)(a)(ii); G.S. 15A-286(7); United States v. Hammond, 286 F.3d 189 (4th Cir. 2002); United States v. Feekes, 879 F.2d 1562 (7th Cir. 1989).

59. G.S. 15A-291(a).

60. G.S. 15A-292.

61. G.S. 15A-291(a).

62. G.S. 15A-293(a).

63. G.S. 15A-294(i); 18 U.S.C. § 2518(11)(b).

Wiretap proceedings are highly confidential. Like other proceedings involving investigative orders, they are ex parte.[64] Any orders that result are sealed.[65] The target is usually informed of the existence of an order within ninety days of the termination of monitoring, though the application and order itself need not be served on the target at that time.[66]

Because wiretapping is so intrusive, both federal and state statutes impose certain constraints on wiretapping orders. Such orders may last no longer than necessary to achieve investigative goals, and in any event no longer than thirty days, though they may be renewed under certain circumstances.[67] They must require investigators to adopt procedures designed to minimize the amount of non-relevant content they intercept.[68] And they may require the submission of periodic progress reports to the court.[69]

---

64. G.S. 15A-293(a); 18 U.S.C. § 2518(3).

65. G.S. 15A-293(d); 18 U.S.C. § 2518(8)(b).

66. G.S. 15A-294(d), (d1) ("Within a reasonable time, but no later than 90 days after the filing of an application for an order or the termination of the period of an order or the extensions thereof," unless delayed by court order, the target must be informed of the fact that a surveillance order was entered and provided with certain other information; the application and order need not be disclosed at this point, but the contents of any intercepted communications are not admissible unless the application and order are provided to the target under G.S. 15A-294(f) and 18 U.S.C. § 2518(9)); 18 U.S.C. § 2518(8)(d).

67. G.S. 15A-293(c) ("No order entered under this Article may authorize the interception of any wire, oral, or electronic communication for any period longer than is necessary to achieve the objective of the authorization, nor in any event longer than 30 days."); 18 U.S.C. § 2518(5).

68. G.S. 15A-293(c); 18 U.S.C. § 2518(5). Neither statute specifies how this is to be accomplished, and courts have generally upheld efforts at minimization, such as listening to the first two minutes of every phone call and then ending monitoring if the call is not relevant. *See* 2 WAYNE R. LAFAVE ET AL., CRIMINAL PROCEDURE § 4.6(h) (3d ed. 2007). Some courts have suggested that an applicant should disclose whether he or she intends to use civilians to monitor the wiretap, a practice that is especially common when the conversations to be intercepted are likely to be in a language other than English. *See, e.g.*, United States v. Lopez, 300 F.3d 46, 54 (1st Cir. 2002) (holding that "the government must disclose its intention to use civilian monitors" so that the court can craft an order ensuring minimization). Both statutes specifically address the issue of minimization when the communications are not in English, providing that "[i]n the event the intercepted communication is in a code or foreign language, and an expert in that foreign language or code is not reasonably available during the interception period, minimization may be accomplished as soon as practicable after the interception." G.S. 15A-293(c). *See also* 18 U.S.C. § 2518(5) (similar).

69. G.S. 15A-293(d); 18 U.S.C. § 2518(6).

B. Non-Content

While the legal requirements for wiretap orders are relatively clear, the framework under which law enforcement may obtain access to real-time non-content information is less clear.

1. Location Information

As noted above in section II.B.3 of this chapter, law enforcement officers are frequently interested in obtaining access to information that may reveal a person's physical location. Just as courts have disagreed about how to handle requests for historical GPS and cellular tower information, they have also differed with respect to requests for such information in real time. Requests for real-time location information are sometimes described as requests to "ping" a suspect's cellular phone.[70]

a. Constitutional Protection

Some courts believe that people who use electronic communications services, such as cellular telephones, voluntarily disclose their location to the service provider in the course of obtaining service and so may claim no reasonable expectation of privacy in location information. Other courts believe that location information is private in nature and that a user's expectation of privacy should not be relinquished by the incidental disclosure of location information in the course of using an electronic communication device. A few courts have tried to chart a middle course, finding long-term tracking of location information to require a warrant but not short-term tracking. The cases summarized below reflect the divergence of judicial opinion on this issue.

Readers interested in this topic should also review section II.B.3 of this chapter, above, regarding access to historical location information. Courts

---

70. *See, e.g.*, United States v. Caraballo, 963 F. Supp. 2d 341, 346 (D. Vt. 2013) ("This investigative technique, commonly referred to as cell phone 'pinging,' consists of the cell phone carrier surreptitiously accessing by satellite the cell phone's GPS location, or if unavailable, its location in terms of its proximity to the nearest cell phone tower."); United States v. Williford, 961 F. Supp. 2d 740 (D. Md. 2013) (using the term to describe law enforcement obtaining real-time location information from suspect's cellular service provider). A federal Drug Enforcement Administration agent explained pinging as follows in *United States v. Barajas*, 710 F.3d 1102, 1104 n.1 (10th Cir. 2013): "a first-party [ping] would be contacting [the carrier], asking them to do a GPS query on . . . the target telephone being used by [the suspect]. [The carrier] would return with the GPS coordinates for the location of that telephone within a certain radius, depending on the telephone's physical location and distance from cell towers. . . . [T]he request is done electronically through a secure website that [the carrier] has set up."

that have found such access to implicate the Fourth Amendment likely would rule the same way with respect to real-time access. The converse may not necessarily follow; that is, a court that believes that access to historical location information is not a constitutional concern might view real-time access as more intrusive and so as implicating the Fourth Amendment.

Case Summaries on Constitutional Protection of Real-Time Location Information

State v. Tracey, 152 So. 3d 504, 522 (Fla. 2014) (officers obtained a pen register order, not based on probable cause, and used it to obtain access to cell site location information (CSLI) that helped them to apprehend a drug suspect; the state supreme court ruled that real-time CSLI is "invasive," protected by the Fourth Amendment, and requires a warrant; it ruled that the third-party doctrine did not apply because "[w]hile a person may voluntarily convey personal information to a business or other entity for personal purposes, such disclosure cannot reasonably be considered to be disclosure for all purposes to third parties not involved in that transaction"; the court also ruled that the duration of the surveillance is irrelevant, as a distinction between long-term and short-term surveillance is "not a workable analysis").

United States v. Powell, 943 F. Supp. 2d 759, 770, 777 (E.D. Mich. 2013) (collecting cases and stating that "[t]he majority of jurisdictions require the government to make a probable-cause showing to obtain real-time cell-site location data," while "[t]he minority of jurisdictions do not accord any protection to cell-site information, or they authorize the use of such information on a showing of less than probable cause"; concluding that, for long-term location tracking, "Fourth Amendment concerns are implicated" and that a showing of probable cause is required; following *Skinner*, below, as to short-term location tracking; and rejecting the claim that any statute purports to permit the disclosure of prospective location information on a showing of less than probable cause).

United States v. Caraballo, 963 F. Supp. 2d 341, 360 (D. Vt. 2013) (noting that the terms of service inform cellular telephone subscribers that their location data may be collected and disclosed; stating that "a cell phone user generally has no reasonable expectation of privacy in cell site information communicated for the purpose or making and receiving calls in the ordinary course of the provision of cellular phone service," because such data is voluntarily disclosed to the service provider; withholding judgment on whether there is a reasonable expectation of privacy in location data obtained when a subscriber's phone is pinged at the request of law enforcement rather than in the normal course of business; and ruling that in this case, exigent circumstances supported the warrantless pinging of the defendant's phone).

***In re* Smartphone Geolocation Data Application, 977 F. Supp. 2d 129, 147 (E.D.N.Y. 2013)** (holding that "as to prospective geolocation data, cell phone users who fail to turn off their cell phones do not exhibit an expectation of privacy and such expectation would not be reasonable in any event," given the widespread knowledge of how cellular technology works, and the existence of "standard industry agreements by which users agree to collection of their geolocation data by third parties"; and ruling, as a statutory matter, that prospective location data is available under the SCA "specific and articulable facts" standard, not under the probable cause standard applicable to tracking devices).

United States v. Skinner, 690 F.3d 772 (6th Cir. 2012) (finding no reasonable expectation of privacy in GPS location "data given off" by defendant's cell phone and ruling that the Fourth Amendment was not implicated by short-term tracking; the court reserved ruling on whether long-term tracking might implicate the Fourth Amendment).

b. Statutory Protection

Just as the constitutional status of real-time location information is unclear, so is the status of such information under statutory law. Recall that historical location information is protected by the SCA, but that the SCA allows such information to be obtained with a court order. As to real-time location information, however, courts disagree about whether, and to what extent, the SCA applies to such information. Most courts have ruled that the SCA applies to historical records, not to prospective monitoring—after all, the statute is named the <Stored> Communications Act. These courts generally have concluded that a search warrant is necessary to obtain real-time location information.[71] But a few have ruled that real-time location information

71. These opinions, which generally are in federal cases, typically conclude that allowing access to real-time CSLI turns cell phones into tracking devices and so the federal warrant requirement for tracking devices should apply. But there are other possibilities. First, if the SCA does not apply to prospective information, and if such information is not subject to a reasonable expectation of privacy because of the third-party/voluntary disclosure doctrine, then the information would be totally unprotected. Second, if the disclosure provisions of the SCA do not apply because they relate only to historical information but the general bar to disclosure in 18 U.S.C. § 2702(a)(3) does apply because it is not limited to

is available under the SCA, either because the information is turned into a record by the service provider before it is disclosed to law enforcement or because a hybrid of the SCA and the pen/trap statutes (discussed below in section III.B.2 of this chapter) allow prospective monitoring.[72]

In recent years, several states have adopted statutes that limit law enforcement access to location information. For example, Colorado law provides that "a government entity shall not obtain the location information of an electronic device without a search warrant . . . a subpoena, or a court order," subject to certain exceptions.[73] Illinois law states that "a law enforcement agency shall not obtain current or future location information pertaining to a person or his or her effects without first obtaining a court order based on probable cause."[74] North Carolina has not enacted a similar statutory scheme.

Case Summaries on Statutory Protection for Real-Time Location Information

***In re* Order Authorizing Prospective & Continuous Release of Cell Site Location Records, 31 F. Supp. 3d 889 (S.D. Tex. 2014)** (federal magistrate judge rules that prospective location information is not available under the Stored Communications Act or under the hybrid authority of the SCA and the pen register statutes and notes that "most published opinions" agree and that there are no appellate cases on point; does not address the Fourth Amendment but states that the federal tracking device statute applies and requires a showing of probable cause).

United States v. Espudo, 954 F. Supp. 2d 1029, 1035 (S.D. Cal. 2013) (collecting cases and stating that "[u]sing a combination of statutory and Fourth Amendment analysis, the majority of federal courts examining the requirements for the acquisition of real-time cell site loca-

---

historical "records," there would be an absolute statutory bar to disclosure of real-time non-content information. Perhaps a federal search warrant could overcome such a bar, but under the Supremacy Clause a state search warrant probably would not be able to do so.

72. For a discussion and endorsement of the so-called "hybrid theory," see *United States v. Booker*, No. 1:11-CR-255-1-TWT, 2013 WL 2903562 (N.D. Ga. June 13, 2013) (unpublished) (noting that the federal pen register statute has been amended to allow real-time access to "signaling information"; concluding that "signaling information" includes CSLI; and arguing that while another federal statute prohibits the disclosure of CSLI based "solely" on the pen register statute, CSLI may be disclosed under a combination of the SCA and the pen register statutes, so long as the more stringent "reasonable grounds to believe" standard of the SCA is satisfied).

73. COLO. REV. STAT. § 16-3-303.5(2).

74. 725 ILL. COMP. STAT. 168/10.

tion data mandate that the government make a showing of probable cause"; rejecting the government's argument that prospective location information is available under the SCA or under the hybrid theory; declining to address the Fourth Amendment issue; and ruling that as a statutory matter, prospective location information is available only with a showing of probable cause).

***In re* Smartphone Geolocation Data Application, 977 F. Supp. 2d 129, 147 (E.D.N.Y. 2013)** (holding that "as to prospective geolocation data, cell phone users who fail to turn off their cell phones do not exhibit an expectation of privacy and such expectation would not be reasonable in any event," given the widespread knowledge of how cellular technology works and the existence of "standard industry agreements by which users agree to collection of their geolocation data by third parties"; and ruling, as a statutory matter, that prospective location data is available under the SCA "specific and articulable facts" standard, not the probable cause standard applicable to tracking devices).

***In re* Application for Pen Register, 396 F. Supp. 2d 747, 760 (S.D. Tex. 2005)** (frequently cited opinion by federal magistrate judge rules that prospective CSLI is not available under the SCA: "Unlike other [federal statutes] which regulate methods of real-time surveillance, the SCA regulates access to records and communications in storage. As implied by its full title ('Stored Wire and Electronic Communications and Transactional Records Access'), the entire focus of the SCA is to describe the circumstances under which the government can compel disclosure of existing communications and transaction records in the hands of third party service providers. Nothing in the SCA contemplates a new form of ongoing surveillance in which law enforcement uses co-opted service provider facilities.").

c. Recommended Practices for Officers

Because it is not clear what legal standard applies to requests for real-time location information, a cautious law enforcement officer will try to meet the highest standard that a court reasonably might apply. As noted above, some courts require a showing of probable cause before granting access to location information, so a cautious officer will try to establish probable cause.

It is also unclear what sort of order an officer should seek. The standard of probable cause is associated with search warrants. However, search warrants do not typically contain the limitations and safeguards that normally are imposed on real-time data collection by law enforcement, such as time limits. Also, search warrants are subject to procedural requirements that make little sense when applied to real-time data collection. For example, search warrants must be executed within forty-eight hours and must be returned after they have been executed. But it is not clear when a warrant authorizing the collection of real-time location information has been executed. Is it when law enforcement first accesses the information? When it stops accessing the information?

Because search warrants are an awkward fit for the collection of real-time location information, officers may wish to seek investigative court orders instead. North Carolina's courts have approved the use of such orders in other contexts,[75] and because court orders are inherently flexible, they may be tailored to fit the context of prospective monitoring of location information. The application process would be similar to that for a search warrant, with an officer submitting a written application with a sworn affidavit. The order itself would find probable cause; authorize the real-time collection of location information; set a time limit on such collection; and address whether and when the target will be notified of the collection. The order likely could be sealed under appropriate circumstances.[76]

The procedure described above may be more demanding than courts eventually will require. However, given the uncertainty of the law in this area, it may be wise to err on the side of caution.

d. Stingrays

The discussion above concerns the authority of law enforcement officers to obtain real-time location information from service providers, particularly cell phone companies. Related issues arise when law enforcement seeks to determine a suspect's location using "stingrays," also known as IMSI (International Mobile Subscriber Identity) catchers or cell site simulators. Stingrays are machines that simulate cell towers and connect with the cellular telephones located nearby. Officers may use them to triangulate the location

---

75. *In re* Superior Court Order Dated April 8, 1983, 315 N.C. 378, 380 (1986) (holding that a superior court judge has inherent authority to issue an investigative order compelling the production of bank records relevant to a criminal investigation where the "other options available to the district attorney at the investigatory stage of the proceeding provide inadequate means of obtaining the desired information").

76. A court would likely apply the standard applicable to sealing search warrants. *In re* Investigation into Death of Cooper, 200 N.C. App. 180 (2009) (allowing search warrants to be sealed when necessary to protect strong government interests and when sealing order is narrowly tailored).

of a suspect's phone, and thereby to locate the suspect, without involving the suspect's service provider.

The legal status of stingrays is unclear. At one end of the spectrum, it is possible to argue that neither constitutional principles nor statutory law limits their use. Constitutionally, the argument would be that a stingray simply detects the signals that a suspect's phone voluntarily broadcasts to the world and so does not infringe on any reasonable expectation of privacy.[77] At a minimum, cell phones send their signals to cellular service providers, and one could argue that this destroys any expectation of privacy in the signals under *Smith v. Maryland*. Statutorily, the argument would be that stingrays normally are configured not to collect the content of any communications, so the wiretapping laws do not apply, and that stingrays operate over the air instead of being installed on a particular phone line, so the pen register statutes do not apply.

A middle ground position is that, while there is no Fourth Amendment issue for the reasons given above, a pen register order is required. As discussed more fully in section III.B.2 of this chapter, below, while the state pen register statute applies only to devices attached to telephone lines, the federal pen register statute defines a pen register in part as any "device or process which records or decodes dialing, routing, addressing, or signaling information transmitted by an instrument . . . from which . . . [an] electronic communication is transmitted."[78] Because the federal definition contains no reference to attachment to a phone line, it might apply to stingrays, and state law generally cannot provide less protection than federal law. Some federal agencies apparently have taken the position that a pen register order is the appropriate process to be used when seeking authorization to employ a stingray.[79]

---

77. *Cf.* State v. McGriff, 151 N.C. App. 631, 638 n.1 (2002) (in a case where one neighbor "inadvertently intercepted" another neighbor's conversation on a cordless phone, apparently because of channel overlap, the court strongly suggested that there is no reasonable expectation of privacy in "cordless telephone conversations").

78. 18 U.S.C. § 3127(3).

79. Ryan Gallagher, *FBI Files Unlock History Behind Clandestine Cellphone Tracking Tool*, Slate, Feb. 15, 2013, www.slate.com/blogs/future_tense/2013/02/15/stingray_imsi_catcher_fbi_files_unlock_history_behind_cellphone_tracking.html (discussing the views of the FBI and the United States Department of Justice as set forth in government documents). *But see* David Kravets, *FBI says search warrants not needed to use "stingrays" in public places*, ArsTechnica (Jan. 5, 2015), http://arstechnica.com/tech-policy/2015/01/fbi-says-search-warrants-not-needed-to-use-stringrays-in-public-places/ (suggesting that the FBI has adopted a policy requiring a search warrant before using

Finally, one could argue that because stingrays are essentially tracking devices than enable law enforcement to locate suspects through electronic surveillance, a search warrant based on full probable cause is required. This argument is similar to the constitutional argument discussed above in connection with obtaining real-time access to location information from a service provider.

As always, when the law is unclear, the safest course for an officer is to meet the highest legal standard that a court might reasonably apply. In this case, that standard is probable cause. An officer might use an application and order process that is similar to the one described in section III.B.1.c, above.

There are very few cases and authorities regarding stingrays at this writing. Some of the more useful sources are collected in the margin.[80]

2. Destination of Outgoing/Origin of Incoming Communications

The pen register and trap and trace statutes provide the legal framework for obtaining access to real-time information about the destination of communications coming from an account and the origins of communications coming into the account. The law in this area is relatively settled, though it is complex.

This routing or addressing information is not subject to a reasonable expectation of privacy and so is not protected by the Fourth Amendment.

---

a stingray, except when "the technology is used in public places or other locations at which the FBI deems there is no reasonable expectation of privacy").

80. Fred Clasen-Kelly, *Charlotte Police Investigators Secretly Track Cellphones*, CharlotteObserver.com (Oct. 18, 2014) www.charlotteobserver.com/2014/10/18/5250818/charlotte-police-investigators.html; Linda Lye, ACLU of N. Cal., Stingrays: The Most Common Surveillance Tool the Government Won't Tell You About (2014), *available at* www.aclunc.org/sites/default/files/StingRays_The_Most_Common_Surveillance_Tool_the_Govt_Won%27t_Tell_You_About_0.pdf; State v. Tate, 849 N.W.2d 798, 803, 810 (Wis. 2014) (officers obtained a court order giving them access to a murder suspect's CSLI, then used a "stingray, a device that mimicked a cell tower" to "allow[] officers to locate the phone based on signal strength"; the court ruled that because the order was based on probable cause, it was sufficient to authorize the tracking and the use of the stingray; "[n]o specific statutory authority is necessary" to issue a sufficient order); United States v. Rigmaiden, No. CR 08-814-PHX-DGC, 2013 WL 1932800 (D. Ariz. May 8, 2013) (unpublished) (government concedes that the use of a stingray is a Fourth Amendment search); *In re* Application of the U.S., 890 F. Supp. 2d 747, 750 (S.D. Tex. 2012) (federal magistrate judge rules that use of a stingray may only be authorized by warrant; the pen/trap statute is inadequate because "pen register applications seek information about a particular telephone," while a stingray gathers information about all phones in an area).

The U.S. Supreme Court ruled in *Smith v. Maryland*[81] that the use of a pen register to collect information on the numbers dialed from a suspect's telephone line did not implicate the Fourth Amendment because a telephone subscriber voluntarily conveys the numbers dialed to the telephone company in order to complete the calls, and therefore relinquishes any reasonable expectation of privacy in the numbers. Although *Smith* was decided in the context of telephone calls, the same reasoning presumably applies to emails, text messages, and the like.

In response to *Smith*, Congress enacted the federal pen register statutes,[82] and the General Assembly subsequently enacted North Carolina's own pen register law.[83] As explained below, both the federal and state laws apply to the installation of pen register and trap and trace devices on telephone lines, while only the federal statute applies to the collection of nontelephone routing and addressing information. Because both statutes may be relevant in practice, each will be described briefly below.

The federal statute prohibits the use of a pen register (to collect numbers dialed) or a trap and trace device (to collect numbers from which incoming calls originated) without a court order.[84] Although the statute was originally written in the context of telephone calls, it has been updated. The definition of a pen register now includes any device that "records or decodes dialing, routing, addressing, or signaling information transmitted by an instrument or facility from which a wire or electronic communication is transmitted,"[85] and the definition of a trap and trace device includes similar language. Thus, a pen register order is needed to obtain, for example, a list of all the addresses to which email is sent from a particular account.

Such orders are easily obtained under federal law. A federal prosecutor may obtain an order authorizing the use of a pen register or a trap and trace device by certifying "that the information likely to be obtained by such installation and use is relevant to an ongoing criminal investigation."[86] A federal judge "shall" issue an order upon receipt of an application containing such a certification.[87] The federal statute also allows state law enforcement

81. 442 U.S. 735 (1979).
82. 18 U.S.C. §§ 3121 *et seq.*
83. G.S. 15A-260 *et seq.*
84. 18 U.S.C. § 3121(a).
85. 18 U.S.C. § 3127(3).
86. 18 U.S.C. § 3123(a)(1).
87. *Id.*

officers to submit applications, containing similar certifications, to certain state judges, unless state law provides otherwise.[88]

However, as in the wiretapping context, the federal statute provides a floor, not a ceiling. State law may be more limiting. In fact, North Carolina's statutory provisions, while generally similar to federal law, are more demanding in several regards. First, before a judge may issue an order under the statute, the judge must find that there is "reasonable suspicion to believe" that a crime has been committed.[89] Presumably, in order to do so, the judge must review the facts of the matter rather than simply defer to an officer's certification. Second, the judge must determine that a felony offense, or a Class A1 or Class 1 misdemeanor offense, has been committed; no order may issue in connection with low-level misdemeanors. (Of course, officers might be reluctant to go to the trouble of seeking such an order in connection with a minor offense even if it were lawful to do so.) Finally, the statute provides that the judge "may" issue an order upon finding the foregoing criteria satisfied, suggesting that the judge has the discretion to refuse the order.[90]

North Carolina's pen register statute has not been updated and still defines a pen register as a device that "identif[ies] numbers dialed or otherwise transmitted on the telephone line to which such device is attached."[91] The definition of a trap and trace device is similarly focused only on telephone lines.[92] An appropriate North Carolina court may nonetheless authorize the interception of nontelephone routing information under the federal statutes, which allow state judges to authorize the use of pen registers and trap and trace devices unless prohibited by state law. Because North Carolina's statutes do not *address* the use of pen registers and trap and trace devices to capture nontelephone routing information, they do not *prohibit* the same.

---

88. 18 U.S.C. §§ 3122(a)(2), 3123(a)(2).

89. G.S. 15A-263(a)(1).

90. G.S. 15A-263(a). The use of the term "may" in North Carolina's statute conflicts with the federal statutes' requirement that a state judge "shall" issue a pen register order upon receipt of a proper certification. 18 U.S.C. § 3123(a)(2). Although federal law generally trumps conflicting state law under the Supremacy Clause, it is reasonably clear that the federal pen register statutes were intended to allow states to enact stronger privacy protections than exist under federal law. Thus, in this specific context, the discretion given to judicial officials by state law likely trumps the conflicting federal provision. *Cf.* 18 U.S.C. § 3122(a)(2) (allowing state officers to seek orders from state courts "[u]nless prohibited by State law," i.e., unless state law is more protective of privacy than federal law).

91. G.S. 15A-260(2).

92. G.S. 15A-260(3).

The applicant for a pen register or trap and trace order in North Carolina will normally be a law enforcement officer. The federal pen register statute allows for applications from "a State investigative or law enforcement officer."[93] The state statute likewise refers to applications from a "law enforcement officer."[94] The application must be in writing, on oath or affirmation, and must contain a certification that the information sought is relevant to a criminal investigation.[95] As noted above, the state statute applies to applications regarding telephone lines and requires a finding of reasonable suspicion by the court; thus, factual information beyond the certification should be included in these applications, at least.

Only a superior court judge may issue pen register and trap and trace orders.[96] A pen register or trap and trace order must contain the information set forth in 18 U.S.C. § 3123(b) (and, for orders concerning telephone lines, the information listed in G.S. 15A-263(b)), which generally requires that the order name the subscriber, identify the target of the investigation, and list "the number or other identifier . . . of the telephone line or other facility" to which the order applies. The order lasts for sixty days and may be renewed upon the same showing that is required for initial issuance.[97] The order is presumptively sealed unless the court orders otherwise, and the phone company, or other relevant person or entity, may not disclose its existence to the subscriber.[98] Furthermore, when presented with an order, the phone company or other persons or entities in a position to facilitate the installation of the pen register or the trap and trace device are required to assist as needed and must be compensated for reasonable expenses incurred while assisting.[99]

The federal statute provides for emergency use of a pen register or a trap and trace device without a court order under limited circumstances, provided that an order is obtained within forty-eight hours.[100] There is no comparable provision in the state statute, so at least as to pen registers and

---

93. 18 U.S.C. § 3122(a)(2).

94. G.S. 15A-262.

95. 18 U.S.C. § 3122; G.S. 15A-262.

96. 18 U.S.C. § 3122(a)(2) (state officers may apply to state courts of "competent jurisdiction"); 18 U.S.C. § 3127(2)(b) (defining a court of competent jurisdiction as one authorized by state law to enter pen register orders); G.S. 15A-262 (only superior court judges may issue such orders).

97. 18 U.S.C. § 3123(c); G.S. 15A-263(c).

98. 18 U.S.C. § 3123(d); G.S. 15A-263(d).

99. 18 U.S.C. § 3124; G.S. 15A-264.

100. 18 U.S.C. § 3125.

trap and trace devices on telephone lines, there appears to be no exigent circumstances exception to the court order requirement.

A final issue regarding the use of pen registers and trap and trace devices concerns the problem of so-called post-cut-through dialed digits. The federal pen register statutes require that law enforcement "shall use technology reasonably available to it that restricts the recording or decoding of electronic or other impulses to the dialing, routing, addressing, and signaling information utilized in the processing and transmitting of wire or electronic communications so as not to include the contents of any wire or electronic communications."[101] This appears to be an attempt to address the fact that a pen register may record all digits dialed on a particular telephone line, including digits dialed after a connection is made. Such digits may include account numbers, passwords, and other protected call content, as when a person uses a telephone to check a bank account balance or to make a credit card payment and enters his or her account number. Because such information is content rather than envelope information, it should not be available to investigators except through a wiretap order.

Apparently, however, there is no "technology . . . that restricts" pen registers so that they do not record post-cut-through dialed digits. It appears that courts have not generally focused on, or perhaps even been aware of, this problem and that many pen register orders have been issued without regard to this issue. Recently, however, a number of decisions have addressed this concern. The decisions have generally agreed that it is improper for law enforcement to obtain information about post-cut-through dialed digits using a pen register, but they have disagreed about the legality of work-around approaches, such as having the post-cut-through dialed digits stripped from the data by the service provider or by a "taint team" of officers not involved in the investigation before the data is provided to the investigating officers.[102] No reported North Carolina case addresses the issues surrounding

---

101. 18 U.S.C. § 3121(c).

102. *See, e.g., In re* United States, 622 F. Supp. 2d 411 (S.D. Tex. 2007) (rejecting government's request to collect post-cut-through dialed digits notwithstanding government's promise not to use such digits for investigative purposes and summarizing the dispute about this issue); *In re* United States, 441 F. Supp. 2d 816 (S.D. Tex. 2006) (rejecting a pen register application that sought access to post-cut-through dialed digits); *In re* United States, 515 F. Supp. 2d 325 (E.D.N.Y. 2007) (same); *In re* United States, 632 F. Supp. 2d 202 (E.D.N.Y. 2008) (approving a pen register application that stated that the service provider would record post-cut-through dialed digits and transmit them to law enforcement but that law enforcement would immediately delete them); *In re* United States, No. 08 MC 0595(JO), 2008 WL 5255815 (E.D.N.Y. Dec. 16, 2008) (unpublished) (rejecting a pen register

post-cut-through dialed digits. Although the North Carolina statutes do not contain the federal requirement regarding restricting recording of electronic impulses that constitute the content of communications, 18 U.S.C. § 3121(c) makes that requirement applicable to orders issued "under State law" as well. Even as a matter of state law alone, obtaining such information requires a wiretap order. Specifically, G.S. 15A-287 makes it illegal to "intercept" an electronic communication without a court order, and G.S. 15A-286(13) defines "intercept" as acquiring the content of a communication through the use of an electronic or mechanical device. Thus law enforcement officers should implement, and judges should require, procedures designed to ensure that officers do not receive or review any information about the content of communications. The federal cases discussed above may provide a starting point for crafting such procedures.

3. Other Non-Content

Most law enforcement requests for real-time information about electronic communication focus on location information or the type of information that may be obtained using a pen register or trap and trace device. However, for the sake of completeness, it is worth briefly discussing how requests for real-time access to other non-content information should be analyzed. For example, an officer might request real-time notification of changes to an account's subscriber or payment information in order to stay abreast of any new address, new email address, or new credit card that a suspect uses in connection with an account.

As a constitutional matter, this information likely is not protected by the Fourth Amendment. Because it is voluntarily disclosed by the subscriber to the service provider, it is not subject to a reasonable expectation of privacy under *Smith v. Maryland.*[103]

As a statutory matter, this information does not appear to be protected by, or available under, the pen register or trap and trace statutes, as this information is not the type of routing or signaling information to which those statutes apply. It is unclear whether and how the SCA applies to this information. The SCA generally prohibits service providers from disclosing to law enforcement any "record or other information pertaining to a subscriber to or customer of such service."[104] However, it requires service providers to

---

application to the extent that it would permit the pen register to record post-cut-through dialed digits, even if the digits were not transmitted to law enforcement or were immediately deleted by law enforcement).

103. 442 U.S. 735 (1979).

104. 18 U.S.C. § 2702(a)(3).

disclose to law enforcement non-content records and "other information pertaining to a subscriber to or customer of such service" when an officer obtains a search warrant or a court order, and requires service providers to disclose basic subscriber information to law enforcement with a subpoena.[105] Perhaps these types of process are sufficient to obtain real-time access to non-content information about a subscriber. However, it is also possible to argue that the SCA regulates access to stored, or historical, information rather than real-time information and that the types of process described by the SCA are ill-suited to real-time data collection because they do not involve time limits and other features commonly found in orders authorizing real-time collection.[106]

IV. Summary Chart

The chart on pages 124 and 125 summarizes the law regarding law enforcement access to historical and real-time information about electronic communications. The chart lists both the constitutional and statutory protection available for each category of information. Where a box in the chart is shaded in gray, that box represents the higher, and so governing, legal standard for the type of information in question. Black shading indicates that the law is unsettled.

V. Other Issues

This section discusses assorted additional issues regarding law enforcement access to electronic communications that arise often enough to warrant separate treatment.

A. Emergency Requests

In emergency situations, law enforcement may wish to begin gathering information about a suspect's electronic communications before obtaining whatever judicial authorization would otherwise be needed. This is often permissible. The exigent circumstances doctrine is an exception to the Fourth

105. 18 U.S.C. § 2703.

106. The issue of real-time access to this information under the SCA is similar, if not identical, to the issue of real-time access to location information under the SCA, as discussed in section III.B.1 of this chapter.

Summary Chart: Historical Information

Type of Information	Constitutional Protection	Statutory Protection
Content	Most courts say content is subject to a reasonable expectation of privacy and is protected by the Fourth Amendment. United States v. Warshak, 631 F.3d 266 (6th Cir. 2010). A search warrant is generally required.	Unclear. Courts disagree about the proper interpretation of the Stored Communications Act (SCA), 18 U.S.C. §§ 2701 *et seq.*
Basic Subscriber Information	None. This information is voluntarily shared by the subscriber with the service provider. Smith v. Maryland, 442 U.S. 735 (1979).	Protected by the SCA but may be disclosed pursuant to subpoena; court order based on "specific and articulable facts showing that there are reasonable grounds to believe that the . . . information sought [is] relevant and material to an ongoing criminal investigation," 18 U.S.C. § 2703(d); or search warrant.
Other Non-Content (Except Location Information)	None. This information is voluntarily shared by the subscriber with the service provider. Smith v. Maryland, 442 U.S. 735 (1979).	Protected by the SCA but may be disclosed pursuant to court order based on "specific and articulable facts showing that there are reasonable grounds to believe that the . . . information sought [is] relevant and material to an ongoing criminal investigation," 18 U.S.C. § 2703(d), or search warrant.
Location Information	Unclear. Courts disagree about whether this information is subject to a reasonable expectation of privacy. *Compare In re* Application of the U.S. for Historical Cell Site Data, 724 F.3d 600 (5th Cir. 2013) (no), *with In re* Application of the U.S. for an Order Authorizing the Release of Historical Cell-Site Info., 809 F. Supp. 2d 113 (E.D.N.Y. 2011) (yes).	Protected by the SCA but may be disclosed pursuant to court order based on "specific and articulable facts showing that there are reasonable grounds to believe that the . . . information sought [is] relevant and material to an ongoing criminal investigation," 18 U.S.C. § 2703(d), or search warrant.

Summary Chart: Real-Time/Prospective Information

Type of Information	Constitutional Protection	Statutory Protection
Content	Subject to a reasonable expectation of privacy and protected by the Fourth Amendment. Katz v. United States, 389 U.S. 347 (1967). A search warrant is generally required.	"Super warrant" based on probable cause and necessity required by federal wiretapping and state electronic surveillance statutes. G.S. 15A-286 *et seq.*
Location Information	Unclear. Courts disagree about whether this information is subject to a reasonable expectation of privacy. *Compare* United States v. Skinner, 690 F.3d 772 (6th Cir. 2012) (no), *with* United States v. Powell, 943 F. Supp. 2d 759 (E.D. Mich. 2013) (yes, and asserting that is the majority rule).	Unclear. Courts disagree about the application of the SCA and the pen register/trap and trace statutes to this information.
Destinations of Outgoing/Origins of Incoming Communications	None. This information is voluntarily shared by the subscriber with the service provider. Smith v. Maryland, 442 U.S. 735 (1979).	Protected by federal and state pen register/trap and trace statutes. G.S. 15A-263 requires reasonable suspicion.
Other Non-Content	None. This information is voluntarily shared by the subscriber with the service provider. Smith v. Maryland, 442 U.S. 735 (1979).	Unclear. Courts disagree about the application of the SCA and the pen register/trap and trace statutes to this information.

Amendment's warrant requirement, and many of the statutes that protect electronic communications also have emergency provisions.

Both the federal and state wiretapping laws allow for emergency warrantless wiretapping, so long as an application is submitted soon after the warrantless interception begins.[107] As discussed above in section III.B.2 of

107. 18 U.S.C. § 2518(7) (allowing warrantless wiretapping in an emergency so long as an application is submitted within forty-eight hours). G.S. 15A-291(b) provides that "[t]he Attorney General or the Attorney General's designee may make emergency applications as provided by section 2518 of Chapter 119 of the United States Code." Although somewhat ambiguous in that it refers only to "applications" rather than to wiretapping in advance of an application, the apparent intent of the provision is to mirror the federal procedure.

this chapter, the federal pen register statutes also provide for emergency circumstances, but the state pen register statutes do not. As explained above, that appears to render emergency use of a pen register or a trap and trace device without a court order unlawful as to telephone lines, the only type of communications addressed by the state pen register statutes.

The SCA contains two different provisions relevant to emergency situations. First, it allows service providers, in their discretion, to disclose content and non-content records voluntarily to a government entity if necessary to address a risk of death or serious injury.[108] Second, when the main concern is not that law enforcement needs immediate access to information but that the information is at imminent risk of being deleted or destroyed in the regular course of business while law enforcement seeks the legal authorization that is necessary to access it, the SCA allows law enforcement to submit emergency preservation requests that compel service providers to retain specified information for ninety days.[109]

B. Discovery

Most law enforcement efforts to intercept or to obtain information about electronic communications will take place during investigations of felony offenses. In felony cases, North Carolina's statutory discovery rules generally require the State to provide the defense with the "complete files of all law enforcement agencies, investigatory agencies, and prosecutors' offices involved in the investigation of the crimes committed or the prosecution of the defendant."[110] Typically, applications and court orders concerning electronic surveillance, and any information obtained pursuant to the orders, will be part of the investigating agency's file and therefore must be disclosed to the defense.

There are exceptions to this general rule. For example, the wiretapping statutes contain their own discovery provisions, as discussed above in section III.A of this chapter. Those provisions probably trump the broad open file discovery statutes under the maxim that specific provisions govern general ones.

---

108. 18 U.S.C. §§ 2702(c), (d). Note that law enforcement cannot compel an emergency disclosure—the decision is up to the service provider. However, in practice, most voluntary emergency disclosures by service providers are prompted by requests from law enforcement.

109. 18 U.S.C. § 2703(f). The ninety-day period may be renewed for an additional ninety days if necessary.

110. G.S. 15A-903(a)(1).

There may be other circumstances under which there are valid reasons to delay, or less frequently, to deny, discovery. If an investigation continues even after criminal charges are brought, requiring investigative orders to be produced immediately in discovery might undermine their efficacy. In that situation, the State could ask the issuing official to seal the application and order for a limited period of time, as search warrants may sometimes be sealed.[111] The sealing order could address discovery, for example by providing that any data obtained pursuant to the order be non-discoverable until the application and order are unsealed. In an appropriate case, the State might seek a protective order limiting discovery of already-obtained information.[112]

When law enforcement seeks information, such as cell site location information, for the purpose of locating and apprehending a suspect who is already the subject of an arrest warrant, it is possible to argue that the information is not part of the "investigation of the crimes committed"[113] by the suspect and so is not subject to the statutory discovery rules. [114] While plausible,[115] such an argument is subject to several possible rejoinders. First, a court might interpret "investigation" as including the process of apprehending a suspect. Second, even if a court were to view investigation and apprehension as distinct in theory, it is common for suspects to be questioned after apprehension or to be apprehended while in possession of incriminating evidence, making the line between investigation and apprehension a blurry one in practice. For those reasons, cautious officers and prosecutors may wish to disclose apprehension-related information to the defense or to seek a court ruling on whether such information is discoverable.

---

111. *In re* Investigation into Death of Cooper, 200 N.C. App. 180 (2009) (allowing search warrants to be sealed when necessary to protect strong government interests and when sealing order is narrowly tailored).

112. G.S. 15A-908 (court may limit discovery for good cause).

113. G.S. 15A-903(a)(1).

114. This argument has been made in connection with the controversy over the use of stingrays in Charlotte. *See* Fred Clasen-Kelly, *Secrecy Lifts in CMPD StingRay Phone Tracking*, CHARLOTTE OBSERVER, Feb. 15, 2015, *available at* www.charlotteobserver.com/2015/02/15/5513724/secrecy-lifts-in-cmpd-phone-tracking.html#.VOY1NWjF964) (noting prosecutors' argument, in connection with discovery issues, that in some instances "cellphone surveillance had been used only to find fleeing suspects who had already been charged, not to build a case against them").

115. There is no North Carolina case on point. An out-of-state case of possible relevance is *People v. Roc*, 961 N.Y.S.2d 847, 853 (Sup. Ct. 2013) (describing an officer as being "part of the apprehension team" and "assist[ing] the apprehension team in locating the defendant" but as having "no part in the investigation of the underlying crime").

C. Defense Access

This chapter focuses mostly on law enforcement access to electronic communications. But defendants and their lawyers might want similar access when investigating a case.

In some instances—particularly regarding real-time data collection—that is simply impossible. A criminal defendant cannot legally wiretap the State's witnesses, for example. There is no statutory process for that and such conduct would be criminal. Similarly, there is no procedure for a defendant to obtain a pen register order or a trap and trace order.

But what about defense access to historical information held by service providers? For example, a defendant charged with a sexual offense may seek access to emails that the complainant sent to a friend, on the theory that the emails may bolster the defendant's argument that the encounter was consensual.

If the complainant still has access to the emails, the defendant can subpoena them from her. But if she does not—for example, if she has deleted them—the defendant does not have a clear path to obtain the emails from the complainant's service provider. The SCA generally prohibits service providers from disclosing the contents of electronic communications. While the statute creates an exception for governmental entities with appropriate process, the defendant is not a governmental entity and there is no general exception for compliance with subpoenas or court orders, which are the types of instruments that the defendant would normally employ in pursuing evidence.

A number of defendants have argued that it is unfair to deprive them of access to available evidence, especially in light of the fact that law enforcement may access the same material. Courts generally have held that, fair or not, the specific nondisclosure command of the SCA does not allow criminal defendants—or private civil litigants, for that matter—to access such information.[116] Service providers typically follow these cases and refuse to produce information in response to defendants' subpoenas and court orders.

---

116. Bower v. Bower, 808 F. Supp. 2d 348 (D. Mass. 2011) (ruling that private parties may not use subpoenas to access information held by service providers under the SCA); Christian v. Crispin Audigier, Inc., 717 F. Supp. 2d 965 (C.D. Cal. 2010) (similar); Thayer v. Chiczewski, No. 07 C 1290, 2009 WL 2957317 (N.D. Ill. Sept. 11, 2009) (unpublished) (similar, collecting cases); *In re* Subpoena Duces Tecum to AOL, LLC, 550 F. Supp. 2d 606 (E.D. Va. 2008) (similar); United States v. Amawi, 552 F. Supp. 2d 679 (N.D. Ohio 2008) (applying the SCA to bar a criminal defendant from compelling a service provider to give him his own stored email). A useful law review article discussing this issue is Marc J. Zwillinger & Christian S. Genetski, *Criminal Discovery of Internet Communications under*

A defendant who is dissatisfied with this state of affairs has several options. First, because an email provider can produce stored communications with the consent of the account holder, the defendant can ask the customer to consent. Second, the defendant can seek a court order requiring the customer to consent.[117] Third, the defendant may try to persuade the prosecution to obtain the information on his behalf. Finally, the defendant could argue that the federal statutes are unconstitutional, perhaps on due process grounds, to the extent that they put a class of evidence completely off-limits to him—especially a class of evidence that the prosecution can access. There are no reported decisions addressing the latter argument, perhaps because defendants are often able to make use of the other methods suggested above.

D. Suppression and Other Remedies

When investigators obtain information without following the necessary procedures, a criminal defendant against whom the information may be used may seek to suppress the information or may pursue other remedies. Which remedies are available depends on the nature of the transgression.

Generally, the exclusionary rule will apply when law enforcement violates the Fourth Amendment in obtaining the information. Of course, an increasing number of exceptions to the exclusionary rule have been recognized in recent years, and some may apply to electronic data collection. For example, if an officer in good faith obtains access to location information using a court order based on less than probable cause but a court subsequently rules that location information should be available only with probable cause, the officer's good faith may call into question the applicability of the exclusionary rule.[118]

---

the Stored Communications Act: It's Not a Level Playing Field, 97 J. Crim. L. & Criminology 569 (2007).

117. There might be some question about the voluntariness or validity of consent obtained in this way, but at least one court has ruled that consent obtained as a result of a court order was valid and allowed a service provider to produce information under the SCA. Negro v. Superior Court, 179 Cal. Rptr. 3d 215 (Cal. Ct. App. 2014).

118. The United States Supreme Court ruled that the Fourth Amendment exclusionary rule does not apply to a search that is conducted in good faith based on appellate precedent that was in effect at the time of the search, even if that precedent is later reversed. Davis v. United States, ___ U.S. ___, 131 S. Ct. 2419 (2011). *Davis* is the latest in a series of cases making an officer's good faith an important consideration in the applicability of the exclusionary rule, a series that began with *United States v. Leon*, 468 U.S. 897 (1984) (concerning good faith reliance on a facially valid search warrant). The North Carolina Supreme Court rejected *Leon* under the state constitution in *State v. Carter*, 322 N.C. 709 (1988),

Sufficiently egregious constitutional violations might also give rise to civil liability under 42 U.S.C. § 1983[119] or other provisions of law.

When law enforcement violates a statutory requirement when collecting electronic communication information, the remedy depends on the statute violated:

- Violations of the wiretapping laws generally require suppression.[120] Such violations are also crimes.[121]
- Neither the state nor the federal pen register/trap and trace statutes contain a suppression remedy. Violations of the state statutes might, if sufficiently severe, lead to suppression under the statutory exclusionary rule in G.S. 15A-974. Such violations are also crimes.[122]
- There is no exclusionary remedy in the Stored Communications Act. Some intentional violations are crimes.[123] Violations may also support civil actions.[124]

---

but whether the appellate courts would extend *Carter* to encompass the example in the text is unclear.

119. The cited section generally creates civil liability for those who deprive others of their constitutional rights while acting "under color of" state law. Law enforcement officers have qualified, or limited, immunity from suit under the statute but still may be liable for clear constitutional violations. The details of Section 1983 litigation are beyond the scope of this book.

120. 18 U.S.C. § 2515; G.S. 15A-294(f), (g). Federal case law suggests that suppression is not appropriate in response to minor, technical violations of the wiretap laws. United States v. Donovan, 429 U.S. 413 (1977); United States v. Giordano, 416 U.S. 505 (1974); United States v. Chavez, 416 U.S. 562 (1974). *See generally* 2 WAYNE R. LAFAVE ET AL., CRIMINAL PROCEDURE § 4.6(m) (3d ed. 2007). Interestingly, the federal statute's exclusionary rule applies only to interceptions of "wire or oral" communications, not electronic communications, apparently because, at one time, electronic communications were viewed as less deserving of protection than wire and oral communications. *See* 1 LAFAVE ET AL., cited in full *supra*, at § 4.6(m). However, North Carolina's exclusionary rule encompasses electronic communications as well. *See* G.S. 15A-294(g). Also worth noting is the fact that while only the state may violate the Fourth Amendment, a private person may violate the wiretap statutes; the results of a private person's illegal wiretapping activity must be suppressed in any civil or criminal proceeding. *See, e.g.*, United States v. Crabtree, 565 F.3d 887 (4th Cir. 2009); Rickenbaker v. Rickenbaker, 290 N.C. 373 (1976); Kroh v. Kroh, 152 N.C. App. 347 (2002); State v. Shaw, 103 N.C. App. 268 (1991).

121. 18 U.S.C. § 2511; G.S. 15A-287.

122. 18 U.S.C. § 3121; G.S. 15A-261.

123. 18 U.S.C. § 2701.

124. 18 U.S.C. § 2707. *See also* Freedman v. America Online, Inc., 303 F. Supp. 2d 121 (D. Conn. 2004) (granting partial summary judgment in favor of a civil plaintiff who contended that two officers obtained records of his electronic communications in violation of federal law).

E. Obtaining Information for the Purpose of Locating a Suspect

Law enforcement officers sometimes seek information in order to locate a suspect rather than to gain evidence about an offense. Yet many of the statutes governing law enforcement access to electronic communications appear to have been written with evidence collection in mind. Therefore, the question arises whether there is authority allowing officers to access electronic communication information to locate suspects rather than to collect evidence.

This question obviously arises with many requests for real-time location information. But it is not limited to such requests, as officers may seek all kinds of information to help them locate a suspect. For example, reading the contents of a suspect's emails might allow officers to learn the suspect's future travel plans. Similarly, historical location information, such as information about where the suspect has been recently, may help officers anticipate a suspect's patterns of movement.

A review of the various electronic surveillance statutes shows that some fit more awkwardly than others with this purpose:

- The North Carolina electronic surveillance statute allows wiretapping when it will reveal "communications concerning" the offense under investigation.[125] Similarly, the federal wiretap act allows wiretap applications to be submitted when "interception may provide . . . evidence" of a specified offense.[126]
- Pen register and trap and trace orders may issue under state law only where the results "will be of material aid in determining whether the person named in the affidavit committed the offense."[127] The federal statute is somewhat broader, requiring only certification that the information sought is "relevant to an ongoing criminal investigation."[128]
- A court order is available under the SCA when information sought would be "material to an ongoing criminal investigation."[129]
- A search warrant may issue to seize fruits, instrumentalities, or evidence of a crime or evidence of the "identity of a person participating in an offense."[130]

125. G.S. 15A-293.
126. 18 U.S.C. § 2516(3).
127. G.S. 15A-263(a)(3).
128. 18 U.S.C. § 3122(b)(2).
129. 18 U.S.C. § 2703(d).
130. G.S. 15A-242.

The few courts to have explored this issue have come to different conclusions about how broadly the above provisions should be read.[131] At least as to search warrants, some support for a broad reading of the statute comes from the fact that search warrants may be used to enter a third party's home to execute an arrest warrant—a function that does not involve gathering evidence and that is similar to locating a suspect.[132] Also at least as to search warrants, even if locating a suspect is not a proper statutory purpose, it may be reasonable from a constitutional standpoint and so may be less likely to require suppression as a remedy.

F. Applications for Orders for Information About Subscribers' Contacts and Correspondents

Suppose that a law enforcement officer applies for a court order for subscriber and billing information about a target's cell phone number *and* for subscriber and billing information for every cell phone number that has called, or has been called by, the suspect's cell phone number in the past thirty days. The officer states that information about the suspect's contacts will help her identify the suspect's criminal associates as well as physical locations where the suspect might be found. Should a court grant such an application?

The answer depends in part on the facts of the particular investigation. For example, if there is considerable evidence that the target is running an ongoing, extensive drug conspiracy and frequently uses his telephone to conduct business, there is a stronger argument for granting the request than if the target is being investigated for a sexual assault that took place weeks earlier.

---

131. *In re* Smartphone Geolocation Data Application, 977 F. Supp. 2d 129, 133 (E.D.N.Y. 2013) (after an arrest warrant was issued, officers had difficulty locating the subject and the subject expressly told them by telephone that he would not surrender; officers obtained an order for prospective location information and used the information to arrest the subject; the court ruled that it is proper to issue search warrants for "information that reasonably could facilitate capture of" a suspect, even absent evidence that the subject has fled to avoid prosecution, citing dicta in a Supreme Court case and several older cases); *In re* Application of the U.S., 849 F. Supp. 2d 526, 536, 530 (D. Md. 2011) (federal magistrate judge rules that the government cannot obtain GPS or cellular site location data "to aid in the apprehension of the subject of an arrest warrant" because "the requested location data does not . . . constitute evidence of any crime" and there is no authority in the Stored Communications Act, the All Writs Act, or the court's inherent power to order the release of such data for that purpose).

132. *See generally* State v. Johnson, 310 N.C. 581 (1984) (noting that a search warrant is proper, and in fact necessary, for this purpose under *Steagald v. United States*, 451 U.S. 204 (1981)).

The answer also depends in part on the nature of the information requested. In the above example, the information that is requested is basic subscriber information that is available under a relatively permissive standard. A court might be more inclined to allow access to such information than to, for example, historical location information regarding individuals who have communicated with a suspect.[133]

There are only a few decisions on point, but courts have taken different approaches to such requests, with some rejecting them absent specific information that particular contacts are implicated in the target's unlawful activities,[134] and others allowing such requests so long as they do not involve the disclosure of highly private information.[135] A court also might choose to

---

133. *Cf.* Poolaw v. Marcantel, 565 F.3d 721 (10th Cir. 2009) (police obtained a search warrant to search the home of the parents-in-law of a murder suspect for the suspect or evidence of the crime; the warrant was based on "little more" than the existence of a family relationship; collecting cases, the court ruled that this was plainly inadequate to establish probable cause).

134. *In re* Application of U.S. for an Order Authorizing Use of a Cellular Telephone Digital Analyzer, 885 F. Supp. 197, 202 (C.D. Cal. 1995) ("The proposed order above also seeks to require various telephone companies to provide subscriber information for all persons called using the cellular telephones being analyzed. Such an order would not appear to provide sufficient accountability for the gathering of such subscriber information. 18 U.S.C. §§ 2703(c) and (d), for example, contemplate that a determination will be made in advance that there are specific and articulable facts showing that a particular subscriber's records will be material to an ongoing criminal investigation. The application does provide specific and articulable facts sufficient to justify disclosure of subscribers who are the named subjects of the investigation. As to subscribers whose telephone numbers are dialed from the target cellular telephones, however, additional applications for orders to disclose subscriber information will be required . . . [and must] independently comply with the statutory requirements for issuance of orders of disclosure.").

135. *In re* Search of Info. Associated with Facebook Account, 21 F. Supp. 3d 1, 7 (D.D.C. 2013) (in a case involving multiple homicides at a Navy yard, officers sought a search warrant for virtually all information associated with the suspect's Facebook account, including subscriber information, billing information, activity logs, all posts and pictures, past and present friend lists, "likes," searches, and information about the "identities and whereabouts" of anyone who communicated with the suspect on Facebook; concerned in part that the application "wholly failed to provide any explanation whatsoever for why there was probable cause to search and seize information about third parties," a federal magistrate judge issued the warrant but narrowed its scope by excluding, among other things, "[t]he contents of any communications sent to the [a]ccount" and most information about the Facebook groups of which the suspect was a member; the court also required that information produced by Facebook that was not relevant to the investigation be returned to Facebook or destroyed to prevent over-seizure of information for which there was no probable cause).

allow such requests as to some individuals while denying them as to others. For example, a court might grant access to the subscriber information of individuals who contacted the suspect five times or more in the past thirty days while denying access to those in less frequent contact.

G. Applications for All Account Information

Sometimes a law enforcement officer will apply for a search warrant or other order allowing him or her access to all information a service provider has about a suspect. Whether such a warrant or order is overbroad may depend in part on the facts of the case. Is there reason to believe that the account was used exclusively or primarily for criminal activity? Did the criminal activity begin at a certain point, rendering older information extremely unlikely to be relevant? Was the criminal activity conducted exclusively in conjunction with an identifiable co-conspirator, rendering communications with other individuals probably immaterial? The cases summarized below give a sense of how different courts have approached this issue; there is not yet a consensus. Readers interested in this question may also wish to review the discussion of search warrants generally in chapter 1, and the discussion of applications for information about a suspect's contacts in section V.F, above.

Case Summaries on Applications for All Account Information

***In re* the Search of Information Associated with [redacted]@mac.com that is Stored at Premises Controlled by Apple, Inc., 25 F. Supp. 3d 1, 4 (D.D.C. 2014)** (denying a search warrant application for a particular Apple email account; expressing concern about search warrant applications that "ask for the entire universe of information tied to a particular account, even if [the government] has established probable cause only for certain information"; criticizing the government's two-step procedure of having the service provider disclose a broad swath of information to the government, after which the government officially seizes, i.e., retains, only relevant material; recommending safeguards like having service providers produce only documents containing certain keywords or having a special master or a taint team review materials before giving only relevant items to the case agents; and arguing that irrelevant materials should be returned to the service provider or destroyed).

Commonwealth v. Orie, 88 A.3d 983, 1008–09 (Pa. Super. Ct. 2014) ("[W]e find the . . . warrant for [the defendant's] AOL account . . . seeking, *inter alia*, 'all stored communications and other files . . . between

August 1, 2009 and the present, including all documents, images, recordings spreadsheets or any other data stored in digital format,' was overbroad. The affidavit . . . provided probable cause that evidence of criminal activity could be found therein, and was limited to [a specific time period] but did not justify the search of all communications for that period.").

United States v. Rudtke, No. 11CR4956 WQH, 2014 WL 688800, at *9 (S.D. Cal. Feb. 20, 2014) (unpublished) (rejecting the defendant's overbreadth argument and ruling that "[i]n this case, the facts detailed in the [a]ffidavit . . . combined with reasonable inferences from those facts, provided probable cause to seize and search the entire content of the [target] email account . . . for evidence of" violations of child pornography laws).

***In re* Applications for Search Warrants for Info. Associated with Target Email Accounts/Skype Accounts, Nos. 13-MJ-8163-JPO, 13-MJ-8144-DJW, 13-MJ-8165-DJW, 13-MJ-8166-JPO, 13-MJ-8167-DJW, 2013 WL 4647554, at *8, *9 (D. Kan. Aug. 27, 2013)** (unpublished) (footnote omitted) (the government sought warrants to require electronic communications service providers to produce "the contents of all emails" and other information related to specified target accounts; a federal magistrate judge, following *United States v. Warshak*, 631 F.3d 266 (6th Cir. 2010), concluded that the Fourth Amendment applies to email; although acknowledging conflicting rulings, the judge decided that the requested warrants were overbroad and violated the Fourth Amendment's particularity requirement; the magistrate judge observed that the warrants were not limited to communications as "to the specific crimes being investigated" and did not include any "filtering procedures" for sifting out irrelevant or privileged communications; the court found that "the breadth of the information sought by the government's search warrant for the target accounts—including the content of every email sent to or from the accounts—is best analogized to a warrant asking the post office to provide copies of all mail ever sent by or delivered to a certain address so that the government can open and read all the mail to find out whether it constitutes fruits, evidence or instrumentality of a crime"; as to how to structure search warrants for electronic communications, the court identified "possible options [such as] asking the electronic communications service provider to provide specific limited information such as emails containing certain key words or emails sent to/from certain recipients, appointing a special master with authority to hire an independent vendor to use computerized search techniques to review the information for relevance and privilege, or setting up a filter group or taint-team to review the information for relevance and privilege").

United States v. Bowen, 689 F. Supp. 2d 675 (S.D.N.Y. 2010) (searches of all records within defendants' email accounts were not overbroad), *aff'd on other grounds sub nom.* United States v. Ingram, 490 F. App'x 363 (2d Cir. 2012).

United States v. McDarrah, 351 F. App'x 558 (2d Cir. 2009) (unpublished) (upholding a search warrant for the defendant's AOL email account; although the defendant argued that the warrant was overbroad because it included communications beyond those with the two people that the government knew were involved in the crime, the court ruled briefly that there was a substantial basis for the issuing magistrate to believe that communications with other individuals would also contain evidence of the crime).

H. Extraterritorial Effect of Search Warrants and Court Orders

As discussed above, there are a number of circumstances under which officers must obtain search warrants in order to access information about a suspect's electronic communications. But does a search warrant from a North Carolina judicial official have any effect when served on, for example, a cell phone company incorporated in Delaware? Or an internet service provider headquartered in California?

In practice, it seems that service providers comply with such search warrants, rendering questions about their extraterritorial effect mainly theoretical.[136] In any event, the courts that have considered the question have generally answered it in the affirmative.[137] Most of these decisions have

136. A suspect might attempt to challenge such a warrant after the fact, but would need to establish that he or she had a constitutionally protected privacy interest in the records in order to do so. Furthermore, if a court were to rule that a North Carolina warrant lacks force in other states, it is not clear that seeking and serving such a warrant would violate the Fourth Amendment; a court might view the service provider's decision to produce records in the face of an ineffective warrant as a voluntary disclosure.

137. Lozoya v. State, No. 07-12-00142-CR, 2013 WL 708489, at *2 (Tex. App. Feb. 27, 2013) (unpublished) (holding that a search warrant issued by a Texas magistrate was valid as it related to records held by Sprint in Kansas; warrants for electronic communications information "are not limited to the territorial jurisdiction of the issuing authority"); Hubbard v. MySpace, Inc., 788 F. Supp. 2d 319,

been made under the SCA, and it might be possible to argue that search warrants issued in other contexts should be analyzed differently. However, given the national, even global, nature of modern telecommunications, courts may rule in favor of extraterritorial search warrants simply because the alternatives are potentially so cumbersome.

325, 326 (S.D.N.Y. 2011) (ruling that Georgia judicial officials may issue search warrants directed at service providers located outside the state because "Congress made clear that, in adopting [18 U.S.C. § 2703], it specifically intended to allow federal courts to authorize searches beyond their normal territorial jurisdictions" and that "[i]f federal warrants satisfy Section 2703(a) in these circumstances, the same ought to be true of equivalent state warrants"); *In re* Search of Yahoo, Inc., No. 07-3194-MB, 2007 WL 1539971 (D. Ariz. May 21, 2007) (unpublished) (discussing authority for a federal district judge to issue a search warrant regarding a service provider located in another district). *Cf.* State v. Esarey, 67 A.3d 1001, 1008 n.17 (Conn. 2013) (a Connecticut judge issued a search warrant for information concerning the defendant's Gmail account, reasoning that California Penal Code § 1524.2(c) gives out-of-state warrants effect in California; the defendant moved to suppress but the trial judge denied the motion; the court of appeals affirmed; it observed in a footnote that "it would appear to us that . . . a Connecticut trial judge may, in connection with the investigation of a crime committed here, order a search of electronically stored communications contained on a . . . server located in another state," but fell short of actually so ruling; instead, it avoided the Fourth Amendment issue by concluding that any error was harmless in light of the overwhelming evidence against the defendant).

Chapter 4: Tracking

This chapter considers the use of tracking devices. In the past, radio frequency "beepers" and other devices were used to track suspects. Today, GPS tracking devices are the norm. Such devices are used in a variety of contexts: to monitor certain sex offenders,[1] as a condition of pretrial release,[2] and to track suspects surreptitiously during criminal investigations. This chapter focuses mainly on the surreptitious use of tracking devices to monitor criminal suspects. Cell phone tracking raises somewhat different legal issues and is discussed in detail in chapter 3.

I. Installing a Tracking Device

Typically, officers install tracking devices on suspects' vehicles. Sometimes the devices contain their own power supply, while other times they are connected to the vehicle's battery. Some devices transmit location data in real time over a cellular connection, while others simply record the data to

1. Sections 14-208.40 *et seq.* of the North Carolina General Statutes (hereinafter G.S.).
2. G.S. 15A-534(5).

be reviewed when the device is recovered. Legally, there is little difference in how these various categories of devices are regulated.

A. *Jones* and the Warrant Requirement

The seminal case in this area is *United States v. Jones*.[3] In *Jones*, the United States Supreme Court ruled that "the Government's installation of a GPS device on a target's vehicle, and its use of that device to monitor the vehicle's movements, constitutes a 'search' " for purposes of the Fourth Amendment.[4] Although most Fourth Amendment cases over the past fifty years have determined whether an officer's conduct constitutes a search by asking whether the conduct intrudes on a citizen's reasonable expectation of privacy, the *Jones* majority analyzed the issue differently. It ruled that the key to the case was that "[t]he Government physically occupied private property for the purpose of obtaining information."[5] That is, the government trespassed when it undertook the "physical intrusion" of installing the device. And a trespass "conjoined with . . . an attempt to find something or to obtain information" constitutes a search for Fourth Amendment purposes.[6]

Four Justices concurred in the judgment in *Jones*. They believed that the case was properly analyzed under the traditional expectations of privacy rubric, not the majority's trespass theory. They would have reached the same conclusion, but on the basis that "relatively short-term monitoring of a person's movements on public streets accords with expectations of privacy that our society has recognized as reasonable. . . . But the use of longer term GPS monitoring in investigations of most offenses impinges on expectations of privacy."[7] Justice Sotomayor concurred separately, joining the majority's trespass analysis but also expressing her agreement with the notion that long-term GPS tracking intrudes on a reasonable expectation of privacy. Thus, there appear to be five Justices who believe that long-term GPS tracking constitutes a search even if the tracking device is planted without a trespass. For example, if an undercover officer were to present a suspect with a necklace that contained a tracking device as a "gift," there would be no trespass, but

---

3. 565 U.S. ___, 132 S. Ct. 945 (2012).
4. *Id.* at ___, 132 S. Ct. at 949 (footnote omitted).
5. *Id.* at ___, 132 S. Ct. at 949.
6. *Id.* at ___ n.5, 132 S. Ct. at 951 n.5.
7. *Id.* at ___, 132 S. Ct. at 964 (citations omitted).

at least five Justices likely would nonetheless view long-term monitoring of the device as a Fourth Amendment search.[8]

Jones focused on the issue of whether the use of a tracking device is a search and did not directly address whether it required a warrant. However, the general rule is that "[e]xcept in certain well-defined circumstances, a search . . . is not reasonable unless it is accomplished pursuant to a judicial warrant."[9] Thus, as discussed in greater detail below, while there may be certain emergencies or other unusual circumstances that would justify the use of a tracking device without prior judicial authorization, absent such circumstances, it appears that prior judicial approval is required. The cases summarized below generally support this conclusion.

If officers installed a GPS tracking device on a suspect's vehicle without a warrant prior to *Jones* but the issue is litigated after *Jones*, the State may argue that the officers acted in good faith and that suppression of the evidence is not required. The federal courts generally have accepted this argument,[10] though the status of the good faith exception to the exclusionary rule is unclear in North Carolina.[11] It is also worth noting that a suspect may not

---

8. *Cf.* United States v. Brown, 744 F.3d 474, 476 (7th Cir. 2014) (noting that a tracking device was installed without a trespass where "[a] Jeep's owner decided to cooperate with the police in their investigation of his confederates and authorized the attachment of a tracker"); State v. Lagrone, 985 N.E.2d 66 (Ind. Ct. App. 2013) (ruling that no search took place when officers inserted a tracking device into a package of marijuana opened by UPS, because the package had not yet come into the defendant's possession).

9. Skinner v. Ry. Labor Execs.' Ass'n, 489 U.S. 602, 619 (1989).

10. *See, e.g.*, United States v. Katzin, 769 F.3d 163 (3d Cir. 2014) (en banc) (officers conducted tracking in good faith, in light of pre-*Jones* precedent and other factors, so results of warrantless GPS tracking were not subject to suppression); United States v. Ransfer, 749 F.3d 914 (11th Cir. 2014) (collecting similar cases and ruling that officers' warrantless use of GPS tracking device prior to *Jones* was done in good faith, so the exclusionary rule did not apply).

11. In *State v. Carter*, 322 N.C. 709 (1988), the state supreme court rejected, under the state constitution, the exception to the federal exclusionary rule for good faith reliance on a search warrant. *See generally* United States v. Leon, 468 U.S. 897 (1984). Whether *Carter* means that the state constitution allows no room for any kind of good faith exception is unclear. For a discussion of this issue in a slightly different context, see Jeff Welty, Riley *and Good Faith*, N.C. Crim. L., UNC Sch. of Gov't Blog (July 30, 2014), http://nccriminallaw.sog.unc.edu/riley-and-good-faith/.

have standing to challenge the use of a GPS tracking device on a vehicle if the suspect does not have a sufficient legal interest in the vehicle.[12]

Case Summaries on the Warrant Requirement

United States v. Katzin, 769 F.3d 163, 170 (3d Cir. 2014) (en banc) (cautioning that "law enforcement should carefully consider that a warrant may be required when engaging in [GPS device] installation and surveillance," but ruling that the GPS evidence in the case at bar, which was obtained without a warrant, would be admissible under the good faith exception to the exclusionary rule because it was obtained pre-*Jones*).

State v. Jackson, 435 S.W.3d 819, 826 (Tex. App. 2014) (citations omitted) ("Warrantless searches are per se unreasonable under the Fourth Amendment unless the State can prove that the search was conducted pursuant to a recognized exception to the warrant requirement.... The State has not shown that its warrantless search with the GPS device on Jackson's car met an exception to the warrant requirement. Under this circumstance, we must deem that the State's installation and use of the GPS device was illegal for the purpose of our analysis.").

State v. Mitchell, 323 P.3d 69, 77 (Ariz. Ct. App. 2014) (citations omitted) ("Under *Jones*, the State's trespassory placement and use of the GPS device to monitor Mitchell's movements constituted a search under the Fourth Amendment. Law enforcement did not obtain a search warrant authorizing the GPS placement.... The State has not argued that any exception to the warrant requirement applies to GPS track-

---

12. The vehicle at issue in *Jones* was registered to the defendant's wife but apparently was used by the defendant, and the Court did not suggest that the defendant might lack standing to contest the use of the tracking device. However, in *United States v. Gibson*, 708 F.3d 1256, 1277 (11th Cir. 2013), the court considered whether a defendant who sometimes used, but did not own, a vehicle had standing to contest the use of a GPS tracking device on the vehicle. The court concluded that the defendant had standing to challenge the use of the tracking device only "while the vehicle was in his possession," but that he could not contest tracking that was done while he was "neither the driver nor a passenger," given his lack of a possessory interest in the vehicle. *See also* United States v. Davis, 750 F.3d 1186 (10th Cir. 2014) (considering a challenge to a vehicle stop where the stop was based in part on evidence from a GPS tracking device installed on the vehicle without a warrant, the court ruled that the defendant lacked standing to challenge the use of the GPS tracking device as he neither owned nor regularly drove the vehicle; the defendant was a passenger at the time of the stop).

ing. We conclude, then, that the warrantless placement of the GPS device and its subsequent use to track Mitchell's movements violated the Fourth Amendment.").

Kelly v. State, 82 A.3d 205, 214 (Md. 2013) (citations omitted) ("We accept at the outset of our analysis the State's concession that, under *Jones*, the . . . detectives' attachment and use of the GPS device in this case is a search under the Fourth Amendment. . . . By retrospective application of *Jones*, therefore, the tracking of Petitioner's vehicle without a proper warrant violated the Fourth Amendment.").

State v. White, 4 N.E.3d 426, 432 (Ohio Ct. App. 2013) ("We find the installation of the GPS tracking device by law enforcement in this case without a warrant, for an extended period, is a violation of the vehicle owner/operator's reasonable expectation of privacy and amounts to an unlawful search."), *rev'd on other grounds*, 21 N.E.3d 1112 (Ohio 2014) (ruling that because the officer acted in good faith under the law at the time of his warrantless installation of the tracking device, suppression was not an appropriate remedy).

United States v. Aguiar, 737 F.3d 251 (2d Cir. 2013) (noting that *Jones* held that the installation of a GPS device was a search but did not address the circumstances under which such a search could be performed without a warrant; but citing the general rule that a warrant is required to render searches reasonable).

B. Search Warrant or Court Order?

Both the *Jones* majority and Justice Sotomayor's concurrence note the lack of a valid "warrant." And, as noted above, the general rule is that searches require warrants. However, the statutory procedures associated with search warrants in North Carolina do not fit well with GPS monitoring. For example, Section 15A-249 of the North Carolina General Statutes (hereinafter G.S.) requires an officer to "give appropriate notice of his identity and purpose to the person to be searched," while G.S. 15A-252 provides that "[b]efore undertaking any search or seizure pursuant to the warrant, the officer must read the warrant and give a copy of the warrant application and affidavit to the person to be searched, or the person in apparent control of the premises or vehicle to be searched." Following these procedures would alert the suspect to the tracking device and would render it impossible to obtain useful information from the device. (By comparison, federal law expressly provides a procedure for obtaining search warrants tailored to the use of tracking devices.[13])

Because of the lack of fit between the statutory procedure and the manner in which tracking devices are used, it may be preferable to use an ex parte court order, under the court's inherent authority, to obtain advance judicial approval for GPS tracking. Our appellate courts have endorsed the use of investigative court orders in other contexts.[14] Alternatively, an officer could seek a search warrant but ask a judge to approve deviations from the statutory notification procedures. Presumably a judge has the authority to approve such variances in appropriate circumstances.[15]

As to the content of the warrant or order, it should:

- Include a finding of probable cause and a statement authorizing the installation and monitoring of the tracking device, including authorization to enter private property to install the device, if needed.
- Set a time limit on monitoring, for example, thirty days unless extended in a subsequent order. The relevant Federal Rule of

---

13. *See* Fed. R. Crim. P. 41.

14. *See In re* Superior Court Order Dated Apr. 8, 1983, 315 N.C. 378, 380 (1986) (holding that a superior court judge has inherent authority to issue an investigative order compelling the production of bank records relevant to a criminal investigation where the "other options available to the district attorney at the investigatory stage of the proceeding provide inadequate means of obtaining the desired information"). Other states have allowed court orders to substitute for warrants in appropriate circumstances involving GPS tracking. *See* State v. Sveum, 787 N.W.2d 317, 334 (Wis. 2010) (ruling that "[a]n order meeting the parameters of a search warrant" was an appropriate vehicle for obtaining judicial approval for tracking).

15. *Cf. In re* Investigation into Death of Cooper, 200 N.C. App. 180 (2009) (holding that judges may seal search warrant applications in appropriate cases). The state court of appeals has recognized that under some circumstances, compliance with the knock and announce requirement may be excused. State v. Prevette, 43 N.C. App. 450, 458 (1979) (holding that exigent circumstances "excuse[d] the officers from the knock and announce requirement"). Courts in other states have dealt with similar concerns. State v. Winningham, 1 N.E.3d 501, 507 (Ohio Ct. App. 2013) (ruling that although search warrant authorizing thirty days of GPS tracking arguably violated state law requiring search warrants to be executed within three days, suppression was not required as the warrant was reasonable, "the rule was not drafted in contemplation of such a situation," and "[a]t this time, there exists no provision in the Rules of Criminal Procedure that contemplates the type of warrant required by the *Jones* decision").

Criminal Procedure provides for a forty-five-day renewable period of monitoring.[16]

- Address whether and how the subject is to be notified of the use of the device. For example, the order could provide for service of the order upon the cessation of monitoring. The federal rule provides for service within ten days of the completion of monitoring, unless the judge finds a reason to do otherwise.[17]
- Finally, the order could require the officer to notify the issuing judge once installation and/or monitoring are complete. This would be akin to the return requirement for search warrants. The federal rule provides that "[w]ithin 10 days after the use of the tracking device has ended, the officer executing the warrant must return it to the judge designated in the warrant."[18]

C. Selecting a Judicial Official

All judges, clerks, and magistrates have the authority to issue search warrants.[19] Nothing in *Jones* or in any other case or statute expressly precludes any of those judicial officials from issuing tracking warrants or orders. Nonetheless, at least for now, officers probably should present applications for tracking warrants or orders to superior court judges. There are several reasons for this.

First, tracking warrants or orders raise unsettled legal issues that are best addressed by a judge. Magistrates and clerks may have less legal training and may have limited access to legal resources. Second, as described above, an order authorizing tracking may require terms and conditions that differ from standard search warrants, and existing case law regarding investigative court orders refers only to the inherent authority of superior court judges.[20] Third, only superior court judges may issue orders permitting other forms of electronic surveillance, such as pen registers.[21] Finally, obtaining

---

16. Fed. R. Crim. P. 41. *See also Winningham*, 1 N.E.3d at 507 (concluding that tracking under search warrant was lawful in part because "[t]he judge did not give [officers] an open-ended license to monitor [the suspect], but allowed such an investigation to continue for 30 days").
17. Fed. R. Crim. P. 41.
18. Fed. R. Crim. P. 41(f)(2)(B).
19. G.S. 15A-243.
20. *See In re* Superior Court Order Dated Apr. 8, 1983, 315 N.C. 378 (1986).
21. G.S. 15A-263.

authorization from a superior court judge reduces the likelihood of problems arising regarding tracking outside the jurisdiction of the issuing official.[22] Our appellate courts may later determine that other types of judicial officials may authorize tracking, but until they do so, the safest course is to address tracking requests to superior court judges.

D. Exceptions to the Warrant Requirement

Although a warrant or an equivalent court order normally is required to install a tracking device, the Fourth Amendment allows for exceptions to the warrant requirement, several of which might be relevant in the tracking context. The exceptions that are most likely to arise are explored in detail below, though other exceptions might be implicated in unusual circumstances.[23]

1. Exigent Circumstances

The exigent circumstances exception to the warrant requirement applies when there is probable cause to conduct a search and an immediate need to do so that renders it impractical to obtain a warrant.[24] Courts have recognized that exigent circumstances may obviate the need for a search warrant for a tracking device.[25] For example, exigent circumstances might exist in a child abduction case where officers develop probable cause to believe that a specific individual is holding the child captive, that there is an imminent danger to the child, and that installing a tracking device on the suspect's car will quickly lead the officers to the child.[26]

---

22. *See infra* section II.A.

23. For example, the potential applicability of the border search exception is discussed in Rob Von Kaenel, *3 Exceptions to Warrants for GPS Tracking*, Police (July 5, 2012), www.policemag.com/blog/technology/story/2012/07/legal-exceptions-for-gps-tracking.aspx.

24. *See generally* Robert L. Farb, Arrest, Search, and Investigation in North Carolina 217 (UNC School of Government, 4th ed. 2011).

25. *See, e.g.*, United States v. Wilfong, 528 F. App'x 814 (10th Cir. 2013) (indicating that the exigent circumstances doctrine likely would allow the warrantless use of a GPS tracking device to find and arrest a fleeing felon). *Cf.* United States v. Shovea, 580 F.2d 1382, 1387 (10th Cir. 1978) ("The utilization of an electronic tracking device, without prior court approval, may be justified by probable cause and exigent circumstances.").

26. Another example would be the use of GPS "darts," "bullets," or "taggers" to track a car that is attempting to avoid a valid stop. For a discussion of this possibility, see Matthew F. Myers, *GPS "Bullets" and the Fourth Amendment*, Wake Forest L. Rev. (Apr. 15, 2014), http://wakeforestlawreview.com/2014/04/gps-bullets-and-the-fourth-amendment/.

2. The Vehicle Exception

Prosecutors and officers sometimes argue that the vehicle exception to the warrant requirement applies to GPS tracking devices that are installed on motor vehicles. The vehicle exception generally allows motor vehicles to be searched without a warrant if there is probable cause to believe that the vehicles contain evidence of a crime.[27] Courts have not been receptive to this argument, often echoing the view of a Wisconsin court that "[t]he installation of [a] GPS device [is] distinguishable from the typical search under the automobile exception because law enforcement's target [is] not evidence *within* the car, which under the exception gives rise to a need to quickly collect evidence . . . before the evidence can be removed from the jurisdiction."[28] And of course, the tracking device in *Jones* was attached to a vehicle and the Supreme Court never suggested that the vehicle exception to the warrant requirement might render the warrantless use of the device permissible under the Fourth Amendment.

3. As a Condition of Supervision

Individuals who are under the supervision of the criminal justice system generally have a reduced expectation of privacy and more limited Fourth Amendment rights than other citizens. As a result, courts have often allowed the warrantless use of GPS tracking devices to aid in the supervision of

---

27. *See generally* Farb, *supra* note 24, at 210.

28. State v. Brereton, 826 N.W.2d 369, 381 (Wis. 2013). *See also* State v. Sullivan, No. 13AP-173, 2014 WL 1347978, at *14, 15 (Ohio Ct. App. Apr. 3, 2014) (unpublished) ("The fact that this case involves an automobile does not automatically entitle the state to the shelter of the automobile exception. . . . The state has not provided any case law expanding the automobile exception to permit warrantless GPS attachment and monitoring. The rationale underlying the automobile exception does not justify the warrantless installation of a GPS device under the facts presented here."), *appeal allowed*, 16 N.E.3d 682 (Ohio 2014); United States v. Sparks, 711 F.3d 58, 62 (1st Cir. 2013) (noting that "[t]hose courts that have found GPS tracking to require a warrant have typically reached that conclusion by rejecting the government's attempts to fit GPS tracking within the Fourth Amendment's automobile exception," and citing cases); United States v. Ortiz, 878 F. Supp. 2d 515, 535 (E.D. Pa. 2012) (noting that the government "candidly acknowledged that no court has expanded the automobile exception to permit warrantless GPS installation and monitoring," and ruling that the exception does not apply because tracking does not seek evidence that is located inside the vehicle).

defendants on pretrial release,[29] sex offenders,[30] probationers,[31] and parolees.[32] However, courts have been more reluctant to allow the surreptitious use of

---

29. G.S. 15A-534(a)(5) authorizes a judicial official to impose "[h]ouse arrest with electronic monitoring" as a condition of pretrial release. At one time, such monitoring may have been accomplished using a radio beeper and a base station, but it is now normally done using GPS monitoring. In *United States v. Clay*, No. 4:12-CR-735-03, 2013 WL 4483405, at *5 (S.D. Tex. May 6, 2013) (unpublished), the court ruled that GPS tracking of a defendant on pretrial release did not violate the Fourth Amendment, in part because "the defendant voluntarily consented to GPS monitoring in order to obtain the benefit of pre-trial release." Whether law enforcement can use the location information obtained through GPS tracking to do more than determine the defendant's compliance with house arrest is discussed below in section II.B of this chapter.

30. *See generally* G.S. 14-208.40 *et seq.* (establishing GPS monitoring regime for certain sex offenders); State v. Jones, ___ N.C. App. ___, 750 S.E.2d 883 (2013) (finding no Fourth Amendment problem with GPS monitoring of sex offenders even in light of *United States v. Jones*, 565 U.S. ___, 132 S. Ct. 945 (2012)); State v. Martin, ___ N.C. App. ___, 735 S.E.2d 238 (2012) (ruling that sex offender had diminished Fourth Amendment rights that were not violated by the imposition of satellite-based monitoring); State v. Dykes, 744 S.E.2d 505 (S.C. 2013) (rejecting due process claim of sex offender subject to GPS monitoring).

31. A court may require a defendant to "[r]emain at his or her residence" as a condition of probation. G.S. 15A-1343(b1)(3c). In such a case, "[t]he offender shall be required to wear a device which permits the supervising agency to monitor the offender's compliance with the condition electronically." *Id.* A judge might also order a defendant to observe a curfew as part of the defendant's probation as an ad hoc condition under G.S. 15A-1343(b1)(10), and might order the defendant to wear a monitoring device to promote compliance with the curfew. The ad hoc condition, at least, may be imposed only if it is "reasonably related to [the defendant's] rehabilitation." G.S. 15A-1343(b1)(10); State v. Cooper, 304 N.C. 180 (1981). In practice, the monitoring device that is used to enforce a house arrest condition or a curfew is a GPS tracking device. Courts in other jurisdictions have often upheld GPS monitoring for probationers, though typically under circumstances where there is something about the defendant or his or her offense that called for it. *See, e.g.*, United States v. Hill, No. 3:12-cr-034, 2013 WL 1811883, at *2 (S.D. Ohio Apr. 29, 2013) (unpublished) ("Placing [the defendant], as a probationer, on GPS monitoring does not violate the Fourth Amendment if the [probation officer] had reasonable suspicion that [the defendant] was violating his terms of release . . . ."); *In re* R.V., 89 Cal. Rptr. 3d 702, 708 (Cal. Ct. App. 2009) (upholding condition of juvenile's probation that he wear a GPS tracking device; the condition was "reasonably related to his past behavior and likely to deter future criminality").

32. *Cf.* United States v. Miller, 530 F. App'x 335, 337 (5th Cir. 2013) (unpublished) (reasonable to impose GPS monitoring as a condition of supervised release on a defendant with a "history of stalking, escape, angry outbursts, and erratic behavior"); United States v. Ringgenberg, 494 F. App'x 685 (8th Cir. 2012) (unpublished) (affirming lower court's decision to impose GPS tracking as a condition of defendant's supervised release after defendant wrote threatening letters to sentencing judge).

tracking devices on supervisees.[33] Furthermore, some courts have suggested that supervisees should be subjected to tracking technologies only if there is an individualized justification for monitoring.[34]

When monitoring is authorized only to ensure compliance with house arrest, a curfew, or similar geographic limitations, questions may arise regarding the propriety of using monitoring data to show something other than a violation of such a limitation, such as that the person subject to monitoring was not only away from home, but was at the scene of a crime. This issue is addressed in section II.B of this chapter, below.

II. Monitoring a Tracking Device

The foregoing discussion has focused mainly on the installation of tracking devices. This section considers two additional legal issues implicated by the subsequent monitoring of such devices.

---

33. This issue often arises when a supervisee is suspected of wrongdoing and an officer places a tracking device on the supervisee's vehicle. The prosecution may contend that warrantless tracking is justified under the theory that the supervisee is required to submit to warrantless searches as a condition of his or her supervision. *See, e.g.*, G.S. 15A-1343(b)(13) (requiring probationers to "[s]ubmit at reasonable times to warrantless searches by a probation officer of the probationer's person and of the probationer's vehicle and premises while the person is present, for purposes directly related to the probation supervision"). This argument has been persuasive to some courts, see *People v. Glass*, No. D063968, 2014 WL 2194502 (Cal. Ct. App. May 27, 2014) (unpublished) (ruling that the warrantless installation of a tracking device on a probationer's vehicle was a search of the vehicle but that the defendant consented to the search and waived his Fourth Amendment rights, given that submitting to warrantless searches was a condition of his probation), but not to others, see *People v. LeFlore*, 996 N.E.2d 678, 691 (Ill. App. Ct. 2013) (although defendant was on parole and required to consent to a search of his person, property, or residence, officers still violated the Fourth Amendment when they surreptitiously installed a GPS tracking device on a vehicle the defendant used; "Defendant's required consent to searches of his person, property, or residence did not include being subjected to continuous and unfettered surveillance of his movements."), *appeal allowed*, 3 N.E.3d 799 (Ill. 2014). As it pertains to North Carolina probationers, even if the installation of a tracking device would be permissible under the statute, the statute requires that the probationer be present for the search, which in most instances would defeat the purpose of installing the tracking device.

34. *See, e.g.*, United States v. Polouizzi, 697 F. Supp. 2d 381 (E.D.N.Y. 2010) (ruling that federal statute requiring the imposition of a mandatory curfew with electronic monitoring on all child pornography defendants released prior to trial violated due process and the Excessive Bail Clause of the Eighth Amendment).

A. Territorial Boundaries

By statute, superior court judges and members of the appellate courts may issue search warrants "valid throughout the State."[35] District court judges may issue search warrants valid within their judicial districts.[36] Magistrates and clerks may issue search warrants valid within their counties.[37] But people suspected of crimes may not stay within a single county, judicial district, or state. Do judicial officials have the authority to permit monitoring of suspects outside those jurisdictional boundaries?

In the federal courts, the issue is settled by statute and by rule. The relevant statute provides that "[i]f a court is empowered to issue a warrant or other order for the installation of a mobile tracking device, such order may authorize the use of that device within the jurisdiction of the court, and outside that jurisdiction if the device is installed in that jurisdiction."[38] Similarly, the Federal Rules of Criminal Procedure state that "a magistrate judge . . . has authority to issue a warrant to install within the district a tracking device; the warrant may authorize use of the device to track the movement of a person or property located within the district, outside the district, or both."[39]

No similar statute or rule exists in North Carolina, and no case addresses the issue. On the one hand, if North Carolina judicial officials only have the power to issue warrants that are valid inside the state, one could argue that any monitoring of a suspect's movements in other states is effectively warrantless monitoring. On the other hand, so long as the officer who installs and monitors the GPS device never leaves North Carolina, perhaps there is no problem with the monitoring, just as there is no problem with wiretapping a telephone line in North Carolina—with a proper order in place—even though calls may come in from another state.

Courts in a few other states have addressed legal issues concerning tracking devices and territorial boundaries, as described in the following case summaries.

Case Summaries on Territorial Boundaries

United States v. Lynn, No. 3:12-cr-00513-BR-1, 2014 WL 1896720, at *1, 4, 6 n.4 (D. Or. May 12, 2014) (unpublished) (Oregon officers obtained a state warrant authorizing them to install a tracking device

---

35. G.S. 15A-243(a).
36. G.S. 7A-291.
37. G.S. 7A-273(4) (magistrates); 7A-180(5) (clerks).
38. 18 U.S.C. § 3117(a).
39. Fed. R. Crim. P. 41(b)(4).

on the defendant's car and to "monitor[] and use the mobile tracking device anywhere in the State of Oregon" for thirty days; the defendant crossed into Washington, but the officers continued to monitor his location periodically; they intercepted him as he re-entered Oregon, stopped him for a traffic violation, and found drugs in his car; the court ruled that monitoring the defendant while in Washington was a search that exceeded the scope of the Oregon warrant but declined to suppress because it concluded that the officers would have waited for the defendant to re-enter Oregon even without the unlawful monitoring and still would have stopped the defendant; in the course of the discussion, the court noted that there was "not any evidence of any practical obstacle to obtaining a warrant from a Washington judicial officer to authorize GPS monitoring of Defendant's movements while in Washington" and that "[t]he government indicates it will not introduce at trial any information . . . gathered while Defendant was in Washington").

United States v. Faulkner, No. 14-05 (JNE/TNL), 2014 WL 3384687, at *2, 6 (D. Minn. July 10, 2014) (unpublished) (Minneapolis officers investigating drug crimes obtained a state warrant authorizing them to install tracking devices on the defendant's vehicles "wherever [they] may be found within the County"; the officers installed a device on one of the defendant's vehicles while it was in a different county; the defendant subsequently argued that "execution of the warrant outside the geographical limitations set forth in the warrant transformed the installation of the GPS tracking device into a warrantless search"; but the court, following *United States v. Hersman,* No. 2:13-cr-00002, 2013 WL 1966047 (S.D. W. Va. May 10, 2013) (unpublished), ruled that the error was a minor, technical error of state law that did not rise to the level of a Fourth Amendment violation and so did not support a suppression remedy).

United States v. Hansen, No. CR13-3010-MWB, 2013 WL 3199988, at *6 (N.D. Iowa June 19, 2013) (unpublished) (an Iowa magistrate issued warrants authorizing GPS tracking of a suspect's vehicle; officers monitored the vehicle as it traveled outside the magistrate's county and outside the state; the court ruled that nothing in Iowa law stated that "monitoring must stop the moment the vehicle leaves the county or, for that matter, the state"; instead, once a tracking device is lawfully installed, "it may be monitored to collect data regardless of whether the target vehicle leaves the county of issuance or the state of Iowa"), *report and recommendation adopted*, No. CR13-3010-MWB, 2013 WL 3940632 (N.D. Iowa July 31, 2013) (unpublished).

State v. Diaz, ID No. 1304006496, 2013 WL 6225103, at *2 n.27 (Del. Super. Ct. Nov. 26, 2013) (unpublished) (Delaware officers obtained a warrant authorizing them to install a tracking device on the defendant's vehicle and to monitor it both inside and outside the state; the reviewing court noted that the state "conceded that a Delaware Superior Court Judge lacks jurisdiction to authorize a search beyond the State's boundaries" and that monitoring of the defendant outside the state was not authorized by the warrant; based on these concessions, the court limited its consideration to the evidence obtained inside the state).

B. Use of Monitoring Data for Purposes Other than Those for Which Monitoring Was Imposed

Finally, questions may arise about whether GPS monitoring data may be used for purposes other than those for which monitoring was originally authorized. This issue may arise when a defendant is subject to a curfew or to house arrest, or is required to stay away from a certain location, and is required to wear a tracking device to ensure compliance with that condition. For example, a defendant may be placed on pretrial release on the condition that he or she remain under house arrest, subject to electronic monitoring.[40] Or a defendant who is sentenced to probation might have a curfew imposed as a condition, or might be required to remain at his or her residence.[41]

In years past, the electronic enforcement of house arrest and curfew orders typically would involve the use of a base station in the defendant's residence and a radio transmitter attached to the defendant, with the base station issuing an alert if it lost touch with the transmitter. Now, GPS tracking devices are generally used instead. Such devices collect far more information than whether the defendant is complying with his or her curfew or house arrest. May an officer use the tracking device to determine a defendant's specific

40. G.S. 15A-534(a)(5) (authorizing such a condition).

41. G.S. 15A-1343(b1)(3c) authorizes a court to require an offender to "[r]emain at his or her residence." The statute provides that "[t]he offender shall be required to wear a device which permits the supervising agency to monitor the offender's compliance with the condition electronically." A judge could also impose a curfew as an ad hoc condition of probation under G.S 15A-1343(b1)(10). Additional circumstances under which a court might order tracking or monitoring of some kind are discussed *supra* in section I.D.3.

location if the defendant violates his or her curfew or house arrest? May an officer use the data collected by the tracking device to place the defendant at the scene of a new crime, even if the defendant's presence did not involve a violation of any location restrictions, such as where a defendant subject to a nighttime curfew was at a crime scene during the day?

No North Carolina case addresses these issues, and the authority in other jurisdictions is scant.[42] At a minimum, it seems likely that a court would conclude that it is reasonable to use data from a tracking device to locate an absconding defendant or to tie the defendant to any additional crimes he or she committed during the time that he or she was supposed to be at home. As a practical matter, a judge concerned with this issue might specify that the curfew or house arrest is to be "enforced by GPS monitoring," rather than "electronic monitoring," as a way of reducing ambiguity about how the condition is to be enforced and clarifying the extent of the reduction in the defendant's expectation of privacy.

---

42. The only case that addresses the issue directly appears to be *United States v. Clay*, No. 4:12-CR-735-03, 2013 WL 4483405, *2 (S.D. Tex. May 6, 2013) ("The specific question before the Court appears to be an issue of first impression in this Circuit or possibly in any federal court in the Country: whether a defendant who voluntarily consents to GPS monitoring as a condition of pre-trial release can prohibit Pretrial Services from disclosing data from the GPS to a police department for investigative purposes. Under the facts of this case, the Court is of the opinion that the data may be disclosed to the authorities."). Other cases of some possible relevance include *Rasnick v. State*, 2 N.E.3d 17 (Ind. Ct. App. 2013) (the probative value of GPS data placing the parolee defendant at the scene of a crime was not outweighed by the prejudicial effect of jury speculation as to why defendant was being monitored); *People v. Roddy*, 2012 WL 1048465, *11 (Cal. Ct. App. Mar. 28, 2012) (unpublished) (the probative value of GPS data indicating that defendant was present at the scene of a vandalism crime was not outweighed by the prejudicial effect of revealing to the jury that defendant was a parolee being monitored by GPS); *State v. Byrd*, 423 S.W.3d 882, 884 (Mo. Ct. App. 2014) (indicating that GPS data collected from probationer defendant's ankle bracelet was introduced at robbery trial, but not conducting substantive analysis); and *People v. Fulton*, 2014 WL 1230208, *2 (Cal. Ct. App. Mar. 26, 2014) (unpublished) (indicating that GPS data placing the parolee defendant at the scene of crimes was admitted into evidence, but not conducting substantive analysis).

Chapter 5: The Admissibility of Electronic Evidence

Even evidence that has been lawfully seized cannot be admitted in court if it cannot satisfy the evidence rules. This chapter considers how the rules of evidence apply to electronic evidence. It focuses on issues that are of particular significance for digital evidence: authentication, the original writing rule (also known as the best evidence rule), and hearsay. Of course, issues of privilege, relevance, and the like may arise with electronic evidence as they may with any form of evidence. Because those issues are not unique to electronic evidence, they are not addressed in this publication.

Like other chapters of this book, this chapter draws heavily on cases decided in other jurisdictions. Fortunately, the rules of evidence are similar across jurisdictions, even sharing a common numbering system based on the federal rules.

I. Authentication

Authentication is widely regarded as the evidentiary consideration that is most different for electronic evidence than it is for traditional evidence.[1] This section reviews important general principles regarding authentication and then applies the principles to several common types of electronic evidence.

A. Authentication Generally

Simply put, authentication is the process of establishing that the piece of evidence in question is what it purports to be, such as an email from the defendant, or a website created by a witness. As explained in the Advisory Committee's Note to Rule 901 of the North Carolina Rules of Evidence, it is a "special aspect of relevancy." To illustrate that point with an example, if a self-incriminating email wasn't actually written by the defendant, it does not tend to establish the defendant's guilt and so should not be admitted at the defendant's trial.

Under N.C. R. EVID. 901(a), "[t]he requirement of authentication . . . is satisfied by evidence sufficient to support a finding that the matter in question is what its proponent claims."[2] This is a low hurdle that courts often

1. *See, e.g.*, G. Michael Fenner, *The Admissibility of Web-Based Evidence*, 47 CREIGHTON L. REV. 63, 64 (2013) ("By and large, the novel question regarding the admissibility of web-based evidence . . . is going to be authentication. . . . Once the evidence is authenticated . . . most of the rest of the evidentiary problems are the common problems lawyers face all the time.").

2. Section 8C-901(a) of the North Carolina General Statutes (hereinafter G.S.).

describe as a prima facie showing.[3] Doubts about authentication generally go to the weight, not the admissibility, of the evidence.[4]

Furthermore, there are many ways to authenticate evidence. N.C. R. EVID. 901 gives several examples of how authentication can be accomplished, such as testimony of a witness who knows what the evidence is under Rule 901(b)(1) and authentication by the distinctive characteristics of the evidence under Rule 901(b)(4). But the Rule itself states that these examples are "[b]y way of illustration only, and not by way of limitation."[5] The following sections of this publication apply these general principles to several common types of digital evidence.

B. Authentication of Electronic Communications

The central concern with authenticating electronic communications is whether the proponent of the evidence has established who authored the communication in question. Sufficient evidence of authorship can be provided in several ways.

---

3. State v. Mercer, 89 N.C. App. 714, 716 (1988) (noting approvingly that "federal courts have held that a *prima facie* showing, by direct or circumstantial evidence, such that a reasonable juror could find in favor of authenticity, is enough"); United States v. Vidacak, 553 F.3d 344, 349 (4th Cir. 2009) (explaining that "[t]he burden to authenticate under [Federal] Rule [of Evidence] 901 is not high—only a *prima facie* showing is required," and stating that all that is needed is evidence "from which the jury could reasonably find that the evidence is authentic"); United States v. Gadson, 763 F.3d 1189, 1203 (9th Cir. 2014) (endorsing the *prima facie* showing standard); United States v. Turner, 718 F.3d 226, 232 (3d Cir. 2013) (stating that the burden of authentication is "slight" and that the court "does not require conclusive proof of a document's authenticity, but merely a prima facie showing of some competent evidence to support authentication," with the ultimate determination of authenticity to be made by the jury); United States v. Fluker, 698 F.3d 988, 999 (7th Cir. 2012) ("Only a prima facie showing of genuineness is required; the task of deciding the evidence's true authenticity and probative value is left to the jury."). *See generally* Fenner, *supra* note 1, at 87–88 (noting that the proponent of evidence need only "make a prima facie showing that the evidence . . . is what he or she claims it is" and that "[t]his is not a particularly high barrier to surmount"); United States v. Hassan, 742 F.3d 104, 133 (4th Cir. 2014) (endorsing the prima facie showing standard in a case involving Facebook and YouTube evidence).

4. Thomas v. Dixson, 88 N.C. App. 337, 344 (1988) ("Authentication does not, however, require strict, mathematical accuracy, and a lack of accuracy will generally go to the weight and not the admissibility of the exhibit.").

5. G.S. 8C-901(b).

1. Rule 901(b)(1): Testimony of a Witness with Knowledge

Occasionally, the proponent is able to call the author of the evidence or someone who saw the author create the evidence. For example, the State might be able to call a witness who saw the defendant compose and send a Tweet about shooting a victim, or a witness to whom the defendant subsequently admitted to sending a threatening email.[6] The leading North Carolina case in this area is *State v. Gray*,[7] where a group of people planned a robbery and communicated about the crime via text message. An officer uncovered, and took pictures of, texts between two of the co-conspirators while searching a phone that belonged to one of them. The State sought to introduce the text messages at the trial of a third co-conspirator. One of the co-conspirators testified at trial that she sent the text messages in question and that the pictures accurately reflected the text messages that she sent. The trial court admitted the messages and the court of appeals affirmed, citing N.C. R. Evid. 901(b)(1). Since the co-conspirator sent the messages herself, she was able to testify about their authorship.

The *Gray* court considered and rejected the defendant's argument that the messages were not adequately authenticated because the State did not call an employee of the telecommunications service provider to explain how the company processes and delivers text messages. Although the court did not explain its reasoning on this point in detail, it is reasonable to assume that the court views modern telecommunications processes as presumptively reliable.

There are a few cases that suggest that Rule 901(b)(1) allows the "personal knowledge" of a recipient of a communication to authenticate the communication as coming from a particular author.[8] That suggestion is probably

---

6. Moore v. State, 763 S.E.2d 670, 674 (Ga. 2014) (ruling that evidence from the defendant's Facebook page was adequately authenticated in part because the defendant "admitted to [his girlfriend] that the Facebook page belonged to him"); Bobo v. State, 285 S.W.3d 270, 275 (Ark. Ct. App. 2008) (ruling that emails sent by the defendant were adequately authenticated in part because the defendant "admitted that she sent emails to [the victim]," even though she disputed the content of the emails).

7. ___ N.C. App. ___, 758 S.E.2d 699, *review allowed*, ___ N.C. ___, 766 S.E.2d 635 (2014).

8. *See, e.g.*, Shea v. State, 167 S.W.3d 98, 105 (Tex. App. 2005) (ruling that emails were properly authenticated under Texas Rule of Evidence 901(b)(1) where a witness testified only "that she was familiar with [the author's] e-mail address and that she had received the six e-mails in question from [the author]"); State v. Koch, 334 P.3d 280, 290 (Idaho 2014) (stating that because a witness testified that she "recognized [the defendant's] number and had previously been in frequent communication with him" at that number, text messages sent from that

mistaken. The recipient of an electronic communication typically does not have first-hand knowledge of who wrote it. Normally, the recipient is making an inference about the identity of the author based on the account from which the communication is sent, the content of the communication, and the like. In other words, the recipient is relying on the characteristics of the communication to identify the author. Such an inference may be entirely reasonable and sufficient to authenticate the communication, as discussed below in connection with Rule 901(b)(4), but it does not constitute personal knowledge under Rule 901(b)(1).

Case Summaries Regarding Rule 901(b)(1)

State v. Gray, ___ N.C. App. ___, 758 S.E.2d 699 (discussed in text, above), *review allowed,* ___ N.C. ___, 766 S.E.2d 635 (2014).

Donati v. State, 84 A.3d 156, 171 (Md. Ct. Spec. App. 2014) (under Maryland Evidence Rule 901(b)(1), "the proponent could admit the e-mail through the testimony of the author of the e-mail or a person who saw the author compose and send the e-mail").

United States v. Fluker, 698 F.3d 988, 999 (7th Cir. 2012) (noting that authentication under Federal Rule of Evidence 901(b)(1) was impossible because neither "[the author] nor anyone who saw [the author] author the emails testified that the emails were actually sent by [the author]").

State v. Webster, 955 A.2d 240 (Me. 2008) (ruling that a transcript of online chats between the defendant and an undercover officer was properly authenticated by the personal knowledge of the undercover officer).

2. Rule 901(b)(4): Distinctive Characteristics

Most often, electronic communications will be authenticated by their distinctive characteristics. That is, the proponent of the evidence will show that it was authored by a specific person by establishing that the communication came from that person's email or social media account; referred to matters known only to that person or of particular interest to that person; contained nicknames, terms, or sayings typically used by that person; and the like.

---

number were properly authenticated under Idaho Rule of Evidence 901(b)(1); the court also ruled that the messages were authenticated under Rule 901(b)(4) of the state rules).

These methods are similar to those used to authenticate traditional means of communication, such as letters.[9]

As to what kind, and what quantity, of such circumstantial evidence is enough to authenticate a communication, the cases nationally "arrive at widely disparate outcomes" and are as "clear as mud."[10] Although the lack of agreement in the case law makes it very difficult to announce general rules, a rough summary of the state of the law follows.

First, the fact that an electronic communication concludes with the name of the purported author (such as "Respectfully yours, Janet Adams") or comes from an account that contains the name of the purported author (such as janetadams@gmail.com) is not alone sufficient to establish the authorship of the communication.[11]

Second, the fact that a communication comes from an account linked to a specific person (such as an account that a witness testifies Janet Adams has used for years or an account linked to Janet Adams through subscriber information obtained from a service provider) is at least important evidence of the authorship of the communication. Depending on the strength of the connection between the purported author and the account, such evidence may in some cases be sufficient to authenticate authorship.[12]

---

9. *See, e.g.*, State v. Young, 186 N.C. App. 343, 354 (2007) (holding that letters were properly authenticated as having been written by the defendant where the defendant told the recipient that he would write to him, the letters used nicknames normally used by the defendant and the recipient, and the letters reflected "intimate knowledge of the crime").

10. Paul W. Grimm et al., *Authentication of Social Media Evidence*, 36 Am. J. Trial Advoc. 433, 441 (2013).

11. Commonwealth v. Purdy, 945 N.E.2d 372, 381 (Mass. 2011) (stating that "[e]vidence that the defendant's name is written as the author of an e-mail or that the electronic communication originates from an e-mail or a social networking Web site such as Facebook or MySpace that bears the defendant's name is not sufficient alone to authenticate the electronic communication as having been authored or sent by the defendant," arguing that "[t]here must be some 'confirming circumstances' sufficient for a reasonable jury to find by a preponderance of the evidence that the defendant authored the e-mails," and finding sufficient confirming circumstances to authenticate a series of e-mails); 2 Kenneth S. Broun et al., McCormick on Evidence § 221, at 57 (6th ed. 2006) (noting in connection with traditional writings that "the purported signature or recital of authorship on the face of a writing will *not* be accepted, without more, as sufficient proof of authenticity to secure the admission of the writing in evidence"); *Id.* § 227, at 73 n.2 ("For purposes of authentication, self-identification of an e-mail is insufficient, just as are the traditional signature and telephonic self-identification.").

12. *Compare* Hollie v. State, 679 S.E.2d 47, 50 (Ga. Ct. App. 2009) ("Though the e-mail transmission in question appears to have come from P.M.'s [the victim's] e-mail address, this alone does not prove its genuineness."), *aff'd*, 696 S.E.2d 642

Third, additional circumstantial authenticate regarding the contents of the communications is often the best way to authenticate authorship. For example, it may be persuasive evidence of authorship if a communication refers to facts or events known only to the author ("Remember that time we kissed behind the Post Office?"), refers to facts or events of particular interest to the author ("I can't wait for the Star Trek convention next week!"), or uses terms or nicknames that are characteristic of the author ("My little tomato, no one can have you if I can't.").[13] Similarly, it may be persuasive evidence of authorship if there is a connection between the communication and a precipitating event in which the author was involved. For example, when a threatening message is sent from the defendant's email address to the defendant's neighbor a few minutes after the two had a verbal altercation, the temporal proximity of the encounter and the email tends to show that the defendant is the author of the email. And it may be persuasive evidence of authentication where there are follow-up communications, linked to the author, referring to or repeating the contents of the original electronic communication, as when the defendant's threatening email is followed up with a face-to-face threat referring to the email.

Case Summaries Regarding Rule 901(b)(4)

SUFFICIENT EVIDENCE OF AUTHENTICITY

Commonwealth v. Johnson, 21 N.E.3d 937, 952 (Mass. Dec. 23, 2014) (ruling, in a harassment case, that the prosecution sufficiently authenticated emails between a defendant and a cooperating witness where the witness testified that the emails were "signed using [the defendant's] typical signature," the witness testified that he had exchanged many emails with the defendant using the same address over the past decade, and the emails referenced the harassing acts at issue in the case).

(Ga. 2010), *with* State v. Andrews, 293 P.3d 1203, 1206 (Wash. Ct. App. 2013) ("[T]estimony as to the defendant's phone number and signature sufficiently authenticated pictures of received text messages.").

13. *See generally* State v. Francis, ___ S.W.3d ___, No. ED 100009, 2014 WL 1686538, at *11 (Mo. Ct. App. Apr. 29, 2014) (collecting cases and stating that authentication may be established by, for example, "an admission by the author that the number from which the message was received is his number and that he has control of that phone," testimony from "the person receiving the message testifying that he regularly receives text messages from the author from this number," or "something distinctive about the text message indicating the author wrote it, such as a personalized signature"); *In re* F.P., 878 A.2d 91 (Pa. Super. Ct. 2005) (instant messages were properly authenticated as having been authored by the defendant where he used his name in the conversation and the content of the conversation referred to a long-running dispute with the victim).

Culp v. State, ___ So. 3d ___, No. CR-13-1039, 2014 WL 6608543 (Ala. Crim. App. Nov. 21, 2014) (holding, in a domestic violence case, that the prosecution sufficiently authenticated threatening emails as having been written by the defendant where the victim testified that she had helped the defendant set up the account from which the emails were sent, each email contained the defendant's picture and screen name, many emails concluded with the defendant's initials, and several emails contained slang terms for drugs that were typically used by the defendant).

State v. Koch, 334 P.3d 280, 289 (Idaho 2014) (collecting cases and ruling, in a child sexual abuse case, that a text message sent to the complainant's mother was properly authenticated as having been authored by the defendant; although "more than just confirmation that the number belonged to the person in question is required when the message's authentication is challenged," the contents of the message in question, including a reference to a recent fight between the defendant's daughter and the complainant, also showed that the defendant was the author; the court also analyzed several other electronic communications, ruling that most, but not all, were adequately authenticated by similar circumstantial evidence).

State v. Wilkerson, ___ N.C. App. ___, 733 S.E.2d 181 (2012) (text messages were sufficiently authenticated as being written by the defendant where a witness reported the defendant's suspicious driving on the victim's street and testified that the defendant appeared to be using a cell phone as he drove; the cell phone from which the messages were sent was found on the defendant's person; the text messages referenced an item stolen from the victim; and cell site data was interpreted by experts to establish that the phone traveled from the area of the defendant's home to the area of the victim's home and back).

Gulley v. State, 423 S.W.3d 569 (Ark. 2012) (sufficient circumstantial evidence authenticated the defendant's authorship of three text messages; messages came from cellular phone number assigned to the defendant; two of the messages referred to facts and circumstances known to the defendant; the third text message announced that the defendant would be dropped off at the victim's house and was followed by his arrival there the night she was killed).

Campbell v. State, 382 S.W.3d 545, 550 (Tex. App. 2012) (noting that "the fact that an electronic communication on its face purports to originate from a certain person's social networking account is generally insufficient standing alone to authenticate that person as the author of the communication"; finding that contents of Facebook messages were authenticated by speech patterns in messages that were consistent with the defendant's patterns of speech, by references to an incident and potential charges a few days after the incident occurred, and by the victim's testimony that, while she once had access to the defendant's account, she did not at the time the messages were sent and did not write the messages).

Tienda v. State, 358 S.W.3d 633 (Tex. Crim. App. 2012) (internal content of MySpace postings, including photographs of the defendant, comments, and music, and a subscriber report listing the owner of two of three accounts as having an email address that contained the defendant's name and zip code and a third account as having an email address that included the defendant's nickname, were sufficient to permit a reasonable juror to find that MySpace postings for all three accounts were created and maintained by the defendant).

State v. Williams, 191 N.C. App. 254 (2008) (unpublished) (instant messages purportedly exchanged between the defendant and the victim were properly authenticated by circumstantial evidence as being authored by the defendant where the victim testified that she and the defendant exchanged instant messages regularly, that the defendant's email address was the one from which the messages originated, and that the content of the messages included details known only to the defendant and the victim).

Dickens v. State, 927 A.2d 32 (Md. Ct. Spec. App. 2007) (authentication requirements were satisfied where threatening text messages were linked to the defendant by direct and circumstantial evidence, including references to facts known by few people, conduct consistent with the contents of the message, and references to seeing the minor child of the defendant and the victim).

State v. Taylor, 178 N.C. App. 395 (2006) (text messages were sufficiently authenticated by circumstantial evidence as being written by the victim where the messages indicated that the author would be driving a car of the same make and model as the victim's and the author twice referred to himself by the victim's name; there was also sufficient authentication of the text messages as being messages to and from a particular cellular phone number where there was expert testimony regarding the service provider database from which the messages were retrieved and the service provider's business practice of storing such messages).

INSUFFICIENT EVIDENCE OF AUTHENTICITY

Smith v. State, 136 So. 3d 424, 434 (Miss. 2014) (ruling, in a murder case, that the prosecution failed to authenticate Facebook messages purportedly sent from the defendant to his wife [and mother of the child victim] as having been composed by the defendant; the court reasoned that social media accounts may easily be hacked or fabricated, so authentication requires more than showing that a message comes from an account with the purported author's "name and photograph"; in this case, "[n]o other identifying information from the Facebook profile, such as date of birth, interests, hometown, or the like, was provided" and the witness did not explain how she identified the messages as coming from the defendant; the court noted that the messages did not appear to be part of a conversation between the two).

State v. Lukowitsch, ___ N.C. App. ___, 752 S.E.2d 258 (2013) (unpublished) ("[T]he trial court properly excluded the content of the text messages because defendant failed to present any evidence to authenticate the text messages as having been sent by [a certain party].").

Rodriguez v. State, 273 P.3d 845 (Nev. 2012) (trial court abused its discretion in admitting text messages that the State claimed were sent by the defendant, a co-defendant, or both, using the victim's cell phone because the State failed to present sufficient evidence corroborating the defendant's identity as the person who sent the messages).

Griffin v. State, 19 A.3d 415 (Md. 2011) (printed pages of a MySpace account allegedly belonging to the defendant's girlfriend upon which appeared a post indicating that "SNITCHES GET STITCHES" were not properly authenticated, and it was prejudicial error to admit them into evidence; the court concluded that because of the risk of camouflaged identities and account manipulation on social networking sites, "a printout of an image from such a site requires a greater degree of authentication than merely identifying the date of birth of the creator and her visage in a photograph on the site in order to reflect that [the defendant's girlfriend] was its creator and the author of the 'snitches get stitches' language").

State v. Eleck, 23 A.3d 818 (Conn. App. 2011) (trial court did not abuse its discretion in excluding evidence of Facebook messages purportedly sent from State's witness's account to the defendant; a reference in the messages to acrimonious history did not sufficiently establish that the State's witness authored the messages such that it was an abuse of discretion to exclude the evidence), *aff'd on other grounds*, 100 A.3d 817 (2014)).

3. Business Records

Courts in some jurisdictions have addressed whether electronic communications may be authenticated as the business records of a social media company or an electronic communications service provider. Those courts have considered Fed. R. Evid. 902(11) or its state equivalents. The federal version of Rule 902(11) designates as self-authenticating "[t]he original or a copy of a domestic record that meets the requirements of [Fed. R. Evid.] 803(6)(A)-(C) [the business records exception to the hearsay rule], as shown by a certification of the custodian or another qualified person that complies with a federal statute or a rule prescribed by the Supreme Court." The rule requires that the proponent of such evidence give the opposing party advance notice of the proponent's intent to offer it.

The Fourth Circuit recently held that screenshots of two defendants' Facebook pages, among other evidence, could be admitted as Facebook's business records.[14] However, a Colorado appellate court reached a contrary result, reasoning that "even though an arguable business relationship exists between Facebook and its users, there was no evidence presented that Facebook substantially relies for any business purpose on information contained in its users' profiles and communications."[15] At least for now, the issue is only of academic interest in North Carolina, as North Carolina has not adopted a version of Rule 902(11) and business records are not self-authenticating in North Carolina's courts.

---

14. United States v. Hassan, 742 F.3d 104, 133 (4th Cir. 2014) (finding no abuse of discretion in district court's decision to admit screenshots of defendants' Facebook pages and YouTube videos posted by defendants as self-authenticating business records).

15. People v. Glover, ___ P.3d ___, No. 13CA0098, 2015 WL 795690 (Colo. App. Feb. 26, 2015) (ruling that the defendant's Facebook messages and profile were not admissible as business records under Colorado's analogue of Fed. R. Evid. 902(11)).

C. Authentication of Tracking Data

As discussed in chapter 3 and elsewhere in this book, GPS data may come into criminal cases in several ways: because law enforcement placed a tracking device on a suspect's vehicle; because a suspect was wearing a GPS tracking bracelet as a condition of probation or pretrial release; because law enforcement seized a cell phone or other device containing GPS data from a suspect; and so on. Although each situation presents slightly different considerations, it is often possible to authenticate such data under N.C. R. Evid. 901(b)(1) (testimony of a witness with knowledge that the data is what it is claimed to be), Rule 901(b)(9) (concerning "[e]vidence describing a process or system used to produce a result and showing that the process or system produces an accurate result"), or some combination of the two.

The leading case in North Carolina is *State v. Jackson*.[16] The defendant committed a sexual assault while wearing a GPS tracking device as a condition of his pretrial release. The supervisor of the electronic monitoring unit testified regarding how the tracking device worked. The defendant argued that the tracking data was not properly authenticated, but the court of appeals ruled to the contrary. However, the court did not analyze the authentication issue in detail—instead focusing mainly on whether the data were inadmissible hearsay—so the opinion is useful mainly for cases that have similar facts.

A few cases from other jurisdictions provide more general guidance. Most courts seem satisfied if a witness who possesses a working familiarity with the GPS system explains how it functions, how the data were collected, and what the data mean.[17] Several cases have focused on the qualifications and experience necessary to authenticate the data. Courts generally have ruled that the witness need not be an expert so long as he or she is familiar with the technology.[18]

---

16. ___ N.C. App. ___, 748 S.E.2d 50 (2013).

17. *See, e.g.*, United States v. Espinal-Almeida, 699 F.3d 588, 612, 613 (1st Cir. 2012) (ruling that data taken from a GPS device seized from a boat used for drug trafficking were properly authenticated by the testimony of the lab analyst who examined the device; the analyst provided a "good amount of testimony about the processes employed by the GPS," allowing the court to apply Fed. R. Evid. 901(b)(9), which permits a witness to describe a process or system and thereby authenticate the result of the process or system; the court ruled that expert testimony was not required to authenticate the data, noting that the analyst was "knowledgeable, trained, and experienced in analyzing GPS devices").

18. *Id. See also* United States v. Brooks, 715 F.3d 1069, 1078 (8th Cir. 2013) (a bank robber was apprehended based on a GPS device that was placed surreptitiously in the loot bag; the trial judge properly took judicial notice of the "accuracy and reliability of GPS technology" generally, and the testimony of an

By contrast, evidence about cell site location information typically is introduced by an expert witness, and courts have disagreed about the extent to which such experts may pinpoint a phone's location, as opposed to identifying a general area in which the phone was located or simply describing the location of the towers to which the phone connected.[19]

---

employee of the security company that supplied the device was sufficient to admit the data generated by the device in question; although the witness apparently lacked a "scientific background," he had worked for the company for eighteen years, "had been trained by the company . . . knew how the device worked, and . . . had demonstrated the device for customers dozens of times"); United States v. Thompson, 393 F. App'x 852 (3d Cir. 2010) (unpublished) (a bank robber was apprehended based on a GPS device that was placed surreptitiously in the loot bag; the GPS data was authenticated at trial by an employee of the security company that supplied the device; he explained how the device worked, and he was properly permitted to testify as a lay witness rather than an expert, given that his knowledge was based on his personal experience with such devices).

19. *Compare* United States v. Evans, 892 F. Supp. 2d 949, 955–57 (N.D. Ill. 2012) (ruling that an FBI agent with extensive training in cell phone investigations could testify as an expert about how cellular networks operate and could testify about which towers interfaced with the defendant's cell phone at various times, but could not estimate the defendant's location using "granulization," a system for determining which of two "closely positioned towers" serves which nearby locations, because granulization does not account for the possibility that a phone may make contact with a tower that is not the closest one due to physical obstructions or network traffic, and because granulization "remains wholly untested by the scientific community"), *and* State v. Payne, 104 A.3d 142, 145–55 (Md. 2014) (ruling that a detective "needed to be qualified as an expert . . . before being allowed to testify . . . [about] the communication path" of the defendants' cell phones, i.e., "the location of cell phone towers through which particular calls were routed and . . . the locations of those towers on a map in relation to the crime scene"; the court noted that "[t]here are a variety of factors affecting to which tower a cell phone will connect, beyond merely the distance" between the phone and the available towers and ruled that the witness "engaged in a process to derive his conclusion [about the location of the defendants' phones] that was beyond the ken of an average person"), *with* United States v. Machado-Erazo, 950 F. Supp. 2d 49, 55–58 (D.D.C. 2013) (ruling that an FBI agent with extensive training in cell phone investigations could testify as an expert to the "general location where a cell phone would have to be located to use a particular cell tower and sector," distinguishing *Evans* as involving an attempt to identify a phone's specific location within an area of overlapping coverage by multiple towers and noting that "many cases" have admitted testimony similar to that at issue in this case), *and* United States v. Jones, 918 F. Supp. 2d 1, 4–6 (D.D.C. 2013) (ruling that an FBI agent with extensive training in cell phone investigations could testify as an expert regarding the location of cell towers in a relevant area, the coverage sectors of the towers, and "where the cell phones must have been when they connected to each tower," because such testimony is "based on reliable methodology" and has been "widely accepted by numerous courts").

D. Authentication of Evidence Seized from a Defendant's Digital Device

Many cases involve evidence that is seized from a digital storage device, such as a computer, disc drive, or cell phone. Child pornography cases may involve images; fraud cases may involve accounting records; and homicide cases may involve information that sheds light on the defendant's motive or the method he or she used to commit the crime. Such evidence normally is authenticated by testimony about the retrieval of the evidence and its preservation, unaltered, until trial.[20] This is similar to the authentication procedure for physical evidence.

A defendant may argue that he did not place the evidence on the digital device—that a virus put it there or that someone else with access to the device was responsible for the presence of the evidence. Such an argument may well be critical to the defendant's culpability and proper for jury consideration, but it is largely irrelevant to authentication, as it does not relate to the identity or genuineness of the evidence. Similarly, in child pornography cases, whether images show real or simulated children may be an important factor in the defendant's guilt or innocence, but it probably should not be viewed as an authentication issue. So long as the images accurately reflect the data obtained from the defendant's digital storage device, they have been authenticated.[21]

---

20. *See generally* United States v. Salcido, 506 F.3d 729, 733 (9th Cir. 2007) ("[T]he government properly authenticated the videos and images . . . by presenting detailed evidence as to the chain of custody [and] how the images were retrieved from the defendant's computers."); Midkiff v. Commonwealth, 694 S.E.2d 576 (Va. 2010) (images retrieved from the defendant's computer were properly authenticated by testimony that they were retrieved by copying the defendant's hard drive and then copying the images in question onto a DVD, from which the images used at trial were generated); Bone v. State, 771 N.E.2d 710 (Ind. Ct. App. 2002) (images were properly authenticated by testimony that they were retrieved from the defendant's computer and printed out).

21. *See, e.g.*, United States v. Edington, 526 F. App'x 584, 591 (6th Cir. 2013) (unpublished) ("The government must produce evidence sufficient to support a finding that the item is what the government claims it is—in this case, a video that the defendant received or possessed. This can be done by offering testimony from an investigator who was present when the video was retrieved and can describe the process used to retrieve it"; the government does not need to show that the video depicts actual children, as that is an issue for the jury to determine); *Salcido*, 506 F.3d at 733 ("While [the defendant] frames [the prosecution's alleged failure to establish that the videos and images in question depicted real, rather than virtual, children] as an issue of authenticity, this argument is more properly considered a challenge to the sufficiency of the evidence.").

E. Authentication of Web Pages

Web pages are often important evidence in criminal cases. Such evidence might include a Facebook wall posting from a defendant admitting guilt; Mapquest directions reflecting the driving distance between the defendant's home and the victim's residence; or a Google Maps printout showing an overhead view of the crime scene. Courts have been skeptical about the origins and authentication of material printed from websites generally.[22] However, the specific authentication issues regarding web pages vary based on the type of page at issue.

For example, social media postings present authorship issues similar to those with electronic communications, discussed above.[23] Different considerations arise with mapping websites like Mapquest and Google Maps. These sites

---

22. *In re* Yopp, 217 N.C. App. 489, 495 (2011) ("internet printout[]" used to show that two banks had merged "was not authenticated as a public record and was inadmissible; the mere fact that a document is printed out from the internet does not endow that document with any authentication whatsoever"); Rankin v. Food Lion, 210 N.C. App. 213, 217 (2011) (plaintiff attempted to use two documents to establish identity of the proper corporate defendant; "[o]ne of these documents appears to consist of a page printed from the website of the North Carolina Secretary of State, while the other appears to consist of an internet posting" about a defendant; these documents were not authenticated and were not admissible); United States v. Jackson, 208 F.3d 633, 638 (7th Cir. 2000) ("[The defendant] needed to show that the web postings in which the white supremacist groups took responsibility for the racist mailings actually were posted by the groups, as opposed to being slipped onto the groups' web sites by [the defendant] herself, who was a skilled computer user"; but the defendant did not do so, and the websites were not authenticated).

23. For additional cases specifically concerning social media postings, see *United States v. Hassan*, 742 F.3d 104, 133 (4th Cir. 2014) (screenshots of Facebook pages were properly authenticated as having been authored by the defendants where investigators had "track[ed] the Facebook pages and Facebook accounts to [the defendants'] mailing and email addresses via internet protocol addresses"); *United States v. Vayner*, 769 F.3d 125, 131 (2d Cir. 2014) ("[W]e conclude that the district court abused its discretion in admitting the VK web page, as it did so without proper authentication under [Federal] Rule [of Evidence] 901. The government did not provide a sufficient basis on which to conclude that the proffered printout was what the government claimed it to be—*Zhyltsou's* profile page—and there was thus insufficient evidence to authenticate the VK page and to permit its consideration by the jury."); *Parker v. State*, 85 A.3d 682 (Del. 2014) (ruling, in an assault case, that Facebook posts were properly authenticated as having been written by the defendant in part because they "referenced the altercation" in question and were created on the same day that the assault took place); and *Moore v. State*, 763 S.E.2d 670 (Ga. 2014) (ruling, in a murder case, that Facebook posts were properly authenticated as having been written by the defendant where the defendant's picture appeared on the Facebook page, the page contained details about the defendant, such as his nickname, hometown, and girlfriend, and

offer maps, driving directions, and driving times. The maps often are admitted based on the testimony of a witness that the maps fairly and accurately represent the area shown.[24] The distance measurements available on the sites may be the subject of judicial notice, though driving times may be hearsay.[25] Finally, information from government websites, like the state prison system's website, may be self-authenticating under Rule 902(5), which provides that "[b]ooks, pamphlets, or other publications purporting to be issued by public authority" are self-authenticating.[26]

II. Original Writing/Best Evidence Rule

A second issue that arises with regard to electronic evidence concerns the original writing or "best evidence" rule. Generally, if a piece of evidence is a writing, a recording, or a photograph and the proponent seeks to prove its contents, N.C. R. Evid. 1002 requires the introduction of the original of the writing, recording, or photograph.

Electronic writings such as emails, text messages, and social media postings are "writings" within the meaning of the original writing requirement. N.C. R. Evid. 1001(1) states that "writings" consist of "letters, words, sounds, or numbers, or their equivalent, set down by handwriting, typewriting, printing, photostating, photographing, magnetic impulse, mechanical or

---

the posts matched the "structure and style" of other communications from the defendant).

24. State v. Brown, 1 So. 3d 504 (La. Ct. App. 2008) (court erred in excluding Mapquest printout depicting crime scene; witness should have been allowed to testify that it fairly and accurately showed the scene; any inaccuracies went to weight, not admissibility).

25. People v. Stiff, 904 N.E.2d 1174 (Ill. App. Ct. 2009) (taking judicial notice of the distance between two residences based on Google Maps); Jianniney v. State, 962 A.2d 229, 230 (Del. 2008) (noting that "many courts have taken judicial notice of facts derived from internet map sites" but ruling that estimates of driving times, as opposed to distances, are hearsay not within any exception).

26. G.S. 8C-902(5). *See, e.g.*, Williams Farms Produce Sales, Inc. v. R & G Produce Co., 443 S.W.3d 250, 259 n.7 (Tex. App. 2014) ("[W]e hold that documents printed from government websites [here, a docket sheet printed from a federal court's website] are self-authenticating."), Firehouse Rest. Group, Inc., v. Scurmont, LLC, No. 4:09-cv-00618-RBH, 2011 WL 3555704, at *4 (D.S.C. Aug. 11, 2011) (unpublished) ("Records from government websites are generally considered admissible and self-authenticating."); Williams v. Long, 585 F. Supp. 2d 679, 689 (D. Md. 2008) ("The printed webpage from the Maryland Judiciary Case Search website is self-authenticating under [Federal] Rule [of Evidence] 902(5).").

electronic recording, or other form of data compilation." Courts have recognized that electronic writings of various kinds meet this definition.[27] Digital photographs also fall within the rule. Thus, in cases in which the contents of a digital writing or photograph are at issue, the proponent must satisfy the original writing requirements.[28]

Some electronic text may not be a writing within the scope of the rule. For example, when a witness seeks to testify about the phone number from which a call originated, based on the witness's observation of the number through caller ID, the opposing party may argue that the caller ID information is a "writing" the content of which the proponent is seeking to prove and that the original writing requirement therefore applies. However, it probably is not, as the number is generated by a computer rather than being "set down by handwriting, typewriting" or the like, as required by the rule.[29]

When it is necessary to comply with the rule, various "originals" may exist. A printout of data stored on an electronic device is an "original."[30] In the case of text messages, the cellular phone displaying the text message also constitutes an "original."[31] Furthermore, even if an "original" is not available,

---

27. *See, e.g.,* State v. Espiritu, 176 P.3d 885 (Haw. 2008) (finding text messages to be a writing).

28. *See* Lorraine v. Markel Am. Ins. Co., 241 F.R.D. 534 (discussing criminal cases in which the proponent sought to prove the content of electronic writings). *See also generally* Hon. Paul W. Grimm et al., *Back to the Future:* Lorraine v. Markel American Insurance Co. *and New Findings on the Admissibility of Electronically Stored Information,* 42 Akron L. Rev. 357 (2009) ("[I]f there is no non-documentary proof of the occurrence, and the only evidence of what transpired is contained in a writing, then the original writing rule applies."). *Cf.* State v. Branch, 288 N.C. 514 (1975) (holding that witness could testify to a conversation he heard even though a recording of the conversation also existed; the conversation, not the content of the recording, was what was at issue).

29. State v. Schuette, 44 P.3d 459, 464 (Kan. 2002) ("Caller ID displays by their nature . . . cannot be printed out or saved on an electronic medium. [The defendant's argument] . . . is akin to contending that a clock must be produced before a witness can testify as to the time he or she observed an accident."). Even if a court were to rule that caller ID information constitutes a "writing," testimony about the writing probably would be admissible under N.C. R. Evid. 1004(1) on the theory that the "original" had been lost or destroyed without bad faith.

30. *See* N.C. R. Evid. 1001(3).

31. *See, e.g.,* State v. Winder, 189 P.3d 580 (Kan. Ct. App. 2008) (unpublished) (excusing production of cell phone containing text message, which the court assumed constituted an original); *Espiritu,* 176 P.3d 885 (trial court properly allowed witness to testify regarding contents of text messages when witness no longer had the cellular phone on which she received the messages; in ruling that the witness no longer had the "actual text messages," the court implicitly

in most instances, a duplicate is admissible to the same extent as an original.[32] A photograph of an electronic writing—for example, a photograph of a text message—may be admitted as a duplicate.[33]

Finally, neither an original nor a duplicate is required in the circumstances described in N.C. R. Evid. 1004. Subsection (1) of Rule 1004 describes the exception that is most likely to arise in criminal cases. It provides that the original is not required, and that a witness may testify to the contents of a writing, if all originals have been lost or destroyed—unless the proponent lost or destroyed the original in bad faith.[34] It is unclear how far courts should inquire into the loss or destruction of originals. For example, if a text message has not been retained on the recipient's phone and the recipient seeks to testify about the contents of the message, must the proponent of the testimony show that it is impossible to recover the contents from the recipient's service provider? From the sender's service provider? From the sender's phone? Case law does not yet answer these questions.[35]

---

concluded that if the witness had retained the phone, that would have constituted an original).

32. *See* N.C. R. Evid. 1003 (stating that a duplicate is admissible except when there is a genuine question about the authenticity of the original or when it would be unfair to admit a duplicate in lieu of the original).

33. *See, e.g.*, Rodriguez v. State, 449 S.W.3d 306, 2014 Ark. App. 660 (Ark. Ct. App. 2014) (ruling that a photograph of a threatening text message was admissible where the witness testified that the message had been deleted from her phone and a representative of the phone company testified that the company does not keep records of the content of text messages; "the photograph of the text was all there was"); State v. Andrews, 293 P.3d 1203 (Wash. Ct. App. 2013) (ruling that a photograph of a text message was properly admitted as a duplicate where defense counsel acknowledged having no reason to doubt the accuracy of the photograph); Dickens v. State, 927 A.2d 32 (Md. Ct. Spec. App. 2007) (photographs of text messages properly admitted).

34. *See, e.g.*, Espiritu, 176 P.3d at 892 (concluding that "bad faith cannot be inferred because the text messages were not printed out when there is no indication that such a printout was even possible").

35. *Cf. Rodriguez*, 449 S.W.3d at 313, 2014 Ark. App. at ___ (ruling that a photograph of a text message was properly admitted notwithstanding the best evidence rule and noting in the course of the discussion that "[t]he State presented an AT & T representative, who testified that the company does not keep records of the content of text messages").

III. Hearsay

The hearsay rule applies to electronic evidence as it does to other evidence. However, certain types of electronic evidence present particular hearsay concerns. This section addresses the provisions of hearsay law that are most likely to arise when dealing with electronic evidence.

A. Statements by the Defendant

When offered by the State, a statement by the defendant is an admission of a party-opponent and therefore will be subject to the hearsay exception for such statements in N.C. R. Evid. 801(d). Thus, a text message, email, or the like that is authenticated as having been written by the defendant may be admitted under the hearsay rules.

If the defendant's statement is threatening, the statement also may be considered a declaration of state of mind within the hearsay exception in N.C. R. Evid. 803(3), or it may be non-hearsay evidence of a verbal act.[36]

B. Evidence That Is Not Hearsay

Several types of electronic evidence are not hearsay. Many courts have recognized that evidence that is produced automatically by a computer is not a statement of a declarant and so simply falls outside the scope of the hearsay rules. Examples include:

- Cell phone records[37]
- Caller ID information[38]
- Logs generated by alarm systems[39]

---

36. *See* State v. Weaver, 160 N.C. App. 61 (2003) (holding that a statement of a bribe was evidence of a verbal act and was not offered for the truth of the matter asserted but, rather, to show that the statement was made).

37. Godoy v. Commonwealth, 742 S.E.2d 407, 411 (Va. Ct. App. 2013) (holding, in a rape case, that the defendant's cell phone records were properly admitted as they were "automatically self-generating" and "not governed by hearsay principles"; the court also noted that the records were not created for the purpose of litigation and so were not testimonial for purposes of Confrontation Clause analysis).

38. Inglett v. State, 521 S.E.2d 241, 245 (Ga. Ct. App. 1999) (finding no hearsay issue because caller ID information is "computer-generated data automatically appearing on the screen of the telephone").

39. State v. Gojcaj, 92 A.3d 1056, 1067 (Conn. App. Ct. 2014) ("[R]ecords that are entirely self-generated by a computer do not trigger the hearsay rule," because they aren't statements made by a declarant; thus, a log showing when an alarm system had been turned on and off was not hearsay).

- Information recorded by red light cameras[40]
- Data recorded by a tracking or monitoring device[41]

Similarly, the telephone number from which a text message was sent has been found not to constitute hearsay because such information is not a statement of a person.[42] Photographs also are not statements and so are not hearsay.[43] It is debatable whether a map constitutes a "statement" or is, like a picture, outside the realm of hearsay. If a map is a statement, it may often be admissible for the non-hearsay purpose of illustrating the testimony of a witness.[44]

C. Business Records

Some electronic evidence may be admitted as business records under N.C. R. Evid. 803(6), which concerns "records of regularly conducted activity" in any form. Courts have sometimes admitted evidence under the business records exception even where the evidence likely is not hearsay at all for the reasons set forth in the preceding section. For example, phone records are

40. People v. Goldsmith, 326 P.3d 239, 249 (Cal. 2014) (ruling that red light camera data, including date, time, and "length of time since the traffic signal light turned red" are "not statements of a person" but are electronically generated and so are not hearsay).

41. State v. Kandutsch, 799 N.W.2d 865, 879 (Wisc. 2011) (distinguishing between "computer-stored records, which memorialize the assertions of human declarants, and computer-generated records, which are the result of a process free of human intervention," and finding that tracking device data are the latter and so are not hearsay).

42. *See* State v. Schuette, 44 P.3d 459 (Kan. 2002); N.C. R. Evid. 801(a) (defining a statement as from "a person").

43. N.C. R. Evid. 801(a) defines a "statement" as "(1) an oral or written assertion or (2) nonverbal conduct of a person, if it is intended by him as an assertion." *See* State v. Patterson, 332 N.C. 409 (1992).

44. State v. Wright, 752 A.2d 1147 (Conn. App. Ct. 2000) (rejecting a defendant's hearsay argument regarding the admission of a map used to show the distance from the location of his arrest to a nearby school; a witness testified that the map was a fair and accurate representation of the area, and the court stated that the map was merely a pictorial representation of the testimony of the witness); Dawson v. Olson, 543 P.2d 499 (Idaho 1975) (map should have been admitted for illustrative purposes, though if offered as substantive evidence, the hearsay rule would apply).

often admitted as business records,[45] and GPS data may also be admitted as a business record.[46]

An issue that arises with business records is whether live testimony is required to establish the foundation for admissibility. According to N.C. R. EVID. 803(6), the foundation for the business records exception must be "shown by the testimony of the custodian or other qualified witness." By way of contrast, the federal business records rule, FED. R. EVID. 803(6), expressly provides that the foundation may be supplied by testimony *or by a written certification* from an appropriate witness. Notwithstanding the use of the term "testimony" in the North Carolina version of the rule, appellate case law supports the use of an affidavit to satisfy the foundational requirements of the business records exception.[47]

---

45. State v. Brewington, 80 N.C. App. 42, 51 (1986) ("The [telephone] records were duly authenticated by the company's custodian for billing records and, if otherwise competent, were admissible under the business records exception to the hearsay rule."); State v. Hunnicutt, 44 N.C. App. 531 (1980) (telephone company's computerized billing and call records were properly admitted as business records). *Cf.* State v. Taylor, 178 N.C. App. 395 (2006) (noting that a telephone representative described how the records of text messages were created and maintained). Of course, the requisite foundation must be established. State v. Price, 326 N.C. 56 (1990) (holding that the trial court erred in allowing a telephone bill to be introduced to show the record of calls without the testimony of a witness about the preparation of the records), *vacated on other grounds*, Price v. North Carolina, 498 U.S. 802 (1990).

46. State v. Jackson, ___ N.C. App. ___, 748 S.E.2d 50 (2013) (the defendant committed a sexual assault while wearing a GPS tracking device as a condition of his pretrial release; the supervisor of the electronic monitoring unit testified regarding how the tracking device worked, and that established the foundation to admit the data from the device as a business record); United States v. Brooks, 715 F.3d 1069, 1079 (8th Cir. 2013) (the defendant robbed a bank and a teller slipped a GPS tracking device into the loot bag; the GPS "tracking reports fell under the business records exception").

47. *See* Simon v. Simon, ___ N.C. App. ___, 753 S.E.2d 475 (2013) (expressly rejecting the argument that the term "testimony" in N.C. R. EVID. 803(6) requires a live witness and holding that the applicability of the business records exception may be established by an affidavit from an appropriate person); *In re* S.W., 175 N.C. App. 719 (2006) (cited approvingly in *In re* S.D.J., 192 N.C. App. 478 (2008)). As authority for the use of an affidavit, *S.W.* cites *Chamberlain v. Thames*, 131 N.C. App. 705 (1998), a civil case that allowed an affidavit to be used under the specific provision regarding the use of affidavits to establish the foundation for the admission of medical and public records in N.C. R. CIV. P. 45(c). Because *Chamberlain* is a civil case applying a particular rule of civil procedure, it may not be a strong precedent for the use of affidavits in criminal cases. However, since *S.D.J.* and *Simon* have followed *S.W.*, the propriety of using affidavits appears to be settled.

The proponent may not avoid the foundation requirements of the business records exception by having a witness read from a business record for which a proper foundation has not been established.[48]

Business records generally are not testimonial, and therefore may be admitted without running afoul of the Confrontation Clause. The North Carolina Court of Appeals recently ruled that this was so even when the business records in question were GPS tracking records compiled by the North Carolina Department of Correction in connection with the monitoring of an individual on post-release supervision.[49]

---

48. *See* State v. Springer, 283 N.C. 627 (1973) (holding that allowing investigator to read from records violated the original writing rule).

49. State v. Gardner, ___ N.C. App. ___, ___, ___ S.E.2d ___, ___, No. COA14-646, 2014 WL 6907482, at *3 (N.C. Ct. App. Dec. 2, 2014) (reasoning that "the GPS evidence admitted in this case was not generated purely for the purpose of establishing some fact at trial. Instead, it was generated to monitor defendant's compliance with his post-release supervision conditions. The GPS evidence was only pertinent at trial because defendant was alleged to have violated his post-release conditions.").

Appendix A

The Stored Communications Act (18 U.S.C. §§ 2701–12)

§ 2701. Unlawful access to stored communications

(a) Offense.—Except as provided in subsection (c) of this section whoever—

(1) intentionally accesses without authorization a facility through which an electronic communication service is provided; or

(2) intentionally exceeds an authorization to access that facility;

and thereby obtains, alters, or prevents authorized access to a wire or electronic communication while it is in electronic storage in such system shall be punished as provided in subsection (b) of this section.

(b) Punishment.—The punishment for an offense under subsection (a) of this section is—

(1) if the offense is committed for purposes of commercial advantage, malicious destruction or damage, or private commercial gain, or in furtherance of any criminal or tortious act in violation of the Constitution or laws of the United States or any State—

(A) a fine under this title or imprisonment for not more than 5 years, or both, in the case of a first offense under this subparagraph; and

(B) a fine under this title or imprisonment for not more than 10 years, or both, for any subsequent offense under this subparagraph; and

(2) in any other case—

(A) a fine under this title or imprisonment for not more than 1 year or both, in the case of a first offense under this paragraph; and

(B) a fine under this title or imprisonment for not more than 5 years, or both, in the case of an offense under this subparagraph that occurs after a conviction of another offense under this section.

(c) Exceptions.—Subsection (a) of this section does not apply with respect to conduct authorized—
  (1) by the person or entity providing a wire or electronic communications service;
  (2) by a user of that service with respect to a communication of or intended for that user; or
  (3) in section 2703, 2704 or 2518 of this title.

§ 2702. Voluntary disclosure of customer communications or records

(a) Prohibitions.—Except as provided in subsection (b) or (c)—
  (1) a person or entity providing an electronic communication service to the public shall not knowingly divulge to any person or entity the contents of a communication while in electronic storage by that service; and
  (2) a person or entity providing remote computing service to the public shall not knowingly divulge to any person or entity the contents of any communication which is carried or maintained on that service—
    (A) on behalf of, and received by means of electronic transmission from (or created by means of computer processing of communications received by means of electronic transmission from), a subscriber or customer of such service;
    (B) solely for the purpose of providing storage or computer processing services to such subscriber or customer, if the provider is not authorized to access the contents of any such communications for purposes of providing any services other than storage or computer processing; and
  (3) a provider of remote computing service or electronic communication service to the public shall not knowingly divulge a record or other information pertaining to a subscriber to or customer of such service (not including the contents of communications covered by paragraph (1) or (2)) to any governmental entity.

(b) Exceptions for disclosure of communications.—A provider described in subsection (a) may divulge the contents of a communication—
  (1) to an addressee or intended recipient of such communication or an agent of such addressee or intended recipient;
  (2) as otherwise authorized in section 2517, 2511(2)(a), or 2703 of this title;

(3) with the lawful consent of the originator or an addressee or intended recipient of such communication, or the subscriber in the case of remote computing service;
(4) to a person employed or authorized or whose facilities are used to forward such communication to its destination;
(5) as may be necessarily incident to the rendition of the service or to the protection of the rights or property of the provider of that service;
(6) to the National Center for Missing and Exploited Children, in connection with a report submitted thereto under section 2258A;
(7) to a law enforcement agency—
  (A) f the contents—
    (i) were inadvertently obtained by the service provider; and
    (ii) appear to pertain to the commission of a crime; or
  [(B) Repealed. Pub.L. 108-21, Title V, § 508(b)(1)(A), Apr. 30, 2003, 117 Stat. 684]
  [(C) Repealed. Pub.L. 107-296, Title II, § 225(d)(1)(C), Nov. 25, 2002, 116 Stat. 2157]
(8) to a governmental entity, if the provider, in good faith, believes that an emergency involving danger of death or serious physical injury to any person requires disclosure without delay of communications relating to the emergency.

(c) Exceptions for disclosure of customer records.—A provider described in subsection (a) may divulge a record or other information pertaining to a subscriber to or customer of such service (not including the contents of communications covered by subsection (a)(1) or (a)(2))—
(1) as otherwise authorized in section 2703;
(2) with the lawful consent of the customer or subscriber;
(3) as may be necessarily incident to the rendition of the service or to the protection of the rights or property of the provider of that service;
(4) to a governmental entity, if the provider, in good faith, believes that an emergency involving danger of death or serious physical injury to any person requires disclosure without delay of information relating to the emergency;

(5) to the National Center for Missing and Exploited Children, in connection with a report submitted thereto under section 2258A; or

(6) to any person other than a governmental entity.

(d) Reporting of emergency disclosures.—On an annual basis, the Attorney General shall submit to the Committee on the Judiciary of the House of Representatives and the Committee on the Judiciary of the Senate a report containing—

(1) the number of accounts from which the Department of Justice has received voluntary disclosures under subsection (b)(8); and

(2) a summary of the basis for disclosure in those instances where—

(A) voluntary disclosures under subsection (b)(8) were made to the Department of Justice; and

(B) the investigation pertaining to those disclosures was closed without the filing of criminal charges.

§ 2703. Required disclosure of customer communications or records

(a) Contents of wire or electronic communications in electronic storage.—A governmental entity may require the disclosure by a provider of electronic communication service of the contents of a wire or electronic communication, that is in electronic storage in an electronic communications system for one hundred and eighty days or less, only pursuant to a warrant issued using the procedures described in the Federal Rules of Criminal Procedure (or, in the case of a State court, issued using State warrant procedures) by a court of competent jurisdiction. A governmental entity may require the disclosure by a provider of electronic communications services of the contents of a wire or electronic communication that has been in electronic storage in an electronic communications system for more than one hundred and eighty days by the means available under subsection (b) of this section.

(b) Contents of wire or electronic communications in a remote computing service.—

(1) A governmental entity may require a provider of remote computing service to disclose the contents of any wire or electronic communication to which this paragraph is made applicable by paragraph (2) of this subsection—

(A) without required notice to the subscriber or customer, if the governmental entity obtains a warrant issued using the procedures described in the Federal Rules of Criminal

Procedure (or, in the case of a State court, issued using State warrant procedures) by a court of competent jurisdiction; or

(B) with prior notice from the governmental entity to the subscriber or customer if the governmental entity—

(i) uses an administrative subpoena authorized by a Federal or State statute or a Federal or State grand jury or trial subpoena; or

(ii) obtains a court order for such disclosure under subsection (d) of this section;

except that delayed notice may be given pursuant to section 2705 of this title.

(2) Paragraph (1) is applicable with respect to any wire or electronic communication that is held or maintained on that service—

(A) on behalf of, and received by means of electronic transmission from (or created by means of computer processing of communications received by means of electronic transmission from), a subscriber or customer of such remote computing service; and

(B) solely for the purpose of providing storage or computer processing services to such subscriber or customer, if the provider is not authorized to access the contents of any such communications for purposes of providing any services other than storage or computer processing.

(c) Records concerning electronic communication service or remote computing service.—

(1) A governmental entity may require a provider of electronic communication service or remote computing service to disclose a record or other information pertaining to a subscriber to or customer of such service (not including the contents of communications) only when the governmental entity—

(A) obtains a warrant issued using the procedures described in the Federal Rules of Criminal Procedure (or, in the case of a State court, issued using State warrant procedures) by a court of competent jurisdiction;

(B) obtains a court order for such disclosure under subsection (d) of this section;

(C) has the consent of the subscriber or customer to such disclosure;

(D) submits a formal written request relevant to a law enforcement investigation concerning telemarketing fraud for the name, address, and place of business of a subscriber or customer of such provider, which subscriber or customer is engaged in telemarketing (as such term is defined in section 2325 of this title); or

(E) seeks information under paragraph (2).

(2) A provider of electronic communication service or remote computing service shall disclose to a governmental entity the—

(A) name;

(B) address;

(C) local and long distance telephone connection records, or records of session times and durations;

(D) length of service (including start date) and types of service utilized;

(E) telephone or instrument number or other subscriber number or identity, including any temporarily assigned network address; and

(F) means and source of payment for such service (including any credit card or bank account number),

of a subscriber to or customer of such service when the governmental entity uses an administrative subpoena authorized by a Federal or State statute or a Federal or State grand jury or trial subpoena or any means available under paragraph (1).

(3) A governmental entity receiving records or information under this subsection is not required to provide notice to a subscriber or customer.

(d) Requirements for court order.—A court order for disclosure under subsection (b) or (c) may be issued by any court that is a court of competent jurisdiction and shall issue only if the governmental entity offers specific and articulable facts showing that there are reasonable grounds to believe that the contents of a wire or electronic communication, or the records or other information sought, are relevant and material to an ongoing criminal investigation. In the case of a State governmental authority, such a court order shall not issue if prohibited by the law of such State. A court issuing an order pursuant to this section, on a motion made promptly by the service provider, may quash or modify such order, if the information or records requested are unusually voluminous in nature or compliance with such order otherwise would cause an undue burden on such provider.

(e) No cause of action against a provider disclosing information under this chapter.—No cause of action shall lie in any court against any provider of wire or electronic communication service, its officers, employees, agents, or other specified persons for providing information, facilities, or assistance in accordance with the terms of a court order, warrant, subpoena, statutory authorization, or certification under this chapter.

(f) Requirement to preserve evidence.—

(1) In general.—A provider of wire or electronic communication services or a remote computing service, upon the request of a governmental entity, shall take all necessary steps to preserve records and other evidence in its possession pending the issuance of a court order or other process.

(2) Period of retention.—Records referred to in paragraph (1) shall be retained for a period of 90 days, which shall be extended for an additional 90-day period upon a renewed request by the governmental entity.

(g) Presence of officer not required.—Notwithstanding section 3105 of this title, the presence of an officer shall not be required for service or execution of a search warrant issued in accordance with this chapter requiring disclosure by a provider of electronic communications service or remote computing service of the contents of communications or records or other information pertaining to a subscriber to or customer of such service.

§ 2704. Backup preservation

(a) Backup preservation.—

(1) A governmental entity acting under section 2703(b)(2) may include in its subpoena or court order a requirement that the service provider to whom the request is directed create a backup copy of the contents of the electronic communications sought in order to preserve those communications. Without notifying the subscriber or customer of such subpoena or court order, such service provider shall create such backup copy as soon as practicable consistent with its regular business practices and shall confirm to the governmental entity that such backup copy has been made. Such backup copy shall be created within two busi-

ness days after receipt by the service provider of the subpoena or court order.

(2) Notice to the subscriber or customer shall be made by the governmental entity within three days after receipt of such confirmation, unless such notice is delayed pursuant to section 2705(a).

(3) The service provider shall not destroy such backup copy until the later of—

(A) the delivery of the information; or

(B) the resolution of any proceedings (including appeals of any proceeding) concerning the government›s subpoena or court order.

(4) The service provider shall release such backup copy to the requesting governmental entity no sooner than fourteen days after the governmental entity›s notice to the subscriber or customer if such service provider—

(A) has not received notice from the subscriber or customer that the subscriber or customer has challenged the governmental entity›s request; and

(B) has not initiated proceedings to challenge the request of the governmental entity.

(5) A governmental entity may seek to require the creation of a backup copy under subsection (a)(1) of this section if in its sole discretion such entity determines that there is reason to believe that notification under section 2703 of this title of the existence of the subpoena or court order may result in destruction of or tampering with evidence. This determination is not subject to challenge by the subscriber or customer or service provider.

(b) Customer challenges.—

(1) Within fourteen days after notice by the governmental entity to the subscriber or customer under subsection (a)(2) of this section, such subscriber or customer may file a motion to quash such subpoena or vacate such court order, with copies served upon the governmental entity and with written notice of such challenge to the service provider. A motion to vacate a court order shall be filed in the court which issued such order. A motion to quash a subpoena shall be filed in the appropriate United States district court or State court. Such motion or application shall contain an affidavit or sworn statement—

(A) stating that the applicant is a customer or subscriber to the service from which the contents of electronic communications maintained for him have been sought; and
(B) stating the applicant›s reasons for believing that the records sought are not relevant to a legitimate law enforcement inquiry or that there has not been substantial compliance with the provisions of this chapter in some other respect.

(2) Service shall be made under this section upon a governmental entity by delivering or mailing by registered or certified mail a copy of the papers to the person, office, or department specified in the notice which the customer has received pursuant to this chapter. For the purposes of this section, the term "delivery" has the meaning given that term in the Federal Rules of Civil Procedure.

(3) If the court finds that the customer has complied with paragraphs (1) and (2) of this subsection, the court shall order the governmental entity to file a sworn response, which may be filed in camera if the governmental entity includes in its response the reasons which make in camera review appropriate. If the court is unable to determine the motion or application on the basis of the parties› initial allegations and response, the court may conduct such additional proceedings as it deems appropriate. All such proceedings shall be completed and the motion or application decided as soon as practicable after the filing of the governmental entity›s response.

(4) If the court finds that the applicant is not the subscriber or customer for whom the communications sought by the governmental entity are maintained, or that there is a reason to believe that the law enforcement inquiry is legitimate and that the communications sought are relevant to that inquiry, it shall deny the motion or application and order such process enforced. If the court finds that the applicant is the subscriber or customer for whom the communications sought by the governmental entity are maintained, and that there is not a reason to believe that the communications sought are relevant to a legitimate law enforcement inquiry, or that there has not been substantial compliance with the provisions of this chapter, it shall order the process quashed.

(5) A court order denying a motion or application under this section shall not be deemed a final order and no interlocutory appeal may be taken therefrom by the customer.

§ 2705. Delayed notice

(a) Delay of notification.—

(1) A governmental entity acting under section 2703(b) of this title may—

(A) where a court order is sought, include in the application a request, which the court shall grant, for an order delaying the notification required under section 2703(b) of this title for a period not to exceed ninety days, if the court determines that there is reason to believe that notification of the existence of the court order may have an adverse result described in paragraph (2) of this subsection; or

(B) where an administrative subpoena authorized by a Federal or State statute or a Federal or State grand jury subpoena is obtained, delay the notification required under section 2703(b) of this title for a period not to exceed ninety days upon the execution of a written certification of a supervisory official that there is reason to believe that notification of the existence of the subpoena may have an adverse result described in paragraph (2) of this subsection.

(2) An adverse result for the purposes of paragraph (1) of this subsection is—

(A) endangering the life or physical safety of an individual;

(B) flight from prosecution;

(C) destruction of or tampering with evidence;

(D) intimidation of potential witnesses; or

(E) otherwise seriously jeopardizing an investigation or unduly delaying a trial.

(3) The governmental entity shall maintain a true copy of certification under paragraph (1)(B).

(4) Extensions of the delay of notification provided in section 2703 of up to ninety days each may be granted by the court upon application, or by certification by a governmental entity, but only in accordance with subsection (b) of this section.

(5) Upon expiration of the period of delay of notification under paragraph (1) or (4) of this subsection, the governmental entity shall serve upon, or deliver by registered or first-class mail to,

the customer or subscriber a copy of the process or request together with notice that—

(A) states with reasonable specificity the nature of the law enforcement inquiry; and

(B) informs such customer or subscriber—

(i) that information maintained for such customer or subscriber by the service provider named in such process or request was supplied to or requested by that governmental authority and the date on which the supplying or request took place;

(ii) that notification of such customer or subscriber was delayed;

(iii) what governmental entity or court made the certification or determination pursuant to which that delay was made; and

(iv) which provision of this chapter allowed such delay.

(6) As used in this subsection, the term "supervisory official" means the investigative agent in charge or assistant investigative agent in charge or an equivalent of an investigating agency›s headquarters or regional office, or the chief prosecuting attorney or the first assistant prosecuting attorney or an equivalent of a prosecuting attorney›s headquarters or regional office.

(b) Preclusion of notice to subject of governmental access.—A governmental entity acting under section 2703, when it is not required to notify the subscriber or customer under section 2703(b)(1), or to the extent that it may delay such notice pursuant to subsection (a) of this section, may apply to a court for an order commanding a provider of electronic communications service or remote computing service to whom a warrant, subpoena, or court order is directed, for such period as the court deems appropriate, not to notify any other person of the existence of the warrant, subpoena, or court order. The court shall enter such an order if it determines that there is reason to believe that notification of the existence of the warrant, subpoena, or court order will result in—

(1) endangering the life or physical safety of an individual;

(2) flight from prosecution;

(3) destruction of or tampering with evidence;

(4) intimidation of potential witnesses; or

(5) otherwise seriously jeopardizing an investigation or unduly delaying a trial.

§ 2706. Cost reimbursement

(a) Payment.—Except as otherwise provided in subsection (c), a governmental entity obtaining the contents of communications, records, or other information under section 2702, 2703, or 2704 of this title shall pay to the person or entity assembling or providing such information a fee for reimbursement for such costs as are reasonably necessary and which have been directly incurred in searching for, assembling, reproducing, or otherwise providing such information. Such reimbursable costs shall include any costs due to necessary disruption of normal operations of any electronic communication service or remote computing service in which such information may be stored.

(b) Amount.—The amount of the fee provided by subsection (a) shall be as mutually agreed by the governmental entity and the person or entity providing the information, or, in the absence of agreement, shall be as determined by the court which issued the order for production of such information (or the court before which a criminal prosecution relating to such information would be brought, if no court order was issued for production of the information).

(c) Exception.—The requirement of subsection (a) of this section does not apply with respect to records or other information maintained by a communications common carrier that relate to telephone toll records and telephone listings obtained under section 2703 of this title. The court may, however, order a payment as described in subsection (a) if the court determines the information required is unusually voluminous in nature or otherwise caused an undue burden on the provider.

§ 2707. Civil action

(a) Cause of action.—Except as provided in section 2703(e), any provider of electronic communication service, subscriber, or other person aggrieved by any violation of this chapter in which the conduct constituting the violation is engaged in with a knowing or intentional state of mind may, in a civil action, recover from the person or entity, other than the United States, which engaged in that violation such relief as may be appropriate.

(b) Relief.—In a civil action under this section, appropriate relief includes—
   (1) such preliminary and other equitable or declaratory relief as may be appropriate;
   (2) damages under subsection (c); and
   (3) a reasonable attorney›s fee and other litigation costs reasonably incurred.

(c) Damages.—The court may assess as damages in a civil action under this section the sum of the actual damages suffered by the plaintiff and any profits made by the violator as a result of the violation, but in no case shall a person entitled to recover receive less than the sum of $1,000. If the violation is willful or intentional, the court may assess punitive damages. In the case of a successful action to enforce liability under this section, the court may assess the costs of the action, together with reasonable attorney fees determined by the court.

(d) Administrative discipline.—If a court or appropriate department or agency determines that the United States or any of its departments or agencies has violated any provision of this chapter, and the court or appropriate department or agency finds that the circumstances surrounding the violation raise serious questions about whether or not an officer or employee of the United States acted willfully or intentionally with respect to the violation, the department or agency shall, upon receipt of a true and correct copy of the decision and findings of the court or appropriate department or agency promptly initiate a proceeding to determine whether disciplinary action against the officer or employee is warranted. If the head of the department or agency involved determines that disciplinary action is not warranted, he or she shall notify the Inspector General with jurisdiction over the department or agency concerned and shall provide the Inspector General with the reasons for such determination.

(e) Defense.—A good faith reliance on—
   (1) a court warrant or order, a grand jury subpoena, a legislative authorization, or a statutory authorization (including a request of a governmental entity under section 2703(f) of this title);
   (2) a request of an investigative or law enforcement officer under section 2518(7) of this title; or
   (3) a good faith determination that section 2511(3) of this title permitted the conduct complained of;

is a complete defense to any civil or criminal action brought under this chapter or any other law.

(f) Limitation.—A civil action under this section may not be commenced later than two years after the date upon which the claimant first discovered or had a reasonable opportunity to discover the violation.

(g) Improper disclosure.—Any willful disclosure of a 'record', as that term is defined in section 552a(a) of title 5, United States Code, obtained by an investigative or law enforcement officer, or a governmental entity, pursuant to section 2703 of this title, or from a device installed pursuant to section 3123 or 3125 of this title, that is not a disclosure made in the proper performance of the official functions of the officer or governmental entity making the disclosure, is a violation of this chapter. This provision shall not apply to information previously lawfully disclosed (prior to the commencement of any civil or administrative proceeding under this chapter) to the public by a Federal, State, or local governmental entity or by the plaintiff in a civil action under this chapter.

§ 2708. Exclusivity of remedies

The remedies and sanctions described in this chapter are the only judicial remedies and sanctions for nonconstitutional violations of this chapter.

§ 2709. Counterintelligence access to telephone toll and transactional records

(a) Duty to provide.—A wire or electronic communication service provider shall comply with a request for subscriber information and toll billing records information, or electronic communication transactional records in its custody or possession made by the Director of the Federal Bureau of Investigation under subsection (b) of this section.

(b) Required certification.—The Director of the Federal Bureau of Investigation, or his designee in a position not lower than Deputy Assistant Director at Bureau headquarters or a Special Agent in Charge in a Bureau field office designated by the Director, may—

(1) request the name, address, length of service, and local and long distance toll billing records of a person or entity if the Director (or his designee) certifies in writing to the wire or electronic communication service provider to which the request is made that the name, address, length of service, and toll billing records

sought are relevant to an authorized investigation to protect against international terrorism or clandestine intelligence activities, provided that such an investigation of a United States person is not conducted solely on the basis of activities protected by the first amendment to the Constitution of the United States; and

(2) request the name, address, and length of service of a person or entity if the Director (or his designee) certifies in writing to the wire or electronic communication service provider to which the request is made that the information sought is relevant to an authorized investigation to protect against international terrorism or clandestine intelligence activities, provided that such an investigation of a United States person is not conducted solely upon the basis of activities protected by the first amendment to the Constitution of the United States.

(c) Prohibition of certain disclosure.—

(1) If the Director of the Federal Bureau of Investigation, or his designee in a position not lower than Deputy Assistant Director at Bureau headquarters or a Special Agent in Charge in a Bureau field office designated by the Director, certifies that otherwise there may result a danger to the national security of the United States, interference with a criminal, counterterrorism, or counterintelligence investigation, interference with diplomatic relations, or danger to the life or physical safety of any person, no wire or electronic communications service provider, or officer, employee, or agent thereof, shall disclose to any person (other than those to whom such disclosure is necessary to comply with the request or an attorney to obtain legal advice or legal assistance with respect to the request) that the Federal Bureau of Investigation has sought or obtained access to information or records under this section.

(2) The request shall notify the person or entity to whom the request is directed of the nondisclosure requirement under paragraph (1).

(3) Any recipient disclosing to those persons necessary to comply with the request or to an attorney to obtain legal advice or legal assistance with respect to the request shall inform such person of any applicable nondisclosure requirement. Any person who

receives a disclosure under this subsection shall be subject to the same prohibitions on disclosure under paragraph (1).

(4) At the request of the Director of the Federal Bureau of Investigation or the designee of the Director, any person making or intending to make a disclosure under this section shall identify to the Director or such designee the person to whom such disclosure will be made or to whom such disclosure was made prior to the request, except that nothing in this section shall require a person to inform the Director or such designee of the identity of an attorney to whom disclosure was made or will be made to obtain legal advice or legal assistance with respect to the request under subsection (a).

(d) Dissemination by bureau.—The Federal Bureau of Investigation may disseminate information and records obtained under this section only as provided in guidelines approved by the Attorney General for foreign intelligence collection and foreign counterintelligence investigations conducted by the Federal Bureau of Investigation, and, with respect to dissemination to an agency of the United States, only if such information is clearly relevant to the authorized responsibilities of such agency.

(e) Requirement that certain congressional bodies be informed.—On a semiannual basis the Director of the Federal Bureau of Investigation shall fully inform the Permanent Select Committee on Intelligence of the House of Representatives and the Select Committee on Intelligence of the Senate, and the Committee on the Judiciary of the House of Representatives and the Committee on the Judiciary of the Senate, concerning all requests made under subsection (b) of this section.

(f) Libraries.—A library (as that term is defined in section 213(1) of the Library Services and Technology Act (20 U.S.C. 9122(1)), the services of which include access to the Internet, books, journals, magazines, newspapers, or other similar forms of communication in print or digitally by patrons for their use, review, examination, or circulation, is not a wire or electronic communication service provider for purposes of this section, unless the library is providing the services defined in section 2510(15)("electronic communication service") of this title.

§ 2710. Wrongful disclosure of video tape rental or sale records

(a) Definitions.—For purposes of this section—

(1) the term "consumer" means any renter, purchaser, or subscriber of goods or services from a video tape service provider;

(2) the term "ordinary course of business" means only debt collection activities, order fulfillment, request processing, and the transfer of ownership;

(3) the term "personally identifiable information" includes information which identifies a person as having requested or obtained specific video materials or services from a video tape service provider; and

(4) the term "video tape service provider" means any person, engaged in the business, in or affecting interstate or foreign commerce, of rental, sale, or delivery of prerecorded video cassette tapes or similar audio visual materials, or any person or other entity to whom a disclosure is made under subparagraph (D) or (E) of subsection (b)(2), but only with respect to the information contained in the disclosure.

(b) Video tape rental and sale records.—

(1) A video tape service provider who knowingly discloses, to any person, personally identifiable information concerning any consumer of such provider shall be liable to the aggrieved person for the relief provided in subsection (d).

(2) A video tape service provider may disclose personally identifiable information concerning any consumer—

(A) to the consumer;

(B) to any person with the informed, written consent (including through an electronic means using the Internet) of the consumer that—

(i) is in a form distinct and separate from any form setting forth other legal or financial obligations of the consumer;

(ii) at the election of the consumer—

(I) is given at the time the disclosure is sought; or

(II) is given in advance for a set period of time, not to exceed 2 years or until consent is withdrawn by the consumer, whichever is sooner; and

(iii) the video tape service provider has provided an opportunity, in a clear and conspicuous manner, for the consumer to withdraw on a case-by-case basis or to withdraw from ongoing disclosures, at the consumer's election;

(C) to a law enforcement agency pursuant to a warrant issued under the Federal Rules of Criminal Procedure, an equivalent State warrant, a grand jury subpoena, or a court order;

(D) to any person if the disclosure is solely of the names and addresses of consumers and if—

(i) the video tape service provider has provided the consumer with the opportunity, in a clear and conspicuous manner, to prohibit such disclosure; and

(ii) the disclosure does not identify the title, description, or subject matter of any video tapes or other audio visual material; however, the subject matter of such materials may be disclosed if the disclosure is for the exclusive use of marketing goods and services directly to the consumer;

(E) to any person if the disclosure is incident to the ordinary course of business of the video tape service provider; or

(F) pursuant to a court order, in a civil proceeding upon a showing of compelling need for the information that cannot be accommodated by any other means, if—

(i) the consumer is given reasonable notice, by the person seeking the disclosure, of the court proceeding relevant to the issuance of the court order; and

(ii) the consumer is afforded the opportunity to appear and contest the claim of the person seeking the disclosure.

If an order is granted pursuant to subparagraph (C) or (F), the court shall impose appropriate safeguards against unauthorized disclosure.

(3) Court orders authorizing disclosure under subparagraph (C) shall issue only with prior notice to the consumer and only if the law enforcement agency shows that there is probable cause to believe that the records or other information sought are relevant to a legitimate law enforcement inquiry. In the case of a State government authority, such a court order shall not issue if prohibited by the law of such State. A court issuing an order pursuant to this section, on a motion made promptly by the video tape service provider, may quash or modify such order if the infor-

mation or records requested are unreasonably voluminous in nature or if compliance with such order otherwise would cause an unreasonable burden on such provider.

(c) Civil action.—
  (1) Any person aggrieved by any act of a person in violation of this section may bring a civil action in a United States district court.
  (2) The court may award—
    (A) actual damages but not less than liquidated damages in an amount of $2,500;
    (B) punitive damages;
    (C) reasonable attorneys› fees and other litigation costs reasonably incurred; and
    (D) such other preliminary and equitable relief as the court determines to be appropriate.
  (3) No action may be brought under this subsection unless such action is begun within 2 years from the date of the act complained of or the date of discovery.
  (4) No liability shall result from lawful disclosure permitted by this section.

(d) Personally identifiable information.—Personally identifiable information obtained in any manner other than as provided in this section shall not be received in evidence in any trial, hearing, arbitration, or other proceeding in or before any court, grand jury, department, officer, agency, regulatory body, legislative committee, or other authority of the United States, a State, or a political subdivision of a State.

(e) Destruction of old records.—A person subject to this section shall destroy personally identifiable information as soon as practicable, but no later than one year from the date the information is no longer necessary for the purpose for which it was collected and there are no pending requests or orders for access to such information under subsection (b)(2) or (c)(2) or pursuant to a court order.

(f) Preemption.—The provisions of this section preempt only the provisions of State or local law that require disclosure prohibited by this section.

§ 2711. Definitions for chapter

As used in this chapter—

  (1) the terms defined in section 2510 of this title have, respectively, the definitions given such terms in that section;

(2) the term "remote computing service" means the provision to the public of computer storage or processing services by means of an electronic communications system;

(3) the term "court of competent jurisdiction" includes—

(A) any district court of the United States (including a magistrate judge of such a court) or any United States court of appeals that—

(i) has jurisdiction over the offense being investigated;

(ii) is in or for a district in which the provider of a wire or electronic communication service is located or in which the wire or electronic communications, records, or other information are stored; or

(iii) is acting on a request for foreign assistance pursuant to section 3512 of this title; or

(B) a court of general criminal jurisdiction of a State authorized by the law of that State to issue search warrants; and

(4) the term "governmental entity" means a department or agency of the United States or any State or political subdivision thereof.

§ 2712. Civil actions against the United States

(a) In general.—Any person who is aggrieved by any willful violation of this chapter or of chapter 119 of this title or of sections 106(a), 305(a), or 405(a) of the Foreign Intelligence Surveillance Act of 1978 (50 U.S.C. 1801 et seq.) may commence an action in United States District Court against the United States to recover money damages. In any such action, if a person who is aggrieved successfully establishes such a violation of this chapter or of chapter 119 of this title or of the above specific provisions of title 50, the Court may assess as damages—

(1) actual damages, but not less than $10,000, whichever amount is greater; and

(2) litigation costs, reasonably incurred.

(b) Procedures.—

(1) Any action against the United States under this section may be commenced only after a claim is presented to the appropriate department or agency under the procedures of the Federal Tort Claims Act, as set forth in title 28, United States Code.

(2) Any action against the United States under this section shall be forever barred unless it is presented in writing to the appropriate Federal agency within 2 years after such claim accrues or unless

action is begun within 6 months after the date of mailing, by certified or registered mail, of notice of final denial of the claim by the agency to which it was presented. The claim shall accrue on the date upon which the claimant first has a reasonable opportunity to discover the violation.

(3) Any action under this section shall be tried to the court without a jury.

(4) Notwithstanding any other provision of law, the procedures set forth in section 106(f), 305(g), or 405(f) of the Foreign Intelligence Surveillance Act of 1978 (50 U.S.C. 1801 et seq.) shall be the exclusive means by which materials governed by those sections may be reviewed.

(5) An amount equal to any award against the United States under this section shall be reimbursed by the department or agency concerned to the fund described in section 1304 of title 31, United States Code, out of any appropriation, fund, or other account (excluding any part of such appropriation, fund, or account that is available for the enforcement of any Federal law) that is available for the operating expenses of the department or agency concerned.

(c) Administrative discipline.—If a court or appropriate department or agency determines that the United States or any of its departments or agencies has violated any provision of this chapter, and the court or appropriate department or agency finds that the circumstances surrounding the violation raise serious questions about whether or not an officer or employee of the United States acted willfully or intentionally with respect to the violation, the department or agency shall, upon receipt of a true and correct copy of the decision and findings of the court or appropriate department or agency promptly initiate a proceeding to determine whether disciplinary action against the officer or employee is warranted. If the head of the department or agency involved determines that disciplinary action is not warranted, he or she shall notify the Inspector General with jurisdiction over the department or agency concerned and shall provide the Inspector General with the reasons for such determination.

(d) Exclusive remedy.—Any action against the United States under this subsection shall be the exclusive remedy against the United States for any claims within the purview of this section.

(e) Stay of proceedings.—

(1) Upon the motion of the United States, the court shall stay any action commenced under this section if the court determines that civil discovery will adversely affect the ability of the Government to conduct a related investigation or the prosecution of a related criminal case. Such a stay shall toll the limitations periods of paragraph (2) of subsection (b).

(2) In this subsection, the terms "related criminal case" and "related investigation" mean an actual prosecution or investigation in progress at the time at which the request for the stay or any subsequent motion to lift the stay is made. In determining whether an investigation or a criminal case is related to an action commenced under this section, the court shall consider the degree of similarity between the parties, witnesses, facts, and circumstances involved in the 2 proceedings, without requiring that any one or more factors be identical.

(3) In requesting a stay under paragraph (1), the Government may, in appropriate cases, submit evidence ex parte in order to avoid disclosing any matter that may adversely affect a related investigation or a related criminal case. If the Government makes such an ex parte submission, the plaintiff shall be given an opportunity to make a submission to the court, not ex parte, and the court may, in its discretion, request further information from either party.

Appendix B

State Wiretapping and Electronic Surveillance Statutes (G.S. 15A-286 through -298)

§ 15A-286. Definitions

As used in this Article, unless the context requires otherwise:

(1) "Aggrieved person" means a person who was a party to any intercepted wire, oral, or electronic communication or a person against whom the interception was directed.

(2) "Attorney General" means the Attorney General of the State of North Carolina, unless otherwise specified.

(3) "Aural transfer" means a transfer containing the human voice at any point between and including the point of origin and the point of reception.

(4) "Chapter 119 of the United States Code" means Chapter 119 of Part I of Title 18, United States Code, being Public Law 90-351, the Omnibus Crime Control and Safe Streets Act of 1968, as amended by the Electronic Communications Privacy Act of 1986.

(5) "Communications common carrier" shall have the same meaning which is given the term "common carrier" by section 153(h) of Title 47 of the United States Code.

(6) "Contents" when used with respect to any wire, oral, or electronic communication means and includes any information concerning the substance, purport, or meaning of that communication.

(7) "Electronic, mechanical, or other device" means any device or apparatus which can be used to intercept a wire, oral, or electronic communication other than:

a. Any telephone or telegraph instrument, equipment, or facility, or any component thereof:

1. Furnished to the subscriber or user by a provider of wire or electronic communication service in the ordinary

course of its business and being used by the subscriber or user in the ordinary course of its business or furnished by the subscriber or user for connection to the facilities of such service and used in the ordinary course of its business; or

2. Being used by a provider of wire or electronic communication service in the ordinary course of its business or by an investigative or law enforcement officer in the ordinary course of the officer's duties.

b. A hearing aid or similar device being used to correct subnormal hearing to not better than normal.

(8) "Electronic communication" means any transfer of signs, signals, writing, images, sounds, data, or intelligence of any nature transmitted in whole or in part by a wire, radio, electromagnetic, photoelectronic, or photooptical system that affects interstate or foreign commerce but does not include:

a. Any wire or oral communication;

b. Any communication made through a tone-only paging device; or

c. Any communication from a tracking device (as defined in section 3117 of Title 18 of the United States Code).

(9) "Electronic communication service" means any service which provides to users thereof the ability to send or receive wire or electronic communications.

(10) "Electronic communication system" means any wire, radio, electronic, magnetic, photooptical, or photoelectronic facilities for the transmission of electronic communications, and any computer facilities or related electronic equipment for the storage of such communications.

(11) "Electronic surveillance" means the interception of wire, oral, or electronic communications as provided by this Article.

(12) "Electronic storage" means:

a. Any temporary, intermediate storage of a wire or electronic communication incidental to the electronic transmission thereof; and

b. Any storage of such communication by an electronic communication service for the purposes of backup protection of the communication.

(13) "Intercept" means the aural or other acquisition of the contents of any wire, oral, or electronic communication through the use of any electronic, mechanical, or other device.

(14) "Investigative or law enforcement officer" means any officer of the State of North Carolina or any political subdivision thereof, who is empowered by the laws of this State to conduct investigations of or to make arrests for offenses enumerated in G.S. 15A-290, and any attorney authorized by the laws of this State to prosecute or participate in the prosecution of those offenses, including the Attorney General of North Carolina.

(15) "Judge" means any judge of the trial divisions of the General Court of Justice.

(16) "Judicial review panel" means a three-judge body, composed of such judges as may be assigned by the Chief Justice of the Supreme Court of North Carolina, which shall review applications for electronic surveillance orders and may issue orders valid throughout the State authorizing such surveillance as provided by this Article, and which shall submit a report of its decision to the Chief Justice.

(17) "Oral communication" means any oral communication uttered by a person exhibiting an expectation that such communication is not subject to interception under circumstances justifying such expectation, but the term does not include any electronic communication.

(18) "Person" means any employee or agent of the United States or any state or any political subdivision thereof, and any individual, partnership, association, joint stock company, trust, or corporation.

(19) "Readily accessible to the general public" means, with respect to a radio communication, that the communication is not:

a. Scrambled or encrypted;
b. Transmitted using modulation techniques whose essential parameters have been withheld from the public with the intention of preserving the privacy of the communication;
c. Carried on a subcarrier or other signal subsidiary to a radio transmission;
d. Transmitted over a communications system provided by a common carrier, unless the communication is a tone-only paging system communication; or

e. Transmitted on frequencies allocated under Part 25, Subpart D, E, or F or Part 94 of the Rules of the Federal Communications Commission as provided by 18 U.S.C. § 2510(16)(E).

(20) "User" means any person or entity who:

a. Uses an electronic communications service; and

b. Is duly authorized by the provider of the service to engage in the use.

(21) "Wire communication" means any aural transfer made in whole or in part through the use of facilities for the transmission of communications by the aid of wire, cable, or other like connection between the point of origin and the point of reception (including the use of such connection in a switching station) furnished or operated by any person engaged in providing or operating such facilities for the transmission of interstate or foreign communications or communications affecting interstate or foreign commerce and the term includes any electronic storage of such communication.

§ 15A-287. Interception and disclosure of wire, oral, or electronic communications prohibited

(a) Except as otherwise specifically provided in this Article, a person is guilty of a Class H felony if, without the consent of at least one party to the communication, the person:

(1) Willfully intercepts, endeavors to intercept, or procures any other person to intercept or endeavor to intercept, any wire, oral, or electronic communication.

(2) Willfully uses, endeavors to use, or procures any other person to use or endeavor to use any electronic, mechanical, or other device to intercept any oral communication when:

a. The device is affixed to, or otherwise transmits a signal through, a wire, cable, or other like connection used in wire communications; or

b. The device transmits communications by radio, or interferes with the transmission of such communications.

(3) Willfully discloses, or endeavors to disclose, to any other person the contents of any wire, oral, or electronic communication, knowing or having reason to know that the information was obtained through violation of this Article; or

(4) Willfully uses, or endeavors to use, the contents of any wire or oral communication, knowing or having reason to know that the

information was obtained through the interception of a wire or oral communication in violation of this Article.

(b) It is not unlawful under this Article for any person to:

(1) Intercept or access an electronic communication made through an electronic communication system that is configured so that the electronic communication is readily accessible to the general public;

(2) Intercept any radio communication which is transmitted:

a. For use by the general public, or that relates to ships, aircraft, vehicles, or persons in distress;

b. By any governmental, law enforcement, civil defense, private land mobile, or public safety communication system, including police and fire, readily available to the general public;

c. By a station operating on any authorized band within the bands allocated to the amateur, citizens band, or general mobile radio services; or

d. By any marine or aeronautical communication system; or

(3) Intercept any communication in a manner otherwise allowed by Chapter 119 of the United States Code.

(c) It is not unlawful under this Article for an operator of a switchboard, or an officer, employee, or agent of a provider of electronic communication service, whose facilities are used in the transmission of a wire or electronic communication, to intercept, disclose, or use that communication in the normal course of employment while engaged in any activity that is a necessary incident to the rendition of his or her service or to the protection of the rights or property of the provider of that service, provided that a provider of wire or electronic communication service may not utilize service observing or random monitoring except for mechanical or service quality control checks.

(d) It is not unlawful under this Article for an officer, employee, or agent of the Federal Communications Commission, in the normal course of his employment and in discharge of the monitoring responsibilities exercised by the Commission in the enforcement of Chapter 5 of Title 47 of the United States Code, to intercept a wire or electronic communication, or oral communication transmitted by radio, or to disclose or use the information thereby obtained.

(e) Any person who, as a result of the person's official position or employment, has obtained knowledge of the contents of any wire, oral, or electronic communication lawfully intercepted pursuant to an electronic surveillance order or of the pendency or existence of or implementation of an electronic surveillance order who shall knowingly and willfully disclose such information for the purpose of hindering or thwarting any investigation or prosecution relating to the subject matter of the electronic surveillance order, except as is necessary for the proper and lawful performance of the duties of his position or employment or as shall be required or allowed by law, shall be guilty of a Class G felony.

(f) Any person who shall, knowingly or with gross negligence, divulge the existence of or contents of any electronic surveillance order in a way likely to hinder or thwart any investigation or prosecution relating to the subject matter of the electronic surveillance order or anyone who shall, knowingly or with gross negligence, release the contents of any wire, oral, or electronic communication intercepted under an electronic surveillance order, except as is necessary for the proper and lawful performance of the duties of his position or employment or as is required or allowed by law, shall be guilty of a Class 1 misdemeanor.

(g) Any public officer who shall violate subsection (a) or (d) of this section or who shall knowingly violate subsection (e) of this section shall be removed from any public office he may hold and shall thereafter be ineligible to hold any public office, whether elective or appointed.

§ 15A-288. Manufacture, distribution, possession, and advertising of wire, oral, or electronic communication intercepting devices prohibited

(a) Except as otherwise specifically provided in this Article, a person is guilty of a Class H felony if the person:

  (1) Manufactures, assembles, possesses, purchases, or sells any electronic, mechanical, or other device, knowing or having reason to know that the design of the device renders it primarily useful for the purpose of the surreptitious interception of wire, oral, or electronic communications; or

  (2) Places in any newspaper, magazine, handbill, or other publication, any advertisement of:

    a. Any electronic, mechanical, or other device knowing or having reason to know that the design of the device renders it primarily useful for the purpose of the surreptitious interception of wire, oral, or electronic communications; or

b. Any other electronic, mechanical, or other device where the advertisement promotes the use of the device for the purpose of the surreptitious interception of wire, oral, or electronic communications.

(b) It is not unlawful under this section for the following persons to manufacture, assemble, possess, purchase, or sell any electronic, mechanical, or other device, knowing or having reason to know that the design of the device renders it primarily useful for the purpose of the surreptitious interception of wire, oral, or electronic communications:

(1) A communications common carrier or an officer, agent, or employee of, or a person under contract with, a communications common carrier, acting in the normal course of the communications common carrier's business, or

(2) An officer, agent, or employee of, or a person under contract with, the State, acting in the course of the activities of the State, and with the written authorization of the Attorney General.

(c) An officer, agent, or employee of, or a person whose normal and customary business is to design, manufacture, assemble, advertise and sell electronic, mechanical and other devices primarily useful for the purpose of the surreptitious interceptions of wire, oral, or electronic communications, exclusively for and restricted to State and federal investigative or law enforcement agencies and departments.

§ 15A-289. Confiscation of wire, oral, or electronic communication interception devices

Any electronic, mechanical, or other device used, sent, carried, manufactured, assembled, possessed, sold, or advertised in violation of G.S. 15A-288 may be seized and forfeited to this State.

§ 15A-290. Offenses for which orders for electronic surveillance may be granted

(a) Orders authorizing or approving the interception of wire, oral, or electronic communications may be granted, subject to the provisions of this Article and Chapter 119 of the United States Code, when the interception:

(1) May provide or has provided evidence of the commission of, or any conspiracy to commit:

a. Any of the drug-trafficking violations listed in G.S. 90-95(h); or

b. A continuing criminal enterprise in violation of G.S. 90-95.1.

(2) May expedite the apprehension of persons indicted for the commission of, or any conspiracy to commit, an offense listed in subdivision (1) of this subsection.

(b) Orders authorizing or approving the interception of wire, oral, or electronic communications may be granted, subject to the provisions of this Article and Chapter 119 of the United States Code, when the interception may provide, or has provided, evidence of any offense that involves the commission of, or any conspiracy to commit, murder, kidnapping, hostage taking, robbery, extortion, bribery, rape, or any sexual offense, or when the interception may expedite the apprehension of persons indicted for the commission of these offenses.

(c) Orders authorizing or approving the interception of wire, oral, or electronic communications may be granted, subject to the provisions of this Article and Chapter 119 of the United States Code, when the interception may provide, or has provided, evidence of any of the following offenses, or any conspiracy to commit these offenses, or when the interception may expedite the apprehension of persons indicted for the commission of these offenses:

(1) Any felony offense against a minor, including any violation of G.S. 14-27.7 (Intercourse and sexual offenses with certain victims; consent no defense), G.S. 14-41 (Abduction of children), G.S. 14-43.11 (Human trafficking), G.S. 14-43.12(Involuntary servitude), G.S. 14-43.13 (Sexual servitude), G.S. 14-190.16 (First degree sexual exploitation of a minor), G.S. 14-190.17 (Second degree sexual exploitation of a minor), G.S. 14-202.1 (Taking indecent liberties with children), G.S. 14-205.2(c) or (d) (Patronizing a prostitute who is a minor or a mentally disabled person), or G.S. 14-205.3(b) (Promoting prostitution of a minor or a mentally disabled person).

(2) Any felony obstruction of a criminal investigation, including any violation of G.S. 14-221.1 (Altering, destroying, or stealing evidence of criminal conduct).

(3) Any felony offense involving interference with, or harassment or intimidation of, jurors or witnesses, including any violation of G.S. 14-225.2 or G.S. 14-226.

(4) Any felony offense involving assault or threats against any executive or legislative officer in violation of Article 5A of Chapter 14 of the General Statutes or assault with a firearm or other deadly weapon upon governmental officers or employees in violation of G.S. 14-34.2.

(5) Any offense involving the manufacture, assembly, possession, storage, transportation, sale, purchase, delivery, or acquisition of weapons of mass death or destruction in violation of G.S. 14-288.8 or the adulteration or misbranding of food, drugs, cosmetics, etc., with the intent to cause serious injury in violation of G.S. 14-34.4.

(d) When an investigative or law enforcement officer, while engaged in intercepting wire, oral, or electronic communications in the manner authorized, intercepts wire, electronic, or oral communications relating to offenses other than those specified in the order of authorization or approval, the contents thereof, and evidence derived therefrom, may be disclosed or used as provided in G.S. 15A-294(a) and (b). Such contents and any evidence derived therefrom may be used in accordance with G.S. 15A-294(c) when authorized or approved by a judicial review panel where the panel finds, on subsequent application made as soon as practicable, that the contents were otherwise intercepted in accordance with this Article or Chapter 119 of the United States Code.

(e) No otherwise privileged wire, oral, or electronic communication intercepted in accordance with, or in violation of, the provisions of this Article or Chapter 119 of the United States Code, shall lose its privileged character.

§ 15A-291. Application for electronic surveillance order; judicial review panel

(a) The Attorney General or the Attorney General's designee may, pursuant to the provisions of section 2516(2) of Chapter 119 of the United States Code, apply to a judicial review panel for an order authorizing or approving the interception of wire, oral, or electronic communications by investigative or law enforcement officers having responsibility for the investigation of the offenses as to which the application is made, and for such offenses and causes as are enumerated in G.S. 15A-290. A judicial review panel shall be composed of such judges as may be assigned by the Chief Justice of the Supreme Court of North Carolina or an Associate Justice acting as the Chief

Justice's designee, which shall review applications for electronic surveillance orders and may issue orders valid throughout the State authorizing such surveillance as provided by this Article, and which shall submit a report of its decision to the Chief Justice. A judicial review panel may be appointed by the Chief Justice or an Associate Justice acting as the Chief Justice's designee upon the notification of the Attorney General's Office of the intent to apply for an electronic surveillance order.

(b) A judicial review panel is hereby authorized to grant orders valid throughout the State for the interception of wire, oral, or electronic communications. Applications for such orders may be made by the Attorney General or the Attorney General's designee. The Attorney General or the Attorney General's designee in applying for such orders, and a judicial review panel in granting such orders, shall comply with all procedural requirements of section 2518 of Chapter 119 of the United States Code. The Attorney General or the Attorney General's designee may make emergency applications as provided by section 2518 of Chapter 119 of the United States Code. In applying section 2518 the word "judge" in that section shall be construed to refer to the judicial review panel, unless the context otherwise indicates. The judicial review panel may stipulate any special conditions it feels necessary to assure compliance with the terms of this act.

(c) No judge who sits as a member of a judicial review panel shall preside at any trial or proceeding resulting from or in any manner related to information gained pursuant to a lawful electronic surveillance order issued by that panel.

(d) Each application for an order authorizing or approving the interception of a wire, oral, or electronic communication must be made in writing upon oath or affirmation to the judicial review panel. Each application must include the following information:

- (1) The identity of the office requesting the application;
- (2) A full and complete statement of the facts and circumstances relied upon by the applicant, to justify his belief that an order should be issued, including:
  - a. Details as to the particular offense that has been, or is being committed;

b. Except as provided in G.S. 15A-294(i), a particular description of the nature and location of the facilities from which or the place where the communication is to be intercepted;
c. A particular description of the type of communications sought to be intercepted; and
d. The identity of the person, if known, committing the offense and whose communications are to be intercepted;

(3) A full and complete statement as to whether or not other investigative procedures have been tried and failed or why they reasonably appear to be unlikely to succeed if tried or to be too dangerous;

(4) A statement of the period of time for which the interception is required to be maintained. If the nature of the investigation is such that the authorization for interception should not automatically terminate when the described type of communication has been obtained, a particular description of facts establishing probable cause to believe that additional communications of the same type will occur thereafter must be added;

(5) A full and complete statement of the facts concerning all previous applications known to the individual authorizing and making adjudication, made to a judicial review panel for authorization to intercept, or for approval of interceptions of wire, oral, or electronic communications involving any of the same persons, facilities, or places specified in the application, and the action taken by that judicial review panel on each such application; and

(6) Where the application is for the extension of an order, a statement setting forth the results thus far obtained from the interception, or a reasonable explanation of the failure to obtain such results.

(e) Before acting on the application, the judicial review panel may examine on oath the person requesting the application or any other person who may possess pertinent information, but information other than that contained in the affidavit may not be considered by the panel in determining whether probable cause exists for the issuance of the order unless the information is either recorded or contemporaneously summarized in the record or on the face of the order by the panel.

§ 15A-292. Request for application for electronic surveillance order

(a) The head of any municipal, county, or State law enforcement agency or any district attorney may submit a written request to the Attorney General that the Attorney General apply to a judicial review panel for an electronic surveillance order to be executed within the requesting agency's jurisdiction. The written requests shall be on a form approved by the Attorney General and shall provide sufficient information to form the basis for an application for an electronic surveillance order. The head of a law enforcement agency shall also submit a copy of the request to the district attorney, who shall review the request and forward it to the Attorney General along with any comments he may wish to include. The Attorney General is authorized to review the request and decide whether it is appropriate to submit an application to a judicial review panel for an electronic surveillance order. If a request for an application is deemed inappropriate, the Attorney General shall send a signed, written statement to the person submitting the request, and to the district attorney, summarizing the reasons for failing to make an application. If the Attorney General decides to submit an application to a judicial review panel, he shall so notify the requesting agency head, the district attorney, and the head of the local law enforcement agency which has the primary responsibility for enforcing the criminal laws in the location in which it is anticipated the majority of the surveillance will take place, if not the same as the requesting agency head, unless the Attorney General has probable cause to believe that the latter notifications should substantially jeopardize the success of the surveillance or the investigation in general. If a judicial review panel grants an electronic surveillance order, a copy of such order shall be sent to the requesting agency head and the district attorney, and a summary of the order shall be sent to the head of the local law enforcement agency with primary responsibility for enforcing the criminal laws in the jurisdiction where the majority of the surveillance will take place, if not the same as the requesting agency head, unless the judicial review panel finds probable cause to believe that the latter notifications would substantially jeopardize the success of the surveillance or the investigation.

(b) This Article does not limit the authority of the Attorney General to apply for electronic surveillance orders independent of, or contrary to, the requests of law enforcement agency heads, nor does it limit the discretion of the Attorney General in determining whether an application is appropriate under any given circumstances.

(c) The Chief Justice of the North Carolina Supreme Court shall receive a report concerning each decision of a judicial review panel.

§ 15A-293. Issuance of order for electronic surveillance; procedures for implementation

(a) Upon application by the Attorney General pursuant to the procedures in G.S. 15A-291, a judicial review panel may enter an ex parte order, as requested or as modified, authorizing the interception of wire, oral, or electronic communications, if the panel determines on the basis of the facts submitted by the applicant that:
  (1) There is probable cause for belief that an individual is committing, has committed, or is about to commit an offense set out in G.S. 15A-290;
  (2) There is probable cause for belief that particular communications concerning that offense will be obtained through such interception;
  (3) Normal investigative procedures have been tried and have failed or reasonably appear to be unlikely to succeed if tried or to be too dangerous; and
  (4) Except as provided in G.S. 15A-294(i), there is probable cause for belief that the facilities from which, or the place where, the wire, oral, or electronic communications are to be intercepted are being used, or are about to be used, in connection with the commission of such offense, or are leased to, listed in the name of, or commonly used by the individual described in subdivision (1) of this subsection.

(b) Each order authorizing the interception of any wire, oral, or electronic communications must specify:
  (1) The identity of the person, if known, whose communications are to be intercepted;
  (2) The nature and location of the communications facilities as to which, or the place where, authority to intercept is granted, and the means by which such interceptions may be made;
  (3) A particular description of the type of communication sought to be intercepted and a statement of the particular offense to which it relates;

(4) The identity of the agency authorized to intercept the communications and of the person requesting the application; and
(5) The period of time during which such interception is authorized, including a statement as to whether or not the interception automatically terminates when the described communication has been first obtained.

(c) No order entered under this Article may authorize the interception of any wire, oral, or electronic communication for any period longer than is necessary to achieve the objective of the authorization, nor in any event longer than 30 days. Such 30-day period begins on the earlier of the day on which the investigative or law enforcement officer first begins to conduct an interception under the order or 10 days after the order is entered. Extensions of an order may be granted, but only upon application for an extension made in accordance with G.S. 15A-291 and the panel making the findings required by subsection (a) of this section. The period of extension shall be no longer than the panel determines to be necessary to achieve the purpose for which it was granted and in no event for longer than 30 days. Every order and extension thereof must contain a provision that the authorization to intercept be executed as soon as practicable, be conducted in such a way as to minimize the interception of communications not otherwise subject to interception under this Article, and terminate upon attainment of the authorized objective, or in any event in 30 days, as is appropriate. In the event the intercepted communication is in a code or foreign language, and an expert in that foreign language or code is not reasonably available during the interception period, minimization may be accomplished as soon as practicable after the interception. An interception under this Article may be conducted in whole or in part by State or federal government personnel, or by an individual operating under a contract with the State or federal government, acting under the supervision of an investigative or law enforcement officer authorized to conduct the interception.

(d) Whenever an order authorizing interception is entered pursuant to this Article, the order may require reports to be made to the issuing judicial review panel showing that progress has been made toward achievement of the authorized objective and the need for continued interception. Such reports must be made at such intervals as the panel may require.

(1) The contents of any wire, oral, or electronic communication intercepted by any means authorized by this Article must be recorded on tape, wire, or electronic or other comparable device. The recording of the contents of any wire, electronic, or oral communication under this subsection must be done in such way as will protect the recording from editing or other alterations. Immediately upon the expiration of the period of the order, or extensions thereof, the recordings must be made available to the judicial review panel and sealed under its direction. Custody of the recordings is wherever the panel orders. They may not be destroyed except upon an order of the issuing panel and in any event must be kept for 10 years. Duplicate recordings may be made for use or disclosure pursuant to the provisions of G.S. 15A-294(a) and (b) for investigations. The contents of any wire, oral, or electronic communication or evidence derived therefrom may not be disclosed or used under G.S. 15A-294(c) unless they have been kept sealed.

(2) Applications made and orders granted under this Article must be sealed by the panel. Custody of the applications and orders may be disclosed only upon a showing of good cause before the issuing panel and may not be destroyed except on its order and in any event must be kept for 10 years.

(3) Any violation of the provisions of this subsection may be punished as for contempt.

(e) The State Bureau of Investigation shall own or control and may operate any equipment used to implement electronic surveillance orders issued by a judicial review panel and may operate or use, in implementing any electronic surveillance order, electronic surveillance equipment in which a local government or any of its agencies has a property interest.

(f) The Attorney General shall establish procedures for the use of electronic surveillance equipment in assisting local law enforcement agencies implementing electronic surveillance orders. The Attorney General shall supervise such assistance given to local law enforcement agencies and is authorized to conduct statewide training sessions for investigative and law enforcement officers regarding this Article.

§ 15A-294. Authorization for disclosure and use of intercepted wire, oral, or electronic communications

(a) Any investigative or law enforcement officer who, by any means authorized by this Article or Chapter 119 of the United States Code, has obtained knowledge of the contents of any wire, oral, or electronic communication, or evidence derived therefrom, may disclose such contents to another investigative or law enforcement officer to the extent that such disclosure is appropriate to the proper performance of the official duties of the officer making or receiving the disclosure.

(b) Any investigative or law enforcement officer, who by any means authorized by this Article or Chapter 119 of the United States Code, has obtained knowledge of the contents of any wire, oral, or electronic communication, or evidence derived therefrom, may use such contents to the extent such use is appropriate to the proper performance of the officers' official duties.

(c) Any person who has received, by any means authorized by this Article or Chapter 119 of the United States Code, any information concerning a wire, oral, or electronic communication, or evidence derived therefrom, intercepted in accordance with the provisions of this Article, may disclose the contents of that communication or such derivative evidence while giving testimony under oath or affirmation in any proceeding in any court or before any grand jury in this State, or in any court of the United States or of any state, or in any federal or state grand jury proceeding.

(d) Within a reasonable time, but no later than 90 days after the filing of an application for an order or the termination of the period of an order or the extensions thereof, the issuing judicial review panel must cause to be served on the persons named in the order or the application and such other parties as the panel in its discretion may determine, an inventory that includes notice of:

(1) The fact of the entry of the order or the application;

(2) The date of the entry and the period of the authorized interception; and

(3) The fact that during the period wire, oral, or electronic communications were or were not intercepted.

(d1) The notification required pursuant to G.S. 15A-294(d) may be delayed if the judicial review panel has probable cause to believe that notification would substantially jeopardize the success of an electronic surveillance or a criminal investigation. Delay of notification shall be only by order of the judicial review panel. The period of delay shall be designated by the judicial review panel and may be extended from time to time until the jeopardy to the electronic surveillance or the criminal investigation dissipates.

(e) The issuing judicial review panel, upon the filing of a motion, may in its discretion, make available to such person or his counsel for inspection, such portions of the intercepted communications, applications, and orders as the panel determines to be required by law or in the interest of justice.

(f) The contents of any intercepted wire, oral, or electronic communication, or evidence derived therefrom, may not be received in evidence or otherwise disclosed in any trial, hearing, or other proceeding in any court of this State unless each party, not less than 20 working days before the trial, hearing, or other proceeding, has been furnished with a copy of the order and accompanying application, under which the interception was authorized.

(g) Any aggrieved person in any trial, hearing, or proceeding in or before any court, department, officer, agency, regulatory body, or other authority of this State, or a political subdivision thereof, may move to suppress the contents of any intercepted wire, oral, or electronic communication, or evidence derived therefrom, on the grounds that:
  (1) The communication was unlawfully intercepted;
  (2) The order of authorization under which it was intercepted is insufficient on its face; or
  (3) The interception was not made in conformity with the order of authorization.

Such motion must be made before the trial, hearing, or proceeding unless there was no opportunity to make such motion or the person was not aware of the grounds of this motion. If the motion is granted, the contents of the intercepted wire, oral, or electronic communication, or evidence derived therefrom, must be treated as having been obtained in violation of this Article.

(h) In addition to any other right to appeal, the State may appeal:
  (1) From an order granting a motion to suppress made under subdivision (1) of this subsection, if the district attorney certifies to the judge granting the motion that the appeal is not taken for purposes of delay. The appeal must be taken within 30 days

after the date the order of suppression was entered and must be prosecuted as are other interlocutory appeals; or

(2) From an order denying an application for an order of authorization, and the appeal may be made ex parte and must be considered in camera and in preference to all other pending appeals.

(i) The requirements of G.S. 15A-293(b)(2) and G.S. 15A-293(a)(4) relating to the specification of the facilities from which, or the place where, the communication is to be intercepted do not apply if:

(1) In the case of an application with respect to the interception of an oral communication:

a. The application is by a State investigative or law enforcement officer and is approved by the Attorney General or his designee;

b. The application contains a full and complete statement as to why the specification is not practical and identifies the person committing the offense and whose communications are to be intercepted; and

c. The judicial review panel finds that the specification is not practical.

(2) In the case of an application with respect to a wire or electronic communication:

a. The application is by a State investigative or law enforcement officer and is approved by the Attorney General or his designee;

b. The application identifies the person believed to be committing the offense and whose communications are to be intercepted, and the applicant makes a showing that there is probable cause to believe that the person's actions could have the effect of thwarting interception from a specified facility;

c. The judicial review panel finds that the showing has been adequately made; and

d. The order authorizing or approving the interception is limited to interception only for such time as it is reasonable to presume that the person identified in the application is or was reasonably proximate to the instrument through which the communication will be or was transmitted.

(j) An interception of a communication under an order with respect to which the requirements of G.S. 15A-293(b)(2) and G.S. 15A-293(a)(4) do not apply by reason of subdivision (i)(1) of this section shall not begin until the place where the communication is to be intercepted is ascertained by the person implementing the interception order. A provider of wire or electronic communications service that has received an order as provided for in subdivision (i)(2) of this section may move the court to modify or quash the order on the grounds that its assistance with respect to the interception cannot be performed in a timely or reasonable fashion. The court, upon notice to the government, shall decide such a motion expeditiously.

§ 15A-295. Reports concerning intercepted wire, oral, or electronic communications

In January of each year, the Attorney General of this State must report to the Administrative Office of the United States Court the information required to be filed by section 2519 of Title 18 of the United States Code, as heretofore or hereafter amended, and file a copy of the report with the Administrative Office of the Courts of North Carolina.

§ 15A-296. Recovery of civil damages authorized

(a) Any person whose wire, oral, or electronic communication is intercepted, disclosed, or used in violation of this Article, has a civil cause of action against any person who intercepts, discloses, uses, or procures any other person to intercept, disclose, or use such communications, and is entitled to recover from any other person:
  (1) Actual damages, but not less than liquidated damages, computed at the rate of one hundred dollars ($100.00) a day for each day of violation or one thousand dollars ($1,000), whichever is higher;
  (2) Punitive damages; and
  (3) A reasonable attorneys' fee and other litigation costs reasonably incurred.

(b) Good faith reliance on a court order or on a representation made by the Attorney General or a district attorney is a complete defense to any civil or criminal action brought under this Article.

§ 15A-297. Conformity to provisions of federal law

It is the intent of this Article to conform the requirements of all interceptions of wire, oral, or electronic communications conducted by investigative or law enforcement officers in this State to provisions of Chapter 119 of the United States Code, except where the context indicates a purpose to provide safeguards even more protective of individual privacy and constitutional rights.

§ 15A-298. Subpoena authority

Pursuant to rules issued by the State Bureau of Investigation, the Director of the State Bureau of Investigation or the Director's designee may issue an administrative subpoena to a communications common carrier or an electronic communications service to compel production of business records if the records:

(1) Disclose information concerning local or long-distance toll records or subscriber information; and

(2) Are material to an active criminal investigation being conducted by the State Bureau of Investigation.

Appendix C

State Pen Register Statutes (G.S. 15A-260 through -264)

§ 15A-260. Definitions

As used in this Article:

(1) "Electronic communication," "electronic communication service," and "wire communication" shall have the meaning as set forth in Section 2510 of Title 18 of the United States Code;

(2) "Pen register" means a device which records or decodes electronic or other impulses which identify numbers dialed or otherwise transmitted on the telephone line to which such device is attached, but the term does not include any device used by a provider or customer of a wire or electronic service for billing, or recording as an incident to billing, for communication services provided by the provider or any device used by a provider or customer of a wire communication service for cost accounting or other like purposes in the ordinary course of its business, nor shall the term include any device which allows the listening or recording of communications transmitted on the telephone line to which the device is attached.

(3) "Trap and trace device" means a device which captures the incoming electronic or other impulses which identify the originating number of an instrument or device from which a wire or electronic communication was transmitted.

§ 15A-261. Prohibition and exceptions

(a) In General.—Except as provided in subsection (b) of this section, no person may install or use a pen register or a trap and trace device without first obtaining a court order as provided in this Article.

(b) Exception.—The prohibition of subsection (a) of this section does not apply to the use of a pen register or a trap and trace device by a provider of wire or electronic communication service:

(1) Relating to the operation, maintenance, or testing of a wire or electronic communication service or to the protection of the

rights or property of the provider, or to the protection of users of that service from abuse of service or unlawful use of service; or

(2) To record the fact that a wire or electronic communication was initiated or completed in order to protect the provider, another provider furnishing service toward the completion of the wire communication, or a user of that service, from fraudulent, unlawful or abusive use of service; or

(3) With the consent of the user of that service.

(c) Penalty—A person who willfully and knowingly violates subsection (a) of this section is guilty of a Class 1 misdemeanor.

§ 15A-262. Application for order for pen register or trap and trace device

(a) Application.—A law enforcement officer may make an application for an order or an extension of an order under G.S. 15A-263 authorizing or approving the installation and use of a pen register or a trap and trace device, in writing under oath or affirmation, to a superior court judge.

(b) Contents of application.—An application under subsection (a) of this section shall include:

(1) The identity of the law enforcement officer making the application and the identity of the law enforcement agency conducting the investigation; and

(2) A certification by the applicant that the information likely to be obtained is relevant to an ongoing criminal investigation being conducted by that agency.

§ 15A-263. Issuance of order for pen register or trap and trace device

(a) In General.—Following application made under G.S. 15A-262, a superior court judge may enter an ex parte order authorizing the installation and use of a pen register or a trap and trace device within the State if the judge finds:

(1) That there is reasonable suspicion to believe that a felony offense, or a Class A1 or Class 1 misdemeanor offense has been committed;

(2) That there are reasonable grounds to suspect that the person named or described in the affidavit committed the offense, if that person is known and can be named or described; and

(3) That the results of procedures involving pen registers or trap and trace devices will be of material aid in determining whether the person named in the affidavit committed the offense.

(b) Contents of Order.—An order issued under this section:
  (1) Shall specify:
    a. The identity, if known, of the person to whom is leased or in whose name is listed the telephone line to which the pen register or trap and trace device is to be attached;
    b. The identity, if known, of the person who is the subject of the criminal investigation;
    c. The number and, if known, physical location of the telephone line to which the pen register or trap and trace device is to be attached and, in the case of a trap and trace device, the geographic limits of the trap and trace order; and
    d. The offense to which the information likely to be obtained by the pen register or trap and trace device relates; and
  (2) Shall direct, upon request of the applicant, the furnishing of information, facilities, or technical assistance necessary to accomplish the installation of the pen register or trap and trace device under G.S. 15A-264.

(c) Time Period and Extension.
  (1) An order issued under this section shall authorize the installation and use of a pen register or a trap and trace device for a period not to exceed 60 days.
  (2) An extension of an order issued under this section may be granted, but only upon an application for an order under G.S. 15A-262 and upon the judicial finding required by subsection (a) of this section. The period of extension shall not exceed 60 days.

(d) Nondisclosure of Existence of Pen Register or a Trap and Trace Device.—An order authorizing or approving the installation and use of a pen register or a trap and trace device shall direct that:
  (1) The order be sealed until otherwise ordered by the judge; and
  (2) The person owning or leasing the line to which the pen register or a trap and trace device is attached, or who has been ordered by the judge to provide assistance to the applicant, not disclose the existence of the pen register or trap and trace device or the existence of the investigation to the listed subscriber, or to any person, unless otherwise ordered by the judge.

The provisions of G.S. 15A-903 and 15A-904 shall apply to this Article.

§ 15A-264. Assistance in installation and use of a pen register or a trap and trace device

(a) Pen Registers.—Upon the request of a law enforcement officer authorized to install and use a pen register under this Article, a provider of wire or electronic communication service, a landlord, a custodian, or other person shall furnish the officer promptly with all information, facilities, or technical assistance necessary to accomplish the installation of the pen register unobtrusively and with a minimum of interference with the communication services, if the assistance is directed by a court order as provided in G.S. 15A-263(b)(2).

(b) Trap and Trace Devices.—Upon the request of a law enforcement officer authorized to receive the results of a trap and trace device under this Article, a provider of a wire or electronic communication service, a landlord, a custodian, or other person shall install the device immediately on the appropriate line and shall furnish the officer all additional information, facilities, or technical assistance, including installation and operation of the device unobtrusively and with a minimum of interference with the communication services, if the installation and assistance are directed by court order as provided in G.S. 15A-263(b)(2). Unless otherwise ordered by the judge, the results of the trap and trace device shall be furnished to the law enforcement officer designated in the court order at reasonable intervals during regular business hours for the duration of the order.

(c) Compensation.—A provider of a wire or electronic communication service, a landlord, a custodian, or other person who furnishes facilities or technical assistance pursuant to this section shall be compensated for the reasonable expenses incurred in providing the facilities and assistance.

(d) No Cause of Action Against a Provider Giving Information or Assistance Under this Article.—No cause of action shall be allowed in any court against any provider of a wire or electronic communication service, its officers, employees, agents, or other specified persons for providing information, facilities, or assistance in accordance with the terms of a court order under this Article.

(e) Defense.—A good faith reliance on a court order or a statutory authorization is a complete defense against any civil or criminal action brought under this Article or any other law.

ISBN-13: 978-156011837
90000
9 781560 118374